Ballots before Bullets
The War Referendum Approach to
Peace in America
1914–1941

Ballots before Bullets

The War Referendum Approach to Peace in America
1914–1941

Ernest C. Bolt, Jr.

University Press of Virginia   Charlottesville

THE UNIVERSITY PRESS OF VIRGINIA
Copyright © 1977 by the Rector and Visitors
of the University of Virginia

First published 1977

Library of Congress Cataloging in Publication Data

Bolt, Ernest C   1936–
  Ballots before bullets.

  Bibliography: p.
  Includes index.
  1. Peace.   2. Referendum—United States.
3. United States—History—1901–1953.   I. Title.
JX1952.B56   327'.172   77-680   ISBN 0-8139-0662-8

Printed in the United States of America

For My Father and Mother
and Mary Frances

Contents

Acknowledgments

I wish to acknowledge the inspiration and assistance of two professors in my development as a historian. Delbert H. Gilpatrick, former longtime historian at Furman University, and Professor John Chalmers Vinson, who introduced me to the war referendum topic at the University of Georgia, provided desirable models as teacher-scholars. Others who facilitated my research include librarians and archivists in Washington, D.C., and Hyde Park, New York, in the Swarthmore College Peace Collection, and in libraries at Duke University, Indiana University, the University of Georgia, and the University of Richmond.

I am grateful to William Jennings Bryan, Jr. for permission to cite and quote from his father's private papers. I also acknowledge that quotations from the Oswald Garrison Villard papers are by permission of the Houghton Library, Harvard University. Permission to quote from the personal papers of Louis L. Ludlow was granted by his son, Louis Ludlow, Jr. Acknowledgment is made also to Mrs. Elizabeth Hughes Gossett for permission to quote from the Charles Evans Hughes papers, to Mrs. William L. White for the William Allen White papers, and Mrs. Ruth Pinchot for the Amos Pinchot papers. Quotations from the papers of Samuel McGowan and the Socialist Party of America are by permission of Duke University Library. Quotations from the Randolph S. Bourne papers are by permission of Columbia University Libraries.

I especially acknowledge the encouragement of my wife Mary Frances and financial support by the Faculty Research Committee and the Faculty Publication Fund of the University of Richmond.

Introduction

AMONG THOSE who have recently lamented the inadvertency of Congress in giving away to the Executive the war powers, former Senator J. William Fulbright has argued that "the Congress has lost the power to declare war as it was written into the Constitution. It has not been so much usurped as given away." [1] Yet few critics of recent American foreign policy or scholars have noted, in their concern over the erosion of congressional roles and powers, earlier efforts of the Congress to "give away" its constitutional power to declare war. From 1914 to 1941 many Americans believed that a popular referendum to declare foreign wars, except in case of attack or invasion, offered the best hope for peace. Admittedly, their search for peace through the war referendum plan was most often unorganized, and interest in it was sporadic. Yet its popularity and persistence, in and out of Congress, has not been well remembered. Historians have often overlooked the war referendum appeal, misrepresented it as requiring a referendum on *any* declaration of war, or have mentioned it only as a foolhardy alternative to collective security in the thirties.

Built upon evidence of remarkable individual, congressional, and organized pacifist interest, the history of the war referendum approach to peace at the same time illustrates both the failure in America's search for peace and points up, better than most historians have realized, some reasons for that failure. This twentieth-century peace plan represented the typically American attempt to reduce the use of force in diplomacy. Relying as it did upon the moral force of public opinion, and based on a limited-defense concept, with most of its partisans committed to continental self-defense only, its popularity in America influenced America's pre-1945 denial of force in foreign affairs. Military defense attitudes of war referendum partisans, therefore, were often important in suggesting why they chose to offer this peace plan. [2]

[1] U.S., Congress, Senate, 90th Cong., 1st sess., *Separation of Powers:* Hearings before the Subcommittee on Separation of Powers of the Committee on the Judiciary, July 19, 20, August 2; and September 13 and 15, 1967, p. 47.

[2] On general treatment of this idea, as well as the one presented in the next paragraph, see John Chalmers Vinson, "Military Force and American Policy, 1919–1939," in Alexander DeConde, ed., *Isolation and Security* (Durham, N.C., 1957), pp. 56–81.

Furthermore, the war referendum plan among its friends demonstrated an unusual faith in "the people" and was the most typical of America's twentieth-century efforts to have greater popular control of diplomacy, revealing a distinct distrust of both executive leadership and the Congress. At the same time, it registered strong support among liberals and radicals who favored returning government to the people through this and other "democratic experiments." It also raised the question, relative to its popular control objective, as to how America might achieve the desired balance between democratic rule and demands for swift action and immediate decisions in diplomacy.

It is the aim of this study to present the history of the war referendum approach to peace in light of these themes and questions and to describe heretofore little-known interest in the peace plan. Efforts within the organized peace movement before American intervention in World War I, for example, finally concentrated upon the war referendum plan as an emergency measure. For the most part William Jennings Bryan's leadership of that campaign has not been outlined before. Emphasis in the 1920s was on attempts to gain international agreement to the plan. It was at this time, for example, that Secretary of State Charles Evans Hughes endorsed the plan unofficially in negotiations with France and Germany just before the Ruhr Crisis in Europe. Throughout the study, strong congressional interest in the form of an advisory referendum and a constitutional amendment will be shown. Louis Ludlow, Democratic Indiana congressman and former newspaperman in the congressional press gallery, was prominent in the near successful effort, 1935 to 1941, to approve the plan in the form of a constitutional amendment. In various forms and on several occasions, the war referendum plan reached a vote in the Congress but was consistently rejected as a peace plan. Opposition to the sporadic campaigns, therefore, will be presented with attention to opposition tactics and the leadership of Presidents Woodrow Wilson and Franklin Roosevelt especially.

Some Americans still find popular control of diplomacy and the limited use of force in diplomacy desirable goals. Recent efforts of Congress to reclaim constitutional authority by defining national commitments and by war-powers legislation echo the thinking of some earlier war referendum partisans. Similarly, the war referendum *idea* predates the referendum peace plans of the twentieth century that are the major interest in this study. Earlier, Americans and Europeans had presented ideas basic to the plan and, in some instances, had even offered war referendum proposals.

The earliest European expressions of the war referendum idea were by French philosopher and legislator the marquis de Condorcet and the

German philosopher Immanuel Kant. Condorcet was a commanding figure in the committee of the National Convention charged with drafting the revolutionary Constitution of 1793, the most democratic of all French constitutions. The people would have no direct control over the details of national defense or over ratification of treaties but could veto declarations of war.³ In his treatise on remedies for imperialism in 1795, Immanuel Kant asserted that every state's constitution "ought to be republican" and that "the assent of every citizen is necessary to decide the question 'whether war shall be declared or not.' " His theory that, if given the power, the people would "certainly beware of plunging into an enterprise so hazardous" became typical of most later American war referendum advocates. They, like Kant, believed that the people would always vote against "all the calamities of war." ⁴

In revolutionary America, although writings of English radicals prompted a full consideration of "representation" and the need for a militia instead of standing armies, the war referendum plan itself was not advocated.⁵ Only on two occasions during the Constitutional Convention of 1787 was the matter of war-declaring powers discussed, and separate moves to give the power to the Senate, the president, and the House of Representatives failed. There seemed to be general agreement, finally, that the entire Congress, which represented the people at large, would be a less likely tool for enemy propaganda than either the president or Senate alone.⁶

More thorough attention to this issue followed with the development of the American peace movement and the resort to war in the nineteenth century. In mid-1809, for example, John Foster, of Massachusetts, made the first known reference to the war referendum idea in the United

³Alphonse Aulard, *The French Revolution* (New York, 1910), II, 159–210, discusses the Constitution of 1793 in great detail.

⁴Immanuel Kant, *Perpetual Peace* (1795; Los Angeles, 1932), pp. 24–26.

⁵James Burgh, *Political Disquisitions* (Philadelphia, 1775), I, 3, II, 341–53; Felix Gilbert, *To the Farewell Address: Ideas of Early American Foreign Policy* (Princeton, 1961), p. 36; Gordon Wood, *The Creation of the American Republic, 1776–1787* (Chapel Hill, N.C., 1969).

⁶James Madison, *The Writings of James Madison* (New York, 1900–1910), IV, 227–28. See VI, 88–90, 138–70 for Madison's 1792–93 articles in the *National Gazette* treating, in part, the war power. See also Max Farrand, ed., *The Records of the Federal Convention of 1787* (New Haven, 1911), I, 292, II, 182, 313–20; and C. C. Tansill, "War Powers of the President of the United States," *Political Science Quarterly*, 45 (1930), 1–55. Recent debate on war powers legislation has produced new examination of the discussion at Philadelphia and subsequent history of the war-declaring powers. See, for example, William B. Spong, Jr., "Can Balance Be Restored in the Constitutional War Powers of the President and Congress?" *University of Richmond Law Review*, 6 (1971), 1–47.

States. Speaking before Boston's Ancient and Honorable Artillery Company, he held that justifiable and necessary wars should not be pursued without adequate preparation and careful consideration of costs. Taking as his text Proverbs 24:6, "By wise counsel thou shalt make thy war," Foster suggested that the war decision must be based on "the collected wisdom of a nation." He emphasized the influence and vote of *every* citizen; he believed that nothing should be done in a republic except that "the people love to have it so" and urged that a strong navy and coastal defense, added to a citizen army, would adequately prepare America against attack.[7]

No better statement of some twentieth-century Americans' later attitudes has been made. As America soon endured its next taste of war, men like Foster hailed the New England governors' opposition to President James Madison's assertion of executive control over the militia. Whereas many had previously insisted that "defensive" wars were "just," the War of 1812 gave birth to a peace movement that more fully rejected force as a proper means to settle international problems. Some pacifists claimed that wars were fought by the common man, whose consent was never given, but none went so far as to advocate the war referendum *plan* as a remedy.[8]

As opposition to war continued during the middle of the nineteenth century, a California pacifist furnished another example of the war referendum idea during the American Civil War. Published in English and Spanish, his peace proposal in 1864 required a national referendum on continuing the war. Voters would be prosecuted for failing to vote and, along with those voting to continue the war, would be placed in the army of the United States. The author of this plan feared that a long war would invite foreign invasion and spell the doom of freedom; furthermore, he believed that the people as a whole would vote to end the war if given a chance.[9]

[7]John Foster of Brighton, *A Sermon Preached Before the Ancient and Honourable Artillery Company, in Boston, June 5, 1809; Being the Anniversary of Their Election of Officers* (Boston, 1809), pp. 4–20.

[8]New England's demands for local control of the militia and local determination of when it could be activated foreshadowed twentieth-century demands for popular civilian control of the war decision. On the nineteenth-century peace movements, see Freeman Galpin, *Pioneering for Peace: A Study of American Peace Efforts to 1846* (Syracuse, N.Y., 1933), and on religious pacifism see Peter Brock, *Pacifism in the United States: From the Colonial Era to the First World War* (Princeton, 1968). See also David S. Patterson, *Toward a Warless World: The Travail of the American Peace Movement, 1887–1914* (Bloomington, Ind., 1976).

[9]Robert E. Beasley, *A Plan to Stop the Present and Prevent Future Wars* (Rio Vista, Calif., 1864), 3–4. He also urged a union of states in North and South America to prevent future wars.

During the 1898–1902 debate over imperialism and America's new world responsibilities, the organized anti-imperialist movement to some degree espoused attitudes later held by war referendum advocates. In fact, several individuals within the anti-imperialist movement at the turn of the century appeared later among the leadership in antimilitarist and war referendum campaigns. Although the American Anti-Imperialist League failed in its chief purposes of opposing annexation of large territories following the Spanish-American War and then in securing the election of William Jennings Bryan in 1900, the anti-imperialist argument, which really hinged on defense attitudes, remained prominent for some time.

The League did not want to commit America to *political* responsibilities beyond the continental homeland. Likewise, its members objected to the larger defense commitment necessary under President McKinley's policies of territorial expansion. That the anti-imperialists did not object to economic or trade expansion was clear. Liberal educator David Starr Jordan and Georgia Congressman William H. Fleming were typical. In an 1898 interview the latter stated the anti-imperialist argument simply: "I do not advocate commercial isolation, but I do advocate political isolation." Jordan in 1899 echoed the League's favor of trade expansion to meet the "open door with open door." [10]

Anti-imperialists, furthermore, *were* willing to defend America's new economic interests. They differed with opponents on the size and number of bases, denied the necessity of holding large areas of territory, and opposed political control or responsibility for such areas. Carl Schurz in 1899 typified the League's attitudes when he maintained that trade expansion could come faster "without armies, without war fleets, without bloody conquests, without colonies." During his 1893 opposition to Hawaiian annexation he had suggested almost the same defense concept: "In our compact continental stronghold we are substantially unassailable. We present no vulnerable point of importance. . . . We can defend all our possessions *without* leaving our own continental ground." [11] By 1899 even Schurz was willing to go out of our "impregnable stronghold" to protect economic expansion through small bases. Like other anti-imperialists, he would make limited defense commitments. One of these was Texas Congressman James L. Slayden, who was willing to provide a "good defensive navy," but hoped that avoiding large annexations or political

[10]Fleming, *The Tariff, Civil Service, Income Tax, Imperialism, the Race Problem, and Other Speeches* (Atlanta, 1908), p. 67; Jordan, *The Question of the Philippines* (Palo Alto, Calif., 1899), p. 48.

[11]Schurz, *Speeches, Correspondence, and Political Papers of Carl Schurz*, ed. Frederic Bancroft (New York, 1913), VI, 109–11; idem, "Manifest Destiny," *Harper's New Monthly Magazine*, 87 (1893), 737–46 (author's emphasis).

responsibility abroad would obviate any need for a large army or navy.[12]
The anti-imperialists, therefore, enunciated defense concepts that were
echoed later by peace advocates and "fortress America" partisans in the
twentieth century.

But the comparison does not end there. The anti-imperialists also
believed there was an inherent danger to democracy from the militaristic
imperialism they fought. There was some consideration after 1900 of
making the League's chief aim antimilitarism, and, indeed, during its
weakened condition before the European war it worked against preparedness. Many of its members, including Jane Addams, Andrew Carnegie,
Cincinnati minister Herbert S. Bigelow, David Starr Jordan, and non-
member William Jennings Bryan, were among the leading peace workers
before American intervention in 1917.

Yet it was the organization's emphasis upon honoring "the consent of
the governed" that produced the closest kinship with later war
referendum advocates. Its fight against Philippine annexation, on these
terms, featured suggestions of a national referendum on imperialism, a
proposal overlooked by most historians.[13] Carl Schurz, for example, suggested "submitting to a popular vote" the question of annexation of the islands. League President George S. Boutwell echoed this sentiment in
1899, and even after the 1900 election a League pamphlet proposed a
referendum in which the people could decide whether the administration's
Philippine policy should continue.[14]

The anti-imperialists' appeal for a direct referendum on the administration's foreign policy in the Philippines indicated an unusual faith in
popular control. Furthermore, the Anti-Imperialist League contained

[12]Anti-Imperialist League (Boston), *Annual Report, 1910*, p. 19. The League reprinted
Slayden's anti-big navy speech in its *Report, 1907*, p. 5. See also U.S., Congress,
Congressional Record, 59th Cong., 2d sess., pp. 2774–75 (Feb. 12, 1907) and 61st Cong., 2d
sess., pp. 4427, 4429 (Apr. 8, 1910).

[13]Merle Curti relates anti-imperialism and pacifism in *Peace or War: The American
Struggle, 1636–1936* (New York, 1936), pp. 179–82. Among the best recent treatments of
the anti-imperialists are Robert L. Beisner, *Twelve against Empire: The Anti-Imperialists,
1898–1900* (New York, 1968), and E. Berkeley Tompkins, *Anti-Imperialism in the United
States: The Great Debate, 1890–1920* (Philadelphia, 1970). See also Fred Harvey Har-
rington, "The Anti-Imperialist Movement in the United States, 1898–1900," *Mississippi
Valley Historical Review*, 22 (1935), 211–30; William E. Leuchtenburg, "Progressivism and
Imperialism: The Progressive Movement and American Foreign Policy, 1898–1916," ibid.,
39 (1952), 483–504; Walter La Feber, *The New Empire: An Interpretation of American Expansion, 1860–1898* (Ithaca, N.Y., 1963), pp. 411–17.

[14]Schurz, *Papers*, V, 530–31; Anti-Imperialist League, *Annual Report, 1899*, p. 15, *1900*,
pp. 20–21, *1904*, p. 16; James W. Stillman, *Republic or Empire? An Argument in Opposition
to the Establishment of an American Colonial System* (Boston, 1900), pp. 5, 30; E. L.
Godkin, "Come Let Us Reason Together," *Nation*, 67 (1898), 344.

several *later* war referendum plan partisans, namely, Miss Addams, Bigelow, and Jordan. The fact that William Jennings Bryan was unofficial leader of both anti-imperialism and then the first significant war referendum campaign, before American intervention in World War I, is also meaningful. Later interwar advocates of the war referendum plan, like the earlier anti-imperialists, believed their prescription for peace was best. Urging greater democracy and reform at home, economic expansion abroad, and avoidance of unlimited political and military responsibilities in foreign affairs, they also believed that in times of international crisis there would always be an opportunity for rational choice between war and peace. They went beyond the anti-imperialist position and argued, without success, that the American electorate as a whole should make that choice.

I have from the outset made a conscious effort to avoid magnifying the war referendum story out of proportion. As historian Frederic L. Paxson has stated so well, "In proportion as the theme is traced and isolated in its original unity, it becomes unreal. As a single topic, however factually it may be portrayed, it never happened." [15] If this has occurred, I acknowledge full responsibility but at the same time register a plea for tolerance.

[15] *American Democracy and the World War: Pre-War Years, 1913–1917* (Boston, 1936), I, 163.

Ballots before Bullets
The War Referendum Approach to
Peace in America
1914–1941

CHAPTER I

Organized Pacifism and the Shock of War

THE TWENTIETH-CENTURY peace movement in America did not at first incorporate the war referendum plan into peace programs. A national vote on war declarations, either in the form of an advisory referendum or as a permanent reform through a constitutional amendment, had not been favored in the nineteenth-century American peace movement.[1] As America's commitments began to extend beyond the continental United States after the turn of the century, however, an increasingly strong, influential, and diverse peace movement began to consider, among other plans, democratization of foreign affairs. In peace organizations and in the Congress, pleas for increased naval preparedness, collective security through limited international cooperation, and even disarmament had been sporadic heretofore. Likewise, consideration of a referendum approach to peace had earlier been limited to several occasions and a few anti-imperialists. But, especially after 1914, both the adherents of force in diplomacy and traditional isolationist spokesmen, each of whom represented a minority sentiment, began campaigns to win approval of a variety of peace plans within Congress and amid a public that was, as a whole, indifferent.[2]

In addition to the wide variety of peace plans advanced during the period of American neutrality, 1914–17, there were more divergent views about involvement in war than at any time in American history.[3] By April 1917, however, the European emergency produced brief pacifist unity, with the more radical antiwar peace campaign centered upon the war referendum plan as never before. Progressives, Socialists, congressmen, social workers, and others first rallied behind this peace measure to show that true democracy in foreign affairs could prevent war. Failing to secure

[1] Merle E. Curti, *Bryan and World Peace,* Smith College Studies in History, Ser. 16, Nos. 3–4 (Northampton, Mass., 1931), p. 226.

[2] In addition to Curti, who treats the impact of World War I on the peace movement in *Peace or War,* pp. 228–61, recent interest in the peace movement is illustrated by Charles Chatfield, *For Peace and Justice: Pacifism in America, 1914–1941* (Knoxville, Tenn., 1971), and C. Roland Marchand, *The American Peace Movement and Social Reform, 1898–1918* (Princeton, 1972).

[3] William E. Leuchtenburg, *The Perils of Prosperity, 1914–1932* (Chicago, 1958), p. 43; Selig Adler, *The Isolationist Impulse: Its Twentieth Century Reaction* (New York, 1961), p. 35.

reform, they then offered it as at least a way to limit the war already being waged.

Expansion and transformation of the American peace movement was well underway by the fall of 1914, caused primarily by divisions on the use of force to preserve peace and progress. Typical of the new peace organizations that emerged after 1905 and claiming to be more "practical" than the older American Peace Society were the New York Peace Society (1906), the American Society of International Law (1906), and the League for Protection, Progress, and Peace (1908), later called the Practical Peace League. The Carnegie Endowment for International Peace and the World Peace Foundation also appeared in this period. This was the time, according to Roland Marchand, when the peace movement developed from "sentimentalism" to "establishment reform." International lawyers and businessmen entered into the search for peace and made the enterprise more respected and influential.[4]

In this new context of respectability, the Fourth American Peace Congress (1913) met in a drive for unity. The congress was committed to peace through disarmament and international law, and the recent interest in arbitration produced consideration of a significant resolution. Seeking to limit congressional war-declaring powers, the resolution recommended a study on whether an amendment should be proposed to the United States Constitution forbidding Congress to enter war, except in case of invasion, until arbitration had failed. The resolution was presented by the German-American Peace Society and was approved by the national peace congress.[5]

This resolution indicated the delegates' high regard for arbitration, a long-standing approach to peace. But it was also clearly a proposal in the direction of popular control of foreign affairs. It was a cautious but real challenge to the constitutional processes, a call for substantive reform of existing war powers enjoyed by the Congress. A leading figure in this effort and in the German-American Peace Society was Richard Bartholdt, German immigrant and liberal leader of the arbitration group in the House of Representatives from 1893 to 1915. A Republican from Reconstruction days, he was a New York newspaperman when he taught

[4]Marchand, *American Peace Movement,* p. 38. See also Chatfield, *For Peace and Justice,* p. 15.

[5]American Peace Congress Files, Swarthmore College Peace Collection, Swarthmore, Pa. See especially Walter B. Stevens, ed., *Book of the Fourth American Peace Congress* (Saint Louis, 1913), p. 579. In 1906 German-American Peace Society President Dr. Ernst Richard had made a similar suggestion in the article "Constitutional Safeguards against War," *Outlook,* 84 (1906), 29–32. Richard was a founder of the New York Peace Society (1906), led by Andrew Carnegie beginning in 1907.

German to state assemblyman Theodore Roosevelt. Later, as congressman from a strongly German-American Saint Louis district, Bartholdt became convinced that international arbitration, disarmament, and world federation offered the best way to prevent war. As the leader of the Interparliamentary Union movement in the United States, he led several hundred members of Congress into this international peace group and secured its 1904 conference for Saint Louis. Subsequently he and other internationalists in the peace movement influenced President Theodore Roosevelt to call the Second Hague Conference.[6]

Bartholdt's preferences for compulsory arbitration and the use of an international naval force to maintain peace made him a typical spokesman for the new "establishment" peace movement. This group advocated international cooperation and included, in addition to Bartholdt, millionaires Edwin Ginn and Andrew Carnegie, *Independent* editor Hamilton Holt, and New York lawyer Hayne Davis. Davis was a cofounder of both the New York Peace Society (1906) and the North Carolina Peace Society (1907), of which he was the first president. Along with Richmond P. Hobson, Spanish-American War hero and Alabama congressman, Davis in 1908 formed a peace-by-preparedness organization called the League for Protection, Progress, and Peace. It became the Practical Peace League (it was also known as the Peace and Arbitration League) and urged a big navy as the best insurance for peace. During 1914 and especially after the war declarations of that year, the influence of these men increased, with the exception of World Peace Foundation founder Ginn, who died early that year. Davis continued to be the "idea man" for the preparedness group, and his influence upon Bartholdt and Holt, who were spokesmen for many of the same ideas, was significant.[7]

Despite Bartholdt's "establishment" identification, his advocacy of the war referendum plan by 1914 illustrated further transformation within the peace movement generally and suggested his own development of the directions toward popular control noted in the 1913 American Peace Congress. On July 21, 1914, only a year after that peace meeting and just

---

[6] Bartholdt, *From Steerage to Congress* (Philadelphia, 1930), pp. 25, 48–52, 56, 67–68; John Chalmers Vinson, *The Parchment Peace: The United States Senate and the Washington Conference 1921–1922* (Athens, Ga., 1955), pp. 8–9. Bartholdt was earlier editor of the Saint Louis *Tribune* and withdrew his candidacy for reelection to Congress in 1914 (Warren F. Kuehl, *Seeking World Order: The United States and International Organization to 1920* [Nashville, 1969], pp. 70–74).

[7] Vinson, "Military Force, 1919–1939," p. 63; Adler, *Isolationist Impulse,* p. 40; Martin David Dubin, "The Development of the Concept of Collective Security in the American Peace Movement, 1899–1917," Diss. Indiana 1960, pp. 12–14, 39–52. Holt's influence is traced thoroughly in Warren F. Kuehl, *Hamilton Holt* (Gainesville, Fla., 1960), pp. 65–133.

before the European war declarations, Bartholdt added the war referendum, in the form of a proposed constitutional amendment, to his other peace measures. It was only a short step from his support of compulsory arbitration, world federation, and disarmament to this first direct congressional endorsement of the war referendum plan. His resolution proposed "that Congress shall not declare war except to repel invasion or under circumstances calling for measures of self defense" until after a national referendum.[8]

Bartholdt's proposed constitutional amendment and its underlying rationale were not immediately incorporated into congressional debates or peace programs of the newer and more affluent peace organizations. Even after war broke out in Europe, most Americans did not feel threatened. The peace groups, apparently more interested in past programs and the postwar peace, emphasized legal, educational, and "scientific" approaches to peace in programs favoring mediation, arbitration, and preparedness. Not even a new wartime peace group, the League to Enforce Peace, organized in June 1915, showed interest in the war referendum plan.[9] Although illustrating a greater urgency in the peace movement, the League retained "establishment" identification and emphasized peace through law and international arbitration rather than popular controls in foreign affairs.

A better example of the 1914–15 radical trend in the peace movement was the American League to Limit Armament, founded in New York City in December 1914. Although not as internationalist-oriented as the League to Enforce Peace, it was more concerned about immediate peace action. Its contrast with the pro-preparedness National Security League and the League to Enforce Peace, its kinship with the former Anti-Imperialist League, and its sense of urgency promised greater boldness in its plans for preventing American intervention. In addition to editor Oswald Garrison Villard, its membership included liberal educator Nicholas Murray Butler and Boston reformer Erving Winslow, both former members of the Anti-Imperialist League, which had briefly endorsed the proposed referendum idea on imperialism at the turn of the century.[10]

8Original typescript, House Joint Resolution 306, "House Joint Resolutions, Originals, Numbers 1–441," 63d Cong., 1913–1915, Records of the House of Representatives, Record Group 233, National Archives (cited hereafter as RG 233, NA).

9Marchand, *American Peace Movement,* pp. 144–45, 154–56; Kuehl, *Holt,* 108–9. On the League to Enforce Peace see also Ruhl J. Bartlett, *The League to Enforce Peace* (Chapel Hill, N.C., 1944) and Sondra R. Herman, *Eleven against War: Studies in American Internationalist Thought, 1898–1921* (Stanford, Calif., 1969), pp. 55–85.

10"List of Members, April 24, 1915," American League to Limit Armament Files, SCPC; Oswald Garrison Villard, *Fighting Years: Memoirs of a Liberal Editor* (New York, 1939), pp. 248–49.

In the short lifetime of this group, however, there was never official advocacy of the war referendum plan. During late 1914 and 1915 this small peace organization emphasized opposition to what social worker Lillian Wald called the "ugly form" of preparedness. Composed of progressives anxious about continued domestic reform, this group advocated a small defense establishment and opposed making the nation an armed camp. "Put whatever war preparations we make into coast defenses and submarines," they argued, believing that such a policy would "amply defend us at 3000 miles distance from a supposable future enemy." Such a policy would furthermore make a reserve army useless and would prevent more and heavier taxation.[11] These attitudes on national defense, expressed increasingly in 1916 on the preparedness issue, eventually made war referendum spokesmen of several members of the American League to Limit Armament. Among them would be Villard, social workers Lillian Wald and Jane Addams, journalists Paul U. Kellogg and Max Eastman, and other liberals such as Frederic C. Howe and Amos Pinchot.

The close relationship in this new group between interest in domestic reform and antipreparedness caused a particularly successful union of peace work and the woman suffrage movement after war began in Europe. Lillian Wald's Henry Street Settlement was the site of the meeting that resulted in the American League to Limit Armament. Jane Addams became chairwoman of another liberal peace organization, the Emergency Federation of Peace Forces, founded in Chicago in December 1914. Finally, in January 1915 Miss Addams and other prominent social workers and suffragists organized the Woman's Peace Party.

All three of these peace groups attracted antimilitarist progressives who believed that the war in Europe threatened progress at home and necessitated new, more radical peace plans.[12] They continued to prescribe traditional disarmament and arbitration schemes as preventives of war. But to end the war already in progress and to prevent American intervention, they encouraged new ideas. One plan, on which most of them agreed

[11] "The Constructive Program for National Security; a Reply to the President," n.d., American League to Limit Armament Files, SCPC. See also Marchand, *American Peace Movement,* pp. 233, 357; Allen F. Davis, "The Social Workers and the Progressive Party, 1912–1916," *American Historical Review,* 69 (1964), 675–77, 688; and Donald Johnson, *The Challenge to American Freedom: World War I and the Rise of the American Civil Liberties Union* (Lexington, Ky., 1963), pp. 1–5.

[12] Marchand, *American Peace Movement,* pp. 182–265, especially treats the importance of this perspective upon the peace movement and emphasizes leadership by women and social workers as a primary factor in further radicalization of the peace movement. Clarke A. Chambers, *Paul U. Kellogg and the Survey: Voices for Social Welfare and Social Justice* (Minneapolis, 1971), pp. 56–57, treats Kellogg's peace work only briefly. Milton Cantor, *Max Eastman* (New York, 1970), presents Eastman chiefly as a literary radical and has little on his antiwar activism beyond participation in the Union Against Militarism.

despite organizational separateness and inherent diversity, took the form of "constructive mediation" by an international conference of neutrals. But they also offered the basic idea behind Congressman Bartholdt's 1914 war referendum resolution. Many peace activists in these groups favored abolition of secret diplomacy and "adequate machinery" to insure democratic control of foreign policy. By mid-1915 the American League to Limit Armament, the Chicago Emergency Federation of Peace Forces, and the Woman's Peace Party endorsed peace through popular control and antimilitarism.[13] Only the Woman's Peace Party among these, however, presented the war referendum plan as "adequate" insurance of democratic control of foreign policy in 1915.

The Woman's Peace Party, which endorsed the war referendum plan in its 1915 platform, was founded in January 1915 by Mrs. Henry Villard, Mrs. Carrie Chapman Catt, Jane Addams, and others.[14] All agreed that other peace organizations had neglected women as a force for peace work, and despite early disagreement on the woman suffrage plank in the platform, they were committed to more activism in peace work. Mrs. Villard's dissatisfaction with the New York Peace Society, of which she was a member, led to her leadership, on August 29, 1914, of the Woman's Peace Parade in New York City.[15] Such popular, direct actions were commonly utilized by this organization and included personal appeals by party leaders to heads of state in Europe and the United States. President Wilson's disinterest in the party's pleas for neutral mediation led the women to urge formation of a mediation commission representing private citizens. Some leaders of the organization also participated in the Henry Ford Peace Ship adventure in December 1915.[16]

The party also sent representatives to the International Congress of Women, meeting at The Hague, April 28 to May 1, 1915, where they

[13]Jane Addams, *Peace and Bread in Time of War* (New York, 1922), pp. 2–10; Marie Louise Degen, *The History of the Woman's Peace Party,* Johns Hopkins University Studies in Historical and Political Science, Ser. 57, No. 3 (Baltimore, 1939), pp. 35–36; George W. Nasmyth, "Constructive Mediation: An Interpretation of the Ten Foremost Proposals," *Survey,* 33 (1915), 616–20; R. L. Duffus, *Lillian Wald: Neighbor and Crusader* (New York, 1938), p. 151. These groups endorsed Senator Robert La Follette's resolution, Feb. 12, 1915, urging a conference of neutrals (*Cong. Rec.,* 63d Cong., 3d sess., pp. 3631–34 [Feb. 12, 1915]).

[14]Platform, adopted at Washington, D.C., Jan. 10, 1915, Woman's Peace Party Collection, SCPC.

[15]Marchand, *American Peace Movement,* pp. 182–83, 189, 193, 197, 204–5; Chatfield, *For Peace and Justice,* pp. 17–18.

[16]Chatfield, *For Peace and Justice,* p. 18; Marchand, *American Peace Movement,* pp. 210–12; Lella Secor Florence, "The Ford Peace Ship and After," in Julian Bell, ed., *We Did Not Fight, 1914–1918: Experiences of War Resisters* (London, 1935), pp. 97–115.

again demonstrated a more radical approach to peace work. They endorsed voiding of secret treaties, including women and other representatives of "the people" at the peace conference, and further democratization of foreign policy.[17] The fullest expression of their commitment to democratization, however, was advocacy of the war referendum plan in the party's own organizing platform and 1915 literature.[18]

Social workers and other progressives, such as those in the Woman's Peace Party, were not alone in their quandary over the use of military force in diplomacy and the degree of popular control needed in foreign affairs. These were issues that would vex them and other Americans for decades. American socialists, for example, when faced with the problem in 1914 through 1916 resolved it in favor of the war referendum plan. Socialists, usually more concerned with domestic ills, had traditionally opposed war and any other use of force in diplomacy, but they were "poorly prepared" for World War I.[19] Endorsement of the war referendum in the 1916 Socialist Party of America platform, however, was a high-water mark in the early history of the peace proposal.

Allan L. Benson, Philadelphia Socialist and journalist, claimed credit for a war referendum proposal as early as August 1914. This placed his advocacy of the idea, along with that of Congressman Bartholdt, before the outbreak of war in Europe. By January 1915 Benson claimed his plan had been endorsed by the Pennsylvania Grange, the Kansas Farmer's Union, and in principle by most American socialists.[20] At the same time, however, several influential members of the American Socialist Party objected to the war referendum idea. It thus became one of the divisive issues in twentieth-century American socialism.

[17]Jane Addams, Emily G. Balch, and Alice Hamilton, *Women at The Hague: The International Congress of Women and Its Results* (New York, 1915), p. 154; Marchand, *American Peace Movement,* pp. 209–10; Chatfield, *For Peace and Justice,* p. 18. Herman, *Eleven against War,* p. 142, points out that the Woman's Peace Party and the Congress of Women drew heavily upon the program of the British Union of Democratic Control, which advocated greater parliamentary control of foreign policy. See also Daniel Levine, *Jane Addams and the Liberal Tradition* (Madison, Wis., 1971), pp. 204–10, and Degen, *Woman's Peace Party,* pp. 64–150, on the party's connection with the Congress of Women and the Ford expedition. Mercedes M. Randall discusses these events and other peace work in *Improper Bostonian: Emily Greene Balch* (New York, 1964), pp. 132–235.

[18]"Eight Alternatives to War," broadside, WPP Collection, SCPC. Marchand correctly notes the party's greater radicalization and commitment to "the search for a new diplomacy," but he fails to note its early (1915) interest in the war referendum plan (*American Peace Movement,* pp. 206, 208–9). Degen, Chatfield, and Herman also do not mention the party's 1915 advocacy of the plan.

[19]David A. Shannon, *The Socialist Party of America* (New York, 1955), p. 81; Marchand, *American Peace Movement,* pp. 274–75.

[20]*A Way to Prevent War* (Girard, Kan., 1915), pp. i–ii, 102–93.

Extant party correspondence, especially that of Carl D. Thompson and Morris Hillquit, revealed a significant concern over the Socialist peace program in 1915, including opposition to "Benson's war referendum." Throughout 1915 and into the following election year, Hillquit and Thompson confessed serious doubts about the war referendum, the latter objecting to what became Benson's single-minded approach to peace through the war referendum. Thompson simply doubted "its effectiveness in preventing war." But Hillquit felt that Benson's plan, "calling for the direct vote of the people for the sanction of offensive wars," was not radical enough. He believed that Socialists ought to oppose "all offensive wars under any circumstances."[21] Such Socialist division, even on opposition to the proposal, was typical until 1917.

Benson's endorsement of the war referendum, unlike that of Bartholdt, was not hedged by other peace measures or by limited support for the use of force in diplomacy. Publicized in 1915 by articles in *Pearson's Magazine,* editorials in his own *Appeal to Reason,* and his book *A Way to Prevent War,* Benson's proposed war referendum amendment to the Constitution was the positive side of his and other socialists' antipreparedness campaign. He also gave the idea an unusual twist, frequently incorporated into later versions of the plan, in that those voting for war would go to the front lines first.[22]

Socialist reactions to the European war thus included an intensive anti-preparedness battle and the war referendum plan, which the Thompson-Hillquit faction regarded as a threat to socialism's program for reform at home. Benson, believing that the party's program was already too broad, wanted something to stand out "in bold relief to seize the public mind." The single plan of a war referendum was his answer. He hoped the world war would at least provide a chance for the "working class" to take over the "capitalists' " war-making and diplomatic machinery. He believed that a war referendum, coupled with disarmament, would make international courts and police forces unnecessary. Benson's faith in the people, once granted the power never again to declare wars, led him to inform the

[21]Carl D. Thompson to Morris Hillquit, Jan. 13, 21, 1915, Hillquit to Thompson, Jan. 18, 20, 1915, National Office Files, Socialist Party of America Papers, Duke University Library, Durham, N.C. Shannon, *Socialist Party of America,* pp. 90–92, treats Socialist interest in this plan briefly; Marchand, *American Peace Movement,* pp. 290–91, notes the war referendum but does not consider it a distinguishable proposal in relation to peace plans offered by activist peace organizations.

[22]Benson, "Shall We Vote on War?" *Pearson's Magazine,* 33 (1915), 466–74; idem, *Way to Prevent War,* and *New York Times,* Nov. 13, 17, 19, 1915, for Benson's antipreparedness activities.

national party office that a proposal for a war referendum would be the only foreign affairs plank for which he would work the next year.[23]

When nominated in 1916 for the presidency, Benson lived up to his promise to emphasize this peace plan. The Socialist platform on which he campaigned included a war referendum plank, and his candidacy featured circulation of his 1915 war referendum book, *A Way to Prevent War*.[24] Greater interest in antipreparedness, to which issue Benson contributed *Inviting War to America*, division in Socialist leadership, and the continuing popular appeal of Woodrow Wilson, however, produced a poor response from the American voters. Socialist party rolls had decreased by some thirty-five thousand names since 1912, and Benson's 590,000 votes were a decline of one-third from Eugene Debs's record 1912 vote.[25] Benson had obviously failed to seize the initiative on the war issue. On the limited national appeal of the war referendum plan in 1916, a radical pacifist later stated that the Socialist proposal was "too mildly liberal to serve as a rallying point for pacifism and too radical to attract supporters from Woodrow Wilson."[26] Yet Benson's record in 1916 revealed remarkable potential for his key platform plank—the war referendum plan.

Some social progressives, as individuals and in the organized peace movement, meanwhile, had also moved closer toward complete endorsement of the war referendum plan. In a March 1915 article in the *Survey,* the chief organ of social workers, reorganization of the American League to Limit Armament began. Among those signing this appeal for a stronger, more effective antipreparedness campaign were progressives and social workers Jane Addams, Lillian Wald, Paul U. Kellogg, and Frederic C. Howe. Others included Professors Emily Greene Balch (Wellesley) and William I. Hull (Swarthmore), George W. Nasmyth of the World Peace Foundation, and the reverend John Haynes Holmes and Rabbi Stephen S. Wise.[27] Most of these, earlier members of the loosely organized Henry Street Peace Committee, were at the time in the New York–based League to Limit Armament, which lacked funds and as yet had been unable to attract a dynamic president.[28]

[23]Benson to Carl D. Thompson, Jan. 19, 1915, Socialist Party of America Papers.

[24]"Socialist Party Platform Adopted by Party Referendum Closing September 16, 1916," *Socialist Handbook, Campaign 1916,* p. 607, Socialist Party of America Papers; Shannon, *Socialist Party of America,* p. 91.

[25]Shannon, *Socialist Party of America,* pp. 91–92.

[26]Jessie Wallace Hughan, *Three Decades of War Resistance* (New York, 1942), p. 10.

[27]"Towards the Peace That Shall Last," *Survey,* 33, pt. 2 (1915), n. pag., copy in American Union Against Militarism Records (microfilm), SCPC.

[28]Marchand, *American Peace Movement,* pp. 223, 225, 240.

In November these and other liberals organized an Anti-Preparedness Committee in the offices of *Evening Post* editor Oswald Garrison Villard, another member of the pioneer League to Limit Armament. Indicative of the still unsettled character of America's recent organized peace efforts was the appearance of Hamilton Holt in this group.[29] These reorganized antimilitarists soon instituted another, but this time permanent, name change and became the American Union Against Militarism.[30] It was destined to become the leading preintervention peace organization and a prominent supporter of the war referendum. But already it contrasted substantially with Hamilton Holt's own League to Enforce Peace and especially with the prewar "establishment" peace groups.

The greater radicalism of this group was typified by the association of Louis Lochner in it. Lochner was earlier secretary of the Chicago Peace Society, a branch of the older American Peace Society. In 1915 he was forced out because he was a peace activist. By that time he had joined with Jane Addams to organize the Chicago Emergency Federation of Peace Forces, promoted the Woman's Peace Party, and especially supported the plan of an unofficial neutral conference to mediate the European war. This last interest later drew him wholeheartedly into a leadership role in the Ford Peace Ship adventure.[31] Other early members of the American Union Against Militarism included George W. Kirchwey, international lawyer and Dean of Columbia Law School; Max Eastman, Socialist editor of the *Masses;* his sister Crystal Eastman, a young and attractive social worker; and Allan Benson, already the leading Socialist spokesman for the war referendum.[32] Of these, Kirchwey would also eventually choose the more radical, activist side of the peace movement, along with the war referendum plan, and thereby reject the American Peace Society, of which he was president from late 1916 to early 1917.

The widespread impression that Henry Ford financed the Union was denied by its leaders, who maintained that contributions came primarily from members and Quakers. Miss Wald was the Union's first chairwoman, Villard the treasurer, and Charles T. Hallinan its Washington

[29]Minutes, Organization Meeting, Nov. 29, 1915, Minutes, Jan. 3, 1916, AUAM Records, SCPC.

[30]Marchand, *American Peace Movement,* pp. 223–28, 238–43, emphasizes its "muckraking" approach and domination by social workers, journalists, and reformers. See also Chatfield, *For Peace and Justice,* pp. 22–25.

[31]Chatfield, *For Peace and Justice,* p. 16, and Marchand, *American Peace Movement,* p. 148.

[32]"History," typed statement of the American Union Against Militarism, n.d., AUAM Records, SCPC.

publicity director. The relationship between wartime liberal pacifism and the women's rights movement was again apparent from Hallinan's former association with the Woman Suffrage Party. The extent to which organized pacifism was drawing support from Wilsonian progressivism was also clear from the large number of Wilson supporters in this group. In addition to those mentioned, individuals like Ben Lindsey, Ray Stannard Baker, Judge Walter Clark, Arthur Capper, Jeannette Rankin, and Walter Rauschenbusch were looked to for support in the growing antipreparedness campaign conducted by this organization.[33]

In 1916 American Socialist candidates for the presidency and vice presidency assisted the American Union Against Militarism in the antipreparedness fight. Allan Benson and George R. Kirkpatrick were members of the Union, and Benson's *Common Sense about the Navy,* a reprint from *Pearson's Magazine,* was among the organization's publications.[34] The American Union Against Militarism carried out a "Truth about Preparedness" campaign in 1916, sponsoring antipreparedness rallies in New York, Cleveland, Buffalo, Detroit, Chicago, Minneapolis, Des Moines, Kansas City, Saint Louis, Cincinnati, and Pittsburgh. Just as Wilson toured the Midwest on behalf of his defense program early in 1916, Union speakers like Amos Pinchot toured the country to stress the dangers of increased militarism. In six addresses he urged Americans to make their first attack upon domestic problems like poverty, social injustice, and unemployment, achieving thereby what he called "real preparedness," or economic democracy at home. Pinchot and others in the tour opposed "child conscription" and tried to counter any idea that America was near invasion by urging the "impregnability" of coastal defenses. Of course, their opposition centered upon bills before Congress which called for an increased regular army and advances in naval construction.[35]

The press and publicity work of the Union's Washington office also reflected the intensified antipreparedness campaign of 1916. Secretary Hallinan and the office staff prepared a mailing list from existing lists furnished by cooperating peace societies, the Farmers' Grange, labor unions, women's clubs, Quaker meetings, college faculties, and organizations like the Intercollegiate Socialist Society, the American Bar Associa-

[33]Ibid., and "Suggestions for 'General Committee' or 'Advisory Council.' " AUAM Records, SCPC.

[34]Minutes, Jan. 3, 1916, "History," and copy of Benson's anti–big navy article, AUAM Records, SCPC. Charles Chatfield notes that Kirkpatrick's *War—What For?* sold about 150,000 copies between its 1910 publication and its suppression in 1917. His *Think or Surrender* (New York, 1916) sold perhaps 100,000 copies ("World War I and the Liberal Pacifist in the United States," *American Historical Review,* 75 [1970], 1931).

[35]Press Releases, 1916, AUAM Records, SCPC.

tion, the American Library Association, and the National Educational Association. They also used the mailing lists of liberal journals, including Bryan's *Commoner,* the *Public, La Follette's Magazine,* and the most important liberal pacifist organ, the *Survey.* Louis Post, former publisher of the *Public* and at the time Wilson's assistant secretary of labor, and Paul Kellogg of the *Survey* were in the ranks of this organization.[36]

Crystal Eastman reported late in May 1916 that the Anti-Preparedness Committee spent about seventeen thousand dollars in six months on the antipreparedness tour and on operation of the Washington press bureau, which served 1,600 newspapers. The mailing list of 50,000 names of probable supporters resulted in growth of the organization from a committee of 15 in late 1915 to a membership of 6,000, with local committees in twenty-two cities. Miss Eastman maintained that the Committee operated *"the only active nation-wide press service available for the forces fighting militarism,"* distributing over six hundred thousand pieces of literature.[37]

Although the antipreparedness issue brought Socialists into the American Union Against Militarism and caused individual members privately to favor the war referendum plan, the organization itself did not endorse Socialist Benson's 1916 emphasis upon the proposal. In keeping with its general support of popular control in foreign affairs, however, this peace group did favor Pennsylvania Congressman Warren Worth Bailey's suggestion of a popular vote on the administration's attempts to increase the naval establishment and to raise a citizen army of 400,000. In his speech to Congress January 20, 1916, which was reprinted by the Union Against Militarism, Bailey also proposed a popular vote on plans to increase the regular standing army from 108,000 to 141,843 men. In effect, Bailey and the Union wanted a referendum on preparedness.[38]

Reflecting the continuing debate on this issue and the ferment within the American peace movement, another new organization emerged in June 1916. The American Neutral Conference Committee, formed by George W. Kirchwey, Hamilton Holt, Jane Addams, and Rebecca Shelly, was an attempt to unite diverse peace forces around the neutral

---

[36] Minutes, Anti-Preparedness Committee, Jan. 17, 1916, ibid.

[37] Crystal Eastman to James P. Warbasse (of the Executive Committee), May 27, 1916, ibid. (emphasis is hers).

[38] Other congressmen whose antipreparedness views were circulated by the Union in 1916 included Claude Kitchin (Democrat, N.C.), Finly H. Gray (Democrat, Ind.), Frank W. Mondell (Republican, Wyo.), Clyde H. Tavenner (Democrat, Ill.), Martin Dies (Democrat, Texas), and General Isaac R. Sherwood (Democrat, Ohio). Tavenner, Sherwood, and Dies frequently spoke at Union rallies. See *Seven Congressmen on Preparedness* (American Union Against Militarism, 1916), especially p. 11, ibid.

conference plan. In keeping with the more radical, activist trends in the peace movement, this group pressured the Wilson administration and circulated petitions on the neutral conference proposal, on the suggestion that citizens not travel in belligerents' danger zones, and on the war referendum peace plan. It was this last objective of the American Neutral Conference Committee that distinguished it, at this time, from the American Union Against Militarism.[39]

The appearance of Kirchwey and Holt in the Neutral Conference Committee illustrates further the rising tensions among liberals in wartime. Both men were still attempting to identify with progressive sentiment and to select the most practical peace plan. Since 1905 Dean Kirchwey had been dissatisfied with the lack of activism in the American Peace Society, the New York Peace Society, and other organizations, like the Mohonk conferences. He had been a founder of the more "practical" American Society of International Law (1906) and later was a member of the Henry Street peace group (1914), the still more radical, activist organization from which the Neutral Conference Committee eventually emerged.[40] Hamilton Holt's participation in the Neutral Conference Committee, however, was even more typical of the liberal's wartime dilemma. He was then a leading spokesman for the collective security element in the peace movement, especially as presented by the League to Enforce Peace. He, too, had moved into prominence in that more "practical" organization from the role of cofounder of the New York Peace Society (1906). By March 1915 Holt was president of the reorganized Emergency Federation of Peace Forces, he encouraged the Woman's Peace Party, and he endorsed the neutral conference scheme.[41] But his interest in these and other more activist peace groups, including his work with the Neutral Conference Committee in the summer of 1916, had ended by the time the League to Enforce Peace required his withdrawal from such organizations late in 1916.[42]

[39]Copy of Resolution-Petition, n.d., letterheads, n.d., American Neutral Conference Committee Papers, SCPC. Lella Secor was another founder of this committee. See Lella Secor Florence, "The Ford Peace Ship and After," p. 116. According to Oswald Garrison Villard, his mother was active in this group and joined two peace delegations in presenting the neutral conference plan to Wilson Aug. 30, 1916, and Dec. 9, 1916 (*Fighting Years,* p. 319).

[40]Marchand, *American Peace Movement,* pp. 39–41, 86, 169, 181, 225, 280.

[41]Kuehl, *Holt,* pp. 108–9.

[42]Marchand, *American Peace Movement,* p. 181. Marchand lists others who briefly maintained "at least tenuous relations with both the old peace organizations and those on the cutting edge of the transformed peace movement" (page 180). He mentions the American Neutral Conference Committee but does not deal with its origins or support of the war referendum plan.

Actually Holt left the more activist Neutral Conference camp partly because of its increasing emphasis upon the war referendum measure, which contrasted clearly with the idea of collective security favored by the League to Enforce Peace.[43] Whatever the judgment of later historians, many Americans in 1914–16 regarded the League to Enforce Peace as nonactivist and akin to the more affluent and prestigious peace groups. Among the most divisive issues facing progressives was the debate over the use of force and additional popular control in diplomacy. This went to the core of their faith largely because they were still working for direct legislation and increased popular controls in domestic politics when the war broke out. They were committed to peace in order to preserve social progress at home. Gradually their commitment to social progress brought them to more radical peace plans, and the war referendum idea, endorsed increasingly by only the most dynamic peace activists, came to distinguish them more than anything else from the Holt-led collective security element.

Despite disappointments and continuous friction in the peace movement itself, peace work in 1915 and 1916 was not unrewarded. Certainly efforts of the more radical, activist individuals and groups on behalf of antipreparedness, neutral mediation, peace by arbitration, and the war referendum plan received increased attention in Congress and the White House. On occasion the peace worker also reflected the thinking of leading legislators, such as the American Neutral Conference Committee's endorsement of Senator Robert La Follette's 1915 resolution for mediation by a conference of neutrals.[44] An important reward for peace work, therefore, came to be the increased coordination between the peace movement and liberals in Congress. Such collaboration of effort is most clearly indicated by the numerous war referendum resolutions introduced in Congress during the period of American neutrality.

Allan Benson claimed in *A Way to Prevent War* that he had referred his peace plan in 1914 to Senator Robert L. Owen, Oklahoma Democrat.[45] Whether true or not, and it was never confirmed by the progressive senator, Owen did become the second congressman in the

---

[43] Neutral Conference Committee Secretary Shelly (she later spelled it Shelley) explained in a letter to members that Holt's resignation as chairman involved no unpleasantness. Philanthropist George F. Peabody replaced him as Miss Shelly and others began to emphasize the war referendum (Rebecca Shelly to members, form letter, Dec. 30, 1916, American Neutral Conference Committee Papers, SCPC). See also Kuehl, *Holt,* pp. 109–11.

[44] A copy of La Follette's resolution, endorsed by the Committee, is in American Neutral Conference Committee Papers, SCPC.

[45] *Way to Prevent War,* p. 102. His claim that Owen's resolution was presented Dec. 29, 1914, is in error.

twentieth century to introduce a war referendum resolution in Congress. In fact, he introduced two proposed amendments to the Constitution, both in 1915.

Owen's resolution of January 15, 1915, became the model text for several later war referendum resolutions. Unlike Benson's plan, as outlined in detail in *A Way to Prevent War*, Senator Owen's proposed constitutional amendment did not suggest the signing of ballots and the sending of pro-war voters to the front lines first. Neither would he have taken the war-declaring power from Congress, as did Benson's plan. The Owen resolutions of January and December 1915 proposed that "no war of aggression shall be waged by the Army or Navy of the United States, except upon a declaration of war by the Congress of the United States, ratified and approved by a majority of the legal votes cast upon the question in a majority of the Congressional districts of the United States."[46] Like Richard Bartholdt's resolution of July 1914, the Owen proposals died without consideration in the Judiciary Committee.

Owen was a blood relation of the Cherokees and, along with Thomas P. Gore, was a pioneer Oklahoma senator after statehood in 1907. Foreign affairs had never been his major interest. Thus it was his liberal attitudes on popular controls that drew him to the war referendum plan. Since 1910 Owen had sought peace through a personal campaign against a large navy. In 1913 he helped establish the National Popular Government League, an organization to further popular control of government, and was in the forefront of the progressive movement. A domestic analogue to Owen's war referendum interest was suggested in his speech entitled "People's Rule vs. Boss Rule." In his domestic progressivism, Owen supported the initiative, recall, and referendum. It was only a short step from this to his support of peace through arbitration and referendum. A frequent correspondent with William Jennings Bryan, another war referendum spokesman by 1915, Owen believed the republic "was not founded on any so-called 'representative' principle" but on the idea that "the people were sovereign."[47]

[46]Text of resolution from original in File on Senate Joint Resolution 227, 63d Cong., 1913–15, RG 233, NA; later edited as Senate Joint Resolution 10, 64th Cong. The bills were introduced Jan. 15 and Dec. 7, 1915.

[47]On Owen's domestic progressivism and general support of Wilson, see Wyatt W. Belcher, "Political Leadership of Robert L. Owen," *Chronicles of Oklahoma,* 31 (1953–54), 361–71; Edward Elmer Keso, *The Senatorial Career of Robert Latham Owen* (Nashville, n.d.), pp. 7, 149–50; and Owen's *Three Years of Democracy: Shall We Have Peace or War?* (Washington, D.C. 1916). That the war referendum was ever in the program of the National Popular Government League, of which Owen was president and Judson King secretary, is not revealed in the Judson King Papers, Manuscript Division, Library of Congress.

William Jennings Bryan, who first discovered the war referendum in mid-1915, was slow to adopt it despite his typically progressive devotion to direct democracy, his earlier anti-imperialism, and his faith in the people. In response to the war in Europe and to prevent American involvement, he originally urged mediation upon President Wilson. This he continued without success into the spring of 1915.[48] Then Bryan's attention was called in June 1915, about a week after his resignation as secretary of state, to the possibility of a war referendum. This suggestion, the first known notice Bryan had of this peace plan after war began, came from some Oklahoma citizens who believed it would illustrate popular opposition to a declaration of war at that time.[49]

In its requirement for delay and a "reasoned" consideration of any war declaration, the war referendum device was not unlike Bryan's earlier and more familiar cooling-off treaties. It was also somewhat similar to the peace plan that he developed in 1910. In a May address before the Lake Mohonk Conference, he discussed the forces that were then at work to produce peace. "The best force," he argued, was "the world's intellectual progress." As the world became more intelligent, he believed "brain methods" would be substituted for "physical force methods" in the settlement of international disputes.[50] At the Edinburgh World Missionary Conference in June he proposed that representatives of Great Britain, Germany, Japan, and the United States endorse treaties to postpone declarations of war until disputes were "submitted to an impartial international tribunal for investigation and report."[51] But this line of thinking took form primarily in the cooling-off treaties while Bryan was secretary of state.

As Bryan determined after his resignation to carry his peace crusade directly to the people, he indicated more and more interest in applying direct democracy to foreign affairs. In a packed Carnegie Hall peace meeting, just days after receiving the Oklahoma petition for a war

[48]Typical are Bryan to Wilson, Sept. 19, 1914, Apr. 23, 1915, and Wilson to Bryan, Apr. 28, 1915, in William Jennings Bryan Papers, General Correspondence Files, LC.

[49]George W. Cornell to Bryan, June 14, 1915, Bryan Papers. Enclosed was a petition, signed by Oklahoma citizens, in favor of a war referendum. Willard H. Smith cites this letter but fails to note the suggestion of a war referendum ("The Pacifist Thought of William Jennings Bryan," *Mennonite Quarterly Review,* 45 [1971], 66).

[50]Bryan, "The Forces That Make for Peace," *Report of the Sixteenth Annual Meeting of the Lake Mohonk Conference on International Arbitration, May 18th, 19th, and 20th, 1910* (Lake Mohonk, N.Y., 1910), p. 165.

[51]Bryan, "The World Missionary Movement," *Outlook,* 95 (1910), 825. Paolo E. Coletta erroneously equates Bryan's 1910 peace plan with advocacy of the war referendum at that time (*William Jennings Bryan,* Vol. II, *Progressive Politician and Moral Statesman, 1909–1915* [Lincoln, Neb., 1969], pp. 3–4). This 1910 plan, rather, contributed to the intellectual framework which brought Bryan to the war referendum plan in mid-1915.

referendum, Bryan expressed the belief that the American people were not willing to transfer the war-declaring power from Congress. Arguing on the basis of "labor's interest in peace," he opposed transfer of that power to a group of European nations through any such peacekeeping organization as advocated by the recently formed League to Enforce Peace.[52] In his mind the differences between that approach to peace and the approach represented by the war referendum plan were clear, and shortly he would become the best-known and most popular advocate of the plan during World War I.

As talk of preparedness increased, Bryan and other progressives identified advocacy of force in diplomacy with the special interests they had fought so long on domestic issues. During the summer, in speeches across the country, Bryan spoke for "the people" as against the "interests," particularly munitions makers. Finally, in August 1915, he openly proposed in the *Commoner* that war, except in case of invasion, be declared only after a national referendum.[53] His anti-imperialism and his attitudes toward preparedness and popular control had brought him to a proposal he would consistently advocate until his death in 1925.

By October Bryan had decided against a personal trip to Europe in the interest of an early peace, a suggestion made earlier by Richard Bartholdt and German-Americans. When another opportunity for such a trip came, Bryan elected not to join the Ford Peace Ship expedition and the neutral conference venture, remaining in America to conduct his anti-preparedness and war referendum campaign.[54] In an address in Grace

[52]"Two Addresses delivered by William Jennings Bryan at Peace Meetings held in New York, June 19 and 24, 1915," especially "Labor's Interest in Peace," June 19, 1915, pp. 6–7, Speech, Article, and Report File, Bryan Papers. Bryan made this first address following his resignation at the request of Congressman Frank Buchanan (Democrat, Ill.), who was himself an advocate of the war referendum plan in 1917. See also William Jennings Bryan and Mary Baird Bryan, *The Memoirs of William Jennings Bryan* (Philadelphia, 1925), pp. 426–27; Coletta, *William Jennings Bryan*, Vol. III, *Political Puritan, 1915–1925* (Lincoln, Neb., 1969), pp. 3–5; and Curti, *Bryan and World Peace*, p. 223.

[53]*Commoner*, Aug. 1915; see also the issues of Oct. 1915 and Jan. 1916. About this time Secretary of the Navy Josephus Daniels confessed his own concern over the conflict between progressivism and preparedness. "There is no danger of militarism from a relatively strong Navy," he believed, but he feared a "big standing army" might indeed have disastrous effects on America (Daniels to Bryan, Aug. 18, 1915, Bryan Papers). See also Lawrence W. Levine, *Defender of the Faith: William Jennings Bryan, The Last Decade, 1915–1925* (New York, 1965), pp. 50–51, 55; Coletta, *Bryan*, III, 8; Smith, "Pacifist Thought of William Jennings Bryan," p. 70.

[54]Richard Bartholdt to Bryan, Oct. 9, 1915, Bryan Papers. Addams, *Peace and Bread in Time of War*, pp. 26–44, discusses the ill-fated expedition led by Henry Ford, as do Coletta, *Bryan*, III, 23–25, Levine, *Bryan*, pp. 37–39, and Marchand, *American Peace Movement*, pp. 210–11. For more detailed treatment see Peter G. Tuttle, "The Ford Peace Ship: Volunteer Diplomacy in the Twentieth Century," Diss. Yale 1958.

Methodist Church, New York City, on October 17, almost as if Bartholdt or Senator Owen had written the text, he dwelt on the war referendum plan more than ever before. This was Bryan's first public endorsement of the proposal in the East, and he took the opportunity to stress the war referendum's relevance to antipreparedness views. Beginning an appeal that was always important to the war referendum movement, especially in the 1920s and 1930s, Bryan also expressed hope that women could be granted the right to vote and that they would vote for peace if the war referendum idea was accepted.[55]

Bryan's peace plan got a cool reception in the press. The *New York Times* declared: "Mr. Bryan's mind is the Happy Valley, the Fortunate Isles. . . . It is a wonderful possession, unique among the treasures of the world."[56] But the former presidential candidate and secretary of state was not easily turned from policies or principles in which he believed. Especially was this true on this issue, for in addition to his antipreparedness viewpoint, the war referendum plan was too much akin to his concept of democracy and too clearly expressed his faith in the slow-turning of diplomatic wheels. For Bryan peace by referendum had much in common with peace by cooling-off treaties and arbitration.

In 1916, with the preparedness controversy more heated and the growing radicalization of the peace movement more evident, cooperation among Bryan, liberal congressmen, and peace workers on the war referendum increased. This was due also to the continuing disagreement among progressives over the relation between the war and future American domestic reform. A typical example was the split in 1916 between Senator La Follette and President Wilson. La Follette and his supporters in the peace movement had failed to win over the president to the idea of neutral mediation in 1915, and the Wisconsin progressive Republican the next year withdrew from the Wilson coalition, following Jane Addams and others, largely because of Wilson's gradual acceptance of preparedness. This difference, therefore, was partly the basis for his introduction of a resolution on April 29, 1916, proposing an *advisory* war referendum upon any break in diplomatic relations with a European country.[57]

The immediate background for La Follette's war referendum resolution was the *Sussex* crisis of 1916. By April 19, when Wilson informed ranking Republican members of the Senate and House foreign affairs

[55] *New York Times,* Oct. 18, 1915. Curti, *Bryan and World Peace,* p. 226, erred in maintaining this was his earliest public support of the plan.

[56] *New York Times,* Oct. 19, 1915.

[57] *Cong. Rec.,* 64th Cong., 1st sess., p. 7018 (Apr. 29, 1916).

committees and then addressed the Congress concerning his April 18 note to Germany, threatening to break relations, La Follette was clearly ready to oppose the president in some way. According to Secretary of the Interior Franklin K. Lane, 80 percent of the American people wanted peace at any price, but the general American reaction, in and out of Congress, was to support the administration in what most agreed was a grave international crisis.[58]

Within ten days, however, La Follette had introduced his bill. The war referendum represented for him another application of that "Jeffersonian principle of the intelligent electorate" that he considered a firm foundation of democracy.[59] His bill provided, in the event of a break in diplomatic relations, an advisory referendum on the question of war. Unlike other such bills offered in Congress or proposed by private individuals outside, La Follette's resolution was unusually detailed in its provision of machinery for taking the referendum. An advisory vote would proceed only after one percent of the qualified electors of twenty-five states petitioned the Bureau of the Census for such a vote. This agency then would conduct the referendum by mail and report the results to Congress.[60]

The La Follette war referendum bill was referred, due to its title and the sponsor's request, to the Committee on the Census, of which La Follette was a member. On May 3 and again on the fifth, Senator William Stone of Missouri attempted to discharge the Census Committee from consideration of the bill and have it referred to the Committee on Foreign Relations. This effort led to a brief debate in the Senate, both on Stone's discharge motion and, indirectly, on the merits of the war referendum proposal.

Senator Stone urged transfer of the bill to the Foreign Relations Committee since it represented "a question of policy which . . . intimately and directly concerns the most vital interests of this Government in dealing with foreign affairs." Senator Moses E. Clapp of Minnesota, however, urged defeat of the Stone motion, dwelling on the merits of the war referendum plan itself. He pointed out, as did many war referendum advocates, that the president as commander in chief could force the country so far toward war as to make it impossible for Congress to back down without showing the enemy a divided sentiment in the nation. Nevertheless, he would not advocate any measure which might embarrass the pres-

[58] Arthur Link, *Wilson, Vol. IV, Confusions and Crises, 1915–1916* (Princeton, 1964), pp. 222–55.

[59] Edward N. Doan, *The La Follettes and the Wisconsin Idea* (New York, 1947), pp. 80–81, 98; Belle Case La Follette and Fola La Follette, *Robert M. La Follette* (New York, 1953), I, 565–66.

[60] *Cong. Rec.,* 64th Cong., 1st sess., p. 7452 (May 5, 1916).

ident in fulfilling his responsibilities for conduct of America's foreign affairs.[61]

Under La Follette's proposal for an advisory public referendum, responsibility in deciding for war would lie not solely with Congress but with Congress *and* the people. La Follette's viewpoint was a result of pressures by organized pacifism, his German-American constituency, and his genuine belief that a great majority of Americans at that time opposed American entry into the European war. Senator Clapp repeated the contention, then current, that a group of twelve men in Europe could determine war or peace. Like many later war referendum advocates, he believed that peace could come only when that "Broad equation of humanity," including "the womanhood of the nations who must bear their share of the burden and the sacrifice of war," had the power to make that decision.[62]

During this first congressional debate on the war referendum plan, another later supporter of the proposal spoke on the La Follette bill. Senator William E. Borah of Idaho asked whether the results of the plebiscite could be regarded an accurate expression of public opinion, a question he would propose many times in the history of the war referendum idea. Clapp explained again the machinery to be used to obtain the vote and assured Borah that the Senate could indeed rely on the results. But the Senate took no further action on either the Stone transfer motion or La Follette's war referendum bill. Like most later congressional resolutions, it died in committee.[63] La Follette's insistence upon the war referendum plan, both as a democratic reform and as an emergency peace measure, nevertheless, did not end with this effort.

The Hearst papers joined him and urged editorially that only the people should decide on war declarations. La Follette predicted in the next issue of his magazine that the day was coming "when the people, who always pay the full price, are going to have the *final say* over their own destinies. . . . They who do the fighting will do the deciding."[64] To these continuing appeals for the peace plan was added in May 1916 endorsement of his resolution by the Woman's Peace Party.[65]

A new pacifist body in New York and Lansdowne, Pennsylvania, the Collegiate Antimilitarism Committee, also endorsed it. These students

[61] Ibid.

[62] Ibid., p. 7453.

[63] Ibid., pp. 7453–56.

[64] Robert M. La Follette, "Consult the People!" *La Follette's Magazine,* 8, No. 5 (1916), 1 (emphasis La Follette's).

[65] Copy of his resolution, Legislative Committee File, and Minutes, with note "Endorsed, May 11, 1916," WPP Collection, SCPC.

discovered in a straw vote at Columbia University, conducted while the La Follette bill was pending, that 64 percent of those polled favored an advisory war referendum. A similar pacifist body, the Harvard Union for American Neutrality, urged in its platform about this time that "Democracy demands a general referendum before a declaration of war."[66] This test referendum of student opinion was an interesting precedent for similar emergency polls of public opinion in 1917 as well as for Gallup polls on war referendum sentiment in the 1930s.

La Follette continued to urge the war referendum in response to evidence of popular support by liberal pacifists and his German-American constituency. At the Chicago convention he led unsuccessful efforts by Wisconsin Republicans to get the war referendum into the 1916 party platform.[67] But neither major political party followed the 1916 Socialist example by including it in its platform.

Meanwhile, William Jennings Bryan remained active for the proposal. Most of his energies since late 1915 had gone into the antipreparedness battle. He became during that time the unofficial hero of some thirty to fifty antipreparedness congressmen, many of whom represented districts in former Bryan country, in the rural South, Midwest, and West. Led in Congress by Democrats Claude Kitchin (N.C.) and Warren Worth Bailey (Pa.), this group fought every major piece of preparedness legislation. But as in the case of the Gore-McLemore Resolutions, which sought restrictions on American travel and trade in contraband, Bryan was the recognized leader of what appeared to be a congressional revolt against Wilson. He frequently conferred with ex-Populist Senator Thomas P. Gore (Democrat, Okla.), and Congressman Bailey became Bryan's chief spokesman in the House.[68] As a significant feature of this activity, Bryan

[66]Collegiate Antimilitarism Committee Files, SCPC. This figure was based on 456 replies.
[67]Doan, *La Follettes,* pp. 80–81. For the plan in the Progressive platform, see "The 'La Follette Platform,'" *La Follette's Magazine,* 8, No. 6 (1916), 4.
[68]See, for example, Kitchin to Bryan, Sept. 10, 1915, Bryan Papers; Bailey to Samuel A. Witherspoon, Oct. 15, 1915, Box 5, Warren Worth Bailey Papers, Princeton University Library. For comments on the Bryan-led congressional bloc, see Levine, *Bryan,* pp. 39, 42–47, 56–60; Link, *Wilson,* IV, 27–30; Coletta, *Bryan,* III, 25–33; and John Milton Cooper, Jr., *The Vanity of Power: American Isolationism and the First World War, 1914–1917* (Westport, Conn., 1969), pp. 88–93. Monroe P. Billington briefly notes Gore's support of Bryan in 1900, their conferences before the controversy over travel on ships of belligerents, and Gore's Aug. 1917 support of the war referendum plan ("Senator Thomas P. Gore: Southern Isolationist," *Southwestern Social Science Quarterly,* 42 [1962], 381–89, and *Thomas P. Gore: The Blind Senator from Oklahoma* [Lawrence, Kan., 1967], pp. 70, 87). For Senator Vardaman's antipreparedness views see William F. Holmes, *The White Chief: James Kimble Vardaman* (Baton Rouge, La., 1970), pp. 306–9.

began to stress the war referendum plan as never before, making it increasingly popular among certain progressive congressmen.

In the February issue of the *Commoner* he defended Senator Owen's December 1915 war referendum bill in convincing fashion. "Let the people rule," he said. "Nowhere is their rule more needed than in deciding upon war policies—nowhere would their influence be more salutary."[69] In a speech in Columbus, Ohio, in March, Bryan offered the war referendum plan again, approving even the proposal that those voting in favor of war be the first to go to the war front. He added the novel idea that those voting "No" in any future referendum constitute a reserve army. Like many liberal pacifists who supported the war referendum plan, he too wanted women to vote on peace or war.[70]

In an address before the Lake Mohonk Conference on International Arbitration, May 18, 1916, the former secretary of state proposed, once more, a war referendum amendment to the Constitution. Entitled "Present Peace Problems and the Preparedness Program," this address was indicative of Bryan's general antipreparedness views and his specific objections to the League to Enforce Peace. He rejected the League as an improper road to peace since it would entangle America with Europe through alliances. He believed it would invite foreign nations to assist the United States in maintaining peace in the Western Hemisphere. But, more important, it would be a "step down" from a policy based on moral suasion to one based on force. The League, according to Bryan, also violated the Constitution in transferring the war-declaring powers from Congress to foreign nations. "If we are to change the Constitution from what it is now I am in favor of putting the declaring of war in the hands of the people, to be decided by a referendum vote of the American people," he insisted.[71] In an interview and report of a Florida speech that followed this address, Bryan confessed: "I so believe in the right of the people to have what they want that I admit the right of the people to go to war if they really want it. There should be a referendum vote about it, however, and those who voted for war should enlist first, together with the jingo newspaper editors."[72]

[69]*Commoner*, Feb. 1916. Levine, *Bryan*, p. 56, erred in dating Owen's resolution "early in 1916." See *Cong. Rec.*, 64th Cong., 1st sess., p. 91 (Dec. 7, 1915). Coletta notes the 1916 La Follette bill but not Bryan's 1916 support of Owen's war referendum bill (*Bryan*, III, 31).

[70]*Ohio State Journal*, Mar. 6, 1916.

[71]*Report of the Twenty-Second Annual Lake Mohonk Conference on International Arbitration, 1916* (Mohonk Lake, N.Y., 1916), pp. 144–46, especially p. 146.

[72]John Reed, "Bryan on Tour," *Collier's*, May 20, 1916, p. 12. Socialist Reed typified many progressives when he later voted for Wilson, according to Cooper (*Vanity of Power*, p. 123).

Although an opponent of Wilson on preparedness and not a delegate to the Democratic convention in 1916, Bryan attended as a reporter, supported Wilson for a second term, and carried the "dove of peace" to Washington after the convention.[73] On the day following Martin H. Glynn's speech, which produced the slogan "He Kept Us Out of War," during which Bryan wept with emotion, the convention demanded that Bryan continue this peace oratory. He lived up to his reputation and the best hopes of Democratic party leaders when he praised Wilson for maintaining peace. This support, according to Ray Stannard Baker, "reassured the unity of the party," and later Wilson himself thanked Bryan for this and subsequent support during the campaign.[74]

After the election, Bryan, however, continued to press President Wilson to ask the belligerents why they were fighting. By December 3, 1916, Wilson also knew that Bryan wanted to go to Europe on behalf of peace and instructed Ambassador James W. Gerard, to whom Bryan had appealed for assistance, to "show him every courtesy" but to understand that Bryan "represented nobody but himself."[75] Such differences and Bryan's increased association with certain congressmen did not produce a rupture with the president. The Bryans, in fact, had lunch at the White House the day following the opening of Congress.

When the new session began December 5, Bryan had decided not to go to Europe and was in Washington. He was received enthusiastically on the floor of the House, where he urged members to support the war referendum plans then before the Congress and to defeat a Senate measure on compulsory military service.[76] It is conceivable, therefore, that Bryan talked with Wilson about the war referendum plan the next day. That evening, in a dinner honoring the former secretary of state, the president was not among the several hundred friends of Bryan in attendance. At that occasion Bryan delivered a sermon on peace entitled "Democracy's Deeds and Duty," in which he offered several proposals indicating his disappointment over the Democratic platform. "The war

[73]Coletta states that Bryan controlled "two or three million votes" (*Bryan*, III, 37). Bryan had been defeated as a delegate on the Prohibition issue.

[74]Ray Stannard Baker, *Woodrow Wilson: Life and Letters*, Vol. VI, *Facing War, 1915–1917* (Garden City, N.Y., 1937), pp. 252, 254.

[75]Ibid., p. 390. Baker states that Wilson, who had continued to watch and listen to Bryan after his resignation, pushed toward his own peace proposal of Dec. 18, 1916, because of Bryan's plans (ibid., p. 391).

[76]Levine, *Bryan*, p. 84, citing the *Washington Post*, Dec. 6, 1916, clipping in Bryan Papers; Coletta, *Bryan*, III, 43, citing (in error) Baker, *Wilson*, VI, 389–91. Bryan, *Memoirs*, pp. 444, 446, does not comment on his attendance at the opening of Congress, nor does *Cong. Rec.*, 64th Cong., 2d sess. (Dec. 5, 1916).

across the sea" had called for one additional plank, he thought. Believing that the "real safety of our nation lies in the people themselves, and not in their representatives," Bryan proposed, as a future platform plank, a constitutional amendment to "submit every declaration of war to a referendum of the people, except in case of actual invasion of the country." With typical Bryan oratory, he observed: "The men who must give their lives, if need be, and the people who must bear the burden of taxation however oppressive it may become—these men should have a voice in saying whether we should resort to the arbitrament of the sword, or seek some method in which reason and not force will be employed."[77] The speech, which lasted to 1:25 A.M. and was later commended by President Wilson, suggested that Bryan, and an increasing number of Americans, felt the war referendum was just such a method.

Bryan's 1916 efforts thus illustrated the proposal's close relation to antipreparedness, arbitration, and progressive reforms like woman suffrage. His Lake Mohonk speech revealed more clearly than ever that the war referendum plan, in comparison with that of the League to Enforce Peace, offered a different route to peace. Progressives, whether professional or political, divided more and more in 1916 on the basic issue of force in diplomacy. Whereas Bryan and his allies believed that continued liberal reform depended upon antipreparedness and noninter-vention, other liberals, including President Wilson, moved closer to schemes of collective security and advocated increased preparedness. By early 1917 the war referendum plan would provide an even more signifi-cant index of defense attitudes and a clearer dividing line between the two groups.

President Wilson's own earlier hesitation to support the use of force in diplomacy and to join the preparedness movement hinged in part on his dilemma over the future of progressivism in wartime. Indeed, war referendum enthusiasts later pointed to Wilson himself as an early spokesman for the war referendum principle. After outlining the adminis-tration's preparedness program to Congress, Wilson made twelve speeches, January 27 to February 3, 1916, suggesting in several that the European war was one of rulers or governments, not peoples. In Chicago he stated: "This war was brought on by rulers, not by the people; and I

---

[77]"Addresses and Proceedings Incident to the Dinner Tendered by Prominent Democrats and Friends in Honor of Honorable William Jennings Bryan at the Hotel Lafayette, Wash-ington, December 6, 1916," Speech, Article, and Report File, Bryan Papers. Coletta em-phasizes this speech as the occasion for Bryan's launching of a campaign for national Pro-hibition and does not note his reference to the war referendum in this speech (*Bryan*, III, 43, 70). See also Arthur Wallace Dunn, *From Harrison to Harding: A Personal Narrative, Covering a Third of a Century: 1888–1921* (New York, 1922), II, 333–35, 348–49.

thank God that there is no man in America who has the authority to bring war on without the consent of the people." More than once he argued that "no people ever went to war with another people." The president stated in Des Moines that he did not have "even a participating part in the making of war" under the Constitution, which grants this power to the people "through their representatives."[78] During the 1916 campaign he continued to allude to the lack of democratic controls over European war declarations, and in the postwar peace negotiations "open diplomacy" was paramount to his program.[79]

The view that this was "not a people's war," echoed by progressive publicists, actually drew most progressives to support Wilson as well as to increase their faith in the extension of democracy as a road to peace.[80] Progressives, however, differed on the specific means of extending democracy, and most did not turn to the war referendum device. Wilsonianism ultimately included self-determination, open diplomacy, and the League of Nations, but despite the president's own frequent suggestion that wars were brought on by rulers, he never endorsed the war referendum.

A Wilsonian progressive who by 1916 did advocate such a plan was Frederic C. Howe. United States commissioner of immigration at the Port of New York since 1914, he concluded after two years of analysis that World War I was not a "people's war." European politics and diplomacy before the war were remarkable for their lack of democratic controls, unwholesome merging of finances and foreign affairs, and an excess of secret diplomacy. Military preparedness diverted attention from social

[78] Woodrow Wilson, *The Public Papers of Woodrow Wilson: The New Democracy*, ed. Ray Stannard Baker and William E. Dodd (New York, 1926), II, 1–121, especially pp. 61, 49, 81. See also Harley Notter, *The Origins of the Foreign Policy of Woodrow Wilson* (Baltimore, 1937), pp. 568–69, for a similar Nov. 1916 statement.

[79] On one aspect of this problem, see Robert H. Ferrell, "Woodrow Wilson and Open Diplomacy," in George L. Anderson, ed., *Issues and Conflicts: Studies in Twentieth Century American Diplomacy* (Lawrence, Kan., 1959), pp. 193–209. During 1916 Wilson had grown more and more receptive to the idea offered by the League to Enforce Peace and had also cultivated labor's support as Samuel Gompers moved toward the League's peace program. He and Gompers, for example, spoke at the League's Washington convention, May 26, 1916 (Frank L. Grubbs, Jr., "Organized Labor and the League to Enforce Peace," *Labor History*, 14 [1973], 249).

[80] J. A. Thompson, "American Progressive Publicists and the First World War, 1914–1917," *Journal of American History*, 58 (1971), 370. Thompson does not mention the war referendum as one of the preferred progressive methods for democratic control, although he treats several of its supporters and their writings. Examples of indecision by liberal publicists include Oswald Garrison Villard, who had lost confidence in Wilson by April and "tried" to support Hughes (*Fighting Years*, p. 317), and Hamilton Holt, who did not vote although his *Independent* supported Hughes (Herman, *Eleven against War*, p. 79).

legislation; this threat to progressivism could best be controlled by means of greater democracy in foreign affairs. Howe urged promotion of peace through some device withholding from those intrusted with power the exclusive right to decide upon war. "The making of war should be lodged with the people."[81]

Howe's prescription for peace and continued progressive reform reflected many of the hopes and most of the frustrations of the wartime liberal. Earlier he had influenced the aims and methods of the American Union Against Militarism, and by 1916, his rejection of force was even clearer. Having equated American preparedness and European diplomacy with special privilege and imperialism, he believed that popular control of the war-deciding power was basic to any hope for peace. For him the choice was simple: democracy or imperialism.[82] Indeed, Howe pointed up once more the affinity of anti-imperialism, antimilitarism, and demands for popular control of foreign policy.

The Woman's Peace Party also continued to support the war referendum as a part of their antipreparedness activity in 1916. Jane Addams's group surpassed other pacifist organizations in the amount of pressure placed upon Congress in favor of government controls over war industries, support of arbitration and peace conferences, and endorsement of war referendum legislation. The pacifist women fully supported La Follette's advisory war referendum resolution of April 1916 and earlier in the year concluded successfully an effort to get antipreparedness hearings before the Senate and House committees on foreign affairs. The Woman's Peace Party worked with the American Union Against Militarism and the American Neutral Conference Committee for mediation and a conference of neutral nations. These organizations also cooperated in support of world federation as a postwar goal, in proposing Pan-American cooperation to preserve republican forms of government, and in urging an international commission on Asian-American problems. Their programs illustrated again the degree of the liberal pacifists' departure from America's isolationist tradition. Yet they reacted violently against peacekeeping machinery based primarily on force. When they did

[81]*Why War?* (New York, 1916), pp. 3, 290, 300, 314–15. Neil Thorburn fails to note Howe's advocacy of a popular war declaration in discussing this popular antipreparedness tract ("A Progressive and the First World War: Frederic C. Howe," *Mid-America,* 51 [1969], 112). Even Howe, *The Confessions of a Reformer* (New York, 1925), makes no mention of his war referendum and antipreparedness views.

[82]Howe, "Democracy or Imperialism—the Alternative That Confronts Us," *Annals of the Academy of Political and Social Science,* 66 (1916), 250–58, in *Preparedness and America's International Program* (Philadelphia, 1916). Also, Minutes, Nov. 29, 1915, AUAM Records, SCPC.

adopt a limited use of force, it took the form of support of a "navy strong for defense . . . but weak for aggression."[83] In addition to supporting Senator La Follette's bill, the Woman's Peace Party endorsed several other 1916 war referendum resolutions, including that of Representative Clyde Tavenner (Democrat, Ill.). Introduced during Senate debate on La Follette's proposal, the Tavenner bill borrowed the entire La Follette text and contained the same complicated machinery, using the Census Bureau and a system of petitions to initiate the advisory vote on war or peace.[84]

One war referendum proposal not endorsed by the Woman's Peace Party was that of Congressman Denver S. Church (Democrat, Calif.). His bill, introduced January 31, 1916, associated the plan with the pre-preparedness forces for the first time. Although it too died in committee, Church clearly believed that "if we enlarge our navy so it is fully adequate for our defense, and then let the people decide when it shall be placed in action, we will have national honor and national peace for at least a hundred years."[85] Absence of support for this resolution by the Woman's Peace Party clearly hinged on the women's belief that its author had tied it too closely with strong defense policies.

A resolution presented March 13, 1916, by Warren Worth Bailey (Democrat, Pa.), however, may have been in part encouraged by the Woman's Peace Party.[86] His plan did not provide for a war referendum. Rather it called for an expression of popular opinion on *all* "questions of national policy." Public opinion would be expressed at general congressional elections not by a choice of representatives but on policies themselves.[87] Bailey, who at the time was one of William Jennings Bryan's congressional spokesmen, had learned his lessons on popular control well. In 1917 he would urge specifically a referendum on the war decision.

Congressional war referendum resolutions in 1916 fostered a concerted but ineffective petition campaign on the part of liberal pacifists. Some

[83]"Report of First Annual Meeting," *Yearbook of the Women's Peace Party, 1916;* "Congressional Program," adopted Dec. 9, 1916; "Resolutions," adopted Dec. 9, 1916; Legislative Committee, Minutes, Releases, and Reports, 1916–1919; *Chicago Herald,* Apr. 8, 1916, all in WPP Collection, SCPC.

[84]The Tavenner bill on file in the National Archives is a copy of La Follette's Senate bill, edited as his own. See "House Bills, Originals, Numbers 15285–15600, 64th Congress, 1915–1917," RG 233, NA; and *Cong. Rec.,* 64th Cong., 1st sess., p. 7496 (May 5, 1916).

[85]"House Joint Resolutions, Originals, Numbers 1–393, 64th Congress, 1915–1917," RG 233, NA, and *Cong. Rec.,* 64th Cong., 1st sess., p. 1930 (Jan. 31, 1916) and *Appendix,* pp. 353–54. In 1934 Church again proposed this same bill.

[86]Harriet P. Thomas to Jane Addams, Feb. 10, 1917, WPP Collection, SCPC.

[87]*Cong. Rec.,* 64th Cong., 1st sess., p. 4044 (Mar. 13, 1916). Bailey's chief use for his "policy" referendum proposal was to have been a referendum on preparedness.

telegrams in February reflected support of the Church resolution. But hundreds of them, received by the chairman of the House Foreign Affairs Committee April 25 to 27, 1916, reflected the tense atmosphere in the country after the *Sussex* crisis. Senator La Follette's advisory war referendum resolution of April 29, in turn, answered many such popular appeals for caution in relations with Germany.[88] Its appeal being strongest in such times of national crisis, the war referendum plan was of growing importance to liberal pacifism as an emergency reform.

The year 1916, which had opened with concerted efforts by peace workers and congressmen to frustrate the administration's defense appropriations, also featured Socialist party and Democratic and Progressive congressional endorsement of the war referendum plan. William Jennings Bryan had continued to advocate both antipreparedness and the war referendum in 1916. But as yet the fight against preparedness and for other peace proposals, including mediation and a conference of neutral nations, dominated the peace movement as well as congressional peace work. Peace forces within Congress and outside took pride in the fact that Congress in 1916 endorsed the idea of an international conference to discuss plans for a court of arbitration and disarmament.[89] The other basis of pacifist enthusiasm by the end of 1916 was President Wilson's action on December 18, 1916, requesting statements of peace terms and war aims from all belligerents. But reassurance, which sent Jane Addams "into the very heaven of internationalism," was short lived.[90] Peace hopes subsided soon in the face of Germany's evolving decision on resuming unrestricted submarine warfare. It was then, as chances of American intervention increased, that the war referendum plan became for many peace workers the chief emergency measure to keep America out of the war.

<hr/>

[88]Neutrality and War Files, Committee Papers, 64th Cong., Committee on Foreign Affairs, House of Representatives, RG 233, NA. Telegrams came chiefly from Pennsylvania, Oklahoma, North Dakota, and especially from Chicago and Saint Louis.

[89]On the Hensley Resolution amended to the naval appropriations bill passed in Aug. 1916, see Ellen Maury Slayden, *Washington Wife: Journal of Ellen Maury Slayden from 1897–1919* (New York, 1963), pp. x, xi; Lillian Wald, "The Hensley Clause and Disarmament," *Survey,* 37 (1916), 308; Vinson, *Parchment Peace,* pp. 16–19.

[90]Addams, *Peace and Bread in Time of War,* pp. 58–59. On Wilson's peace efforts see Link, *Wilson,* IV, 222–79; idem, *Wilson,* Vol. V, *Campaigns for Progressivism and Peace, 1916–1917* (Princeton, 1965), pp. 165–289; idem, *Wilson the Diplomatist* (Baltimore, 1957), pp. 68–77; Notter, *Foreign Policy of Wilson,* pp. 549–57, 572–97.

CHAPTER II

Search for a Storm Cellar

DURING THE MONTHS of crisis with Germany in 1917, the prospect of an actual decision on war or peace moved the question of a war referendum from theory to fact. Peace workers and certain congressional advocates alike began a frenzied campaign to win the public and Congress to support the measure. It became more than an example to the rest of the world of an expression of antipreparedness. It was now most frequently presented as an emergency peace plan. With a base of existing support in certain peace organizations and the Congress, in addition to the general American consensus behind more democratic control of foreign policy and the continued leadership of William Jennings Bryan, new peace groups like the Emergency Peace Federation, the Committee for Democratic Control, and the Emergency Peace Committee of Washington rallied behind the measure. Conduct of an unofficial test referendum by the American Union Against Militarism especially heightened public interest in the war referendum and also was effective with Congress.

This peace plan became the object of a pacifist search for unity, and, in the process of being presented in the form of nine new war referendum resolutions in Congress, it drew increased but still radical-dominated support in the peace movement, Congress, and the public at large. But for most Americans, typified by several key American Peace Society leaders who rejected the peace plan as the country moved closer to intervention against Germany, the war referendum was impractical. For old friends and new spokesmen, however, it was more than a desire to avoid war that brought them to this peace plan. Apprehension that domestic reform would be sacrificed to war gripped liberal leaders like Bryan, Jane Addams, Amos Pinchot, and Randolph Bourne. The emergency character of their war referendum campaign and their ultimate reliance upon legislation, chiefly in the form of resolutions for an advisory referendum, indicated the intensity of their interest in democratic reform and their fears for America. The war referendum measure became, therefore, an emergency plan to preserve peace and progressivism in the months before April 6, 1917.

Typical of the new peace organizations stressing an advisory war vote during February and March 1917 was the Committee for Democratic

Control. Its temporary and emergency character was evident from its first name—the Emergency Fund Office. But its significance was its members' emphasis on preserving American reform by means of the war referendum device, which, according to this group, would result in an anti-interventionist vote. The New York peace organization included Max Eastman of the American Union Against Militarism, criminologist Winthrop D. Lane, editor of the *Survey,* and Margaret Lane and Crystal Eastman of the Woman's Peace Party. More representative of the Committee's aims, however, were journalist Randolph Bourne and radical reformer Amos Pinchot. Their sincere fears that American intervention would end the social, political, and cultural revolt in which they and others were engaged drove them to the war referendum. It would provide "democratic control" of the "ultimate decision" and assure the peace necessary for continuation of their revolt.[1]

As chairman of the Committee for Democratic Control, Pinchot represented the young peace workers' hopes and fears most clearly. A leading member of the American Union Against Militarism, he took seriously the Union's February call for additional emergency peace groups. He helped organize the committee as a small but significant new organization designed to preserve America's chances to serve as a model for the world. Speaking for his new associates and himself, Pinchot expressed a youthful progressivism that reacted violently to war:

War means the turning of labor from the creating of food to the making of munitions. . . . War means the suppression of civil liberties here, or at the very mildest, the domination of the military element. . . . War would mean the risk of putting our domestic liberties at the mercy of our most reactionary groups. And if our concern is not for our own liberties but for the liberty of the world, let us ask ourselves what democratic contribution could be made to the world after the war by an America in the grip of its most illiberal forces. . . . If worst comes to worst, call for a referendum before we embark on war. Organize for democratic control.[2]

Such fear of war's impact upon American reform, expressed earlier during the preparedness controversy, now reflected the intense desperation of intellectuals, who contributed to what John Milton Cooper, Jr., calls preintervention "idealistic isolationism."[3]

[1]Amos Pinchot to Mrs. George Walton Green, Mar. 26, 1917, Amos R. E. Pinchot Papers, LC. For a list of members see letterhead, Committee for Democratic Control, Box 6, Randolph Silliman Bourne Papers (microfilm), Columbia University Library, New York, N.Y.; Joy Young to Amos Pinchot, Feb. 14, 1917, Amos Pinchot Papers. The name change resulted from confusion between this group and the New York Emergency Peace Federation, understandable given the similar names, objectives, and even membership.

[2]Statement of Amos Pinchot, n.d., Amos Pinchot Papers.

[3]Cooper, *Vanity of Power,* pp. 54–55, 72–76, discusses Randolph Bourne as a major contributor to that viewpoint.

Randolph Bourne's reaction to World War I, especially as American intervention approached, recorded those fears in exact proportion to his own advanced idealism and leadership in a prewar cultural renaissance.[4] His role as the leading antiwar intellectual of the period, which developed from his search for new ideas to challenge the social, political, and cultural status quo, therefore, made his advocacy of the war referendum plan a significant expression of its appeal.

Bourne's association with the Committee for Democratic Control and his war referendum advocacy were a culmination of his response to war. He urged, from within pacifist ranks, that liberalism continue its search for new ideas. This challenge brought a personal break with his teacher and friend John Dewey of Columbia University, and the hunchbacked intellectual's once regular contributions to Herbert Croly's *New Republic* also gradually ceased in 1917. Bourne's antiwar stand, including intellectual and activist support of the war referendum idea, thus became what he called a fight against other intellectuals' "war-liberalism."[5]

Reacting to the formation of the League to Enforce Peace in June 1915, Bourne opposed American participation in any coalition "to guarantee the peace of the world." America might be forced into wars in which it had no concern. To join the League to Enforce Peace, or the "League of Belligerents," as he called it, would "mean our immediate militarization and the *indefinite postponement of democratic reconstruction.*" Democratic and radical movements, cultural as well as social and political, Bourne believed, would be sacrificed to a war society. The greatest hope for pragmatism, reform, and peace lay in reliance on defensive armament along with the cooperation of neutral nations in an effort to curb war by nonmilitary coercion—a League of Neutrals.[6] As preparedness advocates among the liberals, including John Dewey, intensified their efforts for peace by insisting on such proposals as universal military training, Bourne continued to express opposition. This plan, he declared, denied the chance for choice, creativity, or rational control. In short, war was a threat to

[4]Bourne's advocacy of cultural innovation appeared in the *Atlantic,* the *Dial,* and the *New Republic* and in his books *Education and Living* (New York, 1917) and *History of a Literary Radical and Other Essays* (New York, 1920). See also John Adam Moreau, *Randolph Bourne: Legend and Reality* (Washington, D.C., 1966) and *The World of Randolph Bourne,* ed. Lillian Schlissel (New York, 1965).

[5]Bourne's most precise statements on the war referendum were made after American intervention as he drifted into an antistate pessimism; see chapter 4 below. But his activity in the Committee for Democratic Control placed him in the center of preintervention war referendum activities.

[6]Bourne, "Doubts about Enforcing Peace," Box 7, Bourne Papers (emphasis mine). John M. Cooper, Jr., maintains that this paper was Bourne's response to a Dec. 1916 *New Republic* editorial (*Vanity of Power,* p. 72).

pragmatism. Adopting William James's 1910 suggestion that "constructive interests" be found to compete with war's appeals, Bourne offered his own moral equivalent for conscription in the hope of resolving the conflict between war and progressive reform. His plan called for two years national service for youth—in education, social service, or cultural life, rather than military duty. This program, he believed, would assure continued guidance and choice by intelligence.[7]

Bourne's work for peace before 1917, always reflecting an intellectual analysis of war's threat to American reform, included also his effort to furnish an "explanation" for the war.[8] He had been in Europe on the eve of the 1914 war declarations and had expressed disappointment over visible popular enthusiasm for war. Later, in his *New Republic* contributions, he appealed to intellectuals for a social, psychological, and cultural explanation of the European war, especially "the connection between the initiating and directing groups."[9]

Such an analysis of the war helped bring about Bourne's interest in the war referendum plan. Although his diary does not mention his 1916 antipreparedness and antiwar speeches, association with war referendum advocates Max and Crystal Eastman, Amos Pinchot, and W. D. Lane, who joined with Bourne in 1917 to form the Committee for Democratic Control, may have first introduced him to the peace plan.[10] But Bourne was never content just to describe a national disease and then engage in "passivism." He had no use for a peace campaign couched in negative and antiwar emotionalism. Like his suggested League of Neutrals and national youth service, therefore, the war referendum was an alternative to intervention. As the leading intellectual in the Committee for Democratic Control, Bourne's proposals challenged the status quo. The war referendum principle, when applied, would assure choice in wartime,

---

[7]William James, "The Moral Equivalent of War," *International Conciliation,* No. 27 (1910), p. 16; Dewey, "Universal Service as Education," *New Republic,* 6 (1916), 309–10; Bourne, "A Moral Equivalent for Universal Military Service," ibid., 7 (1916), 217–19.

[8]For his other peace activities before 1917, see his two essays on arbitration, his review of Allan Benson's *Inviting War to America* (1916), and his edited symposium of peace proposals: *Report of the Eighteenth Annual Lake Mohonk Conference on International Arbitration, 1912* (Lake Mohonk, N.Y., 1912), p. 180; Bourne, "Arbitration and International Policies," *International Conciliation,* No. 70 (1913), pp. 7–12; idem, "Magic and Scorn," *New Republic,* 9 (1916), 130–31; and Bourne, comp., *Towards an Enduring Peace: A Symposium of Peace Proposals and Programs, 1914–1916* (New York, 1916).

[9]Bourne to Alyse Gregory, July 30, 1914, Box 1, Bourne Papers; Bourne, review of Hugo Munsterberg's *The War and America* (New York, 1914), *New Republic,* 1 (1914), 27; idem, "Continental Cultures," ibid., 1 (1915), 14–16.

[10]Bourne, Diary, 1916, Box 8, Bourne Papers; Daniel Aaron, *Writers on the Left: Episodes in American Literary Communism* (New York, 1961), p. 35.

Bourne believed. It would preserve pragmatism and A.nerican reform.[11]

The Committee's work, directed toward the intellectual community rather than the masses, appeared primarily in editorial advertisemen published in the *New Republic,* the *New York Times,* and midwestern papers. The original $3,000 used by the American Union Against Militarism to start the Emergency Office, later the Committee for Democratic Control, provided funds for their first ads.[12] This group, typically represented by Bourne and Pinchot, was devoted to the "reality" of the pacifist state and saw continued neutrality early in 1917 as the first requirement of a creative America. Their activity, both analytical and activist, was part of the frenzied effort made by intellectuals, social workers, and other peace activists to obtain an advisory referendum on war during the crisis with Germany.

The Emergency Peace Federation was another small group of peace workers who advocated the war referendum as a unifying plan among peace organizations. Organized after a February 2 emergency meeting called by leaders of the American Neutral Conference Committee and seeking to emphasize "the importance of public opinion," it also represented a search for unity by the American Union Against Militarism, the Woman's Peace Party, the American Peace Society, the Church Peace Union, and the Socialist Party of America. Louis Lochner, Emily Greene Balch, and Lella Faye Secor at first dominated the organization, making it, in the process, the most radical, or militant, of new peace organizations endorsing the war referendum before American intervention.[13] The emphasis upon the war referendum was clear from the appeal, made by Miss Secor, secretary of the American Neutral Conference Committee and on behalf of the new Federation, to create a campaign of "writing and telegraphing to their Senators and Congressmen, recommending a referendum vote."[14]

[11]Bourne, "The War and the Intellectuals," *Seven Arts,* 2 (1917), 133–46; idem, *Untimely Papers* (New York, 1919).

[12]Crystal Eastman to Amos Pinchot, June 21, 1917, and Aug. 15, 1917, Amos Pinchot Papers. Max Eastman later called the Committee for Democratic Control "a little publicity battalion" of the American Union Against Militarism (*Love and Revolution: My Journey through an Epoch* [New York, 1964], p. 28). See chapter 4 below for discussion of the Committee's 1917 tactics in the campaign for an advisory referendum.

[13]"History and Organization," Statement of Emily Greene Balch, June 8, 1940, People's Council of America Papers (microfilm), SCPC; Lella Secor to members, Feb. 9, 1917, WPP Collection, SCPC; Lella Secor Florence, "The Ford Peace Ship and After," pp. 119–20; "How Pacifists Mobilized against War," *Survey,* 37 (1917), 551; *New York Times,* Feb. 6, 7, 1917.

[14]Lella Secor to members, Feb. 9, 1917, WPP Collection, SCPC. Neither Chatfield, *For Peace and Justice,* pp. 26–27, nor Marchand, *American Peace Movement,* pp. 249–50, mentions the Federation's support of the war referendum.

This group, whose origins also revealed once more William Jennings Bryan's activities for the war referendum, was ultimately led by Mrs. Henry Villard, chairwoman, Lochner and Balch (vice-chairpersons), and Rebecca Shelly (field secretary). Among its members, in addition to Miss Secor, were Professors Henry W. L. Dana, Harry Overstreet, and David Starr Jordan.[15] Formal organization of the Federation, which itself merged into the People's Council of America after American intervention, apparently grew out of the resignation of some peace workers from the Neutral Conference Committee and from an address by William Jennings Bryan at a New York City "Keep Out of War" meeting February 2. Bryan vigorously repeated his appeals, made since 1915, for arbitration, a neutral conference to mediate the European struggle, and a war referendum. Such oratory, as well as his continued active relations with peace organizations and certain congressmen, set the tone for peace activity during February and March 1917 and especially helped establish the special stress upon the war referendum plan.[16]

Although arranged before public knowledge of Germany's intention to resume unrestricted submarine warfare, the New York meeting, sponsored by the American Neutral Conference Committee, took place the day after that policy was made effective. Out of that crisis and Bryan's subsequent reactions, peace workers organized the Emergency Peace Federation. Indeed, his speech could not be ignored at the time, and so apt were his arguments for the war referendum that they would be repeated in the 1920s and 1930s. Rapid communication facilities, the telegraph, telephone, and railroad networks, he believed, made a referendum practicable. Citing an argument that was central to the thinking of many war referendum advocates, he said, "We now have more faith than they [our forefathers] had in the intelligence of the masses of our country." However, his assertion that the masses were better informed "than our most prominent leaders" when the war power was given to Congress was of less validity. Nevertheless, Bryan considered the time "ripe for an amendment to the Constitution, giving to the people, except in case of actual invasion, a referendum on a declaration of war."[17] Bryan was in

[15]Letterhead, Emergency Peace Federation Papers, SCPC; David Starr Jordan to William Jennings Bryan, Apr. 1, 1917, Bryan Papers.

[16]*New York Times,* Feb. 3, 1917; "How Pacifists Mobilized against War," p. 550; Curti, *Bryan and World Peace,* p. 241. On the day following this speech, Bryan telephoned Senator Henry F. Ashurst that "he would flood Congress with telegrams against war except in case of *actual* invasion" (*A Many-Colored Toga: The Diary of Henry Fountain Ashurst* [Tucson, Ariz., 1962], p. 54).

[17]Bryan, "America and the European War; Address by William Jennings Bryan at

Washington when President Wilson severed diplomatic relations with Germany the next day. In his speech to the peace rally the former secretary of state had praised Wilson's recent peace efforts. With the break, however, Bryan worked hurriedly with Senator La Follette to devise some plan to prevent American intervention. Believing the best chances for peace lay with pressure upon Congress, Bryan began a closer association with his spokesmen there in an effort to get war referendum legislation.[18]

An additional Bryan move was still needed, however, to produce the effort of key peace organizations. It was actually La Follette who suggested that he and Bryan seek to unite Democrats and progressive Republicans behind a war referendum resolution, a move which the Wisconsin Senator felt would help cool things off.[19] But since the break in relations with Germany now made a constitutional amendment impractical, Bryan first urged American citizens to petition Congress for an *advisory* referendum. This call for action was repeated in the *Commoner* and also in a discussion of Bryan's statement in *La Follette's Magazine*.[20] Although Bryan and La Follette alike despaired of their efforts in Congress, it was not long before their direct appeals to the people began to show results. These came in the American Union Against Militarism's test referendum (begun February 7), the formation of a Washington Emergency Peace Committee, and the subsequent activities of the Emergency Peace Federation itself.[21] Despite the loud outcry against Bryan and La Follette, as well as the peace movement in general, their efforts were directed toward the American people. Their appeals thus contrasted with the Pinchot-Bourne appeals made chiefly to other intellectuals. Bryan especially symbolized a faith in the masses that became central to the war referendum cause, and his continued efforts for the

Madison Square Garden, New York City, February 2, 1917," pp. 10–11, typescript in Speech, Article, and Report File, Bryan Papers. The speech was published in 1917 by the Emergency Peace Federation. See Coletta, *Bryan,* III, 50, and Levine, *Bryan,* pp. 84–85, for brief discussions of this speech, which the latter regards Bryan's "most eloquent and moving" appeal for peace.

[18]La Follette and La Follette, *La Follette,* I, 599; Levine, *Bryan,* p. 85; Coletta, *Bryan,* III, 51; Cooper, *Vanity of Power,* p. 171. Legislative aspects of the emergency war referendum campaign of 1917 are discussed below in chapter 3.

[19]Coletta, *Bryan,* III, 51.

[20]*New York Times,* Feb. 4, 1917; *Commoner,* Feb. 1917; La Follette, "Do the People Want War?" *La Follette's Magazine,* 9, No. 2 (1917), 4.

[21]Coletta, *Bryan,* III, 51. The test referendum and Washington peace group are discussed below in chapter 3. Levine, *Bryan,* pp. 86–87, discusses the bitterness of Bryan's life in this period as a result of his peace efforts and the threats and denunciations made against him.

plan gave the peace movement some of the unity it sought during this hectic period.

Uniting around the slogan No War Without Referendum, the Emergency Peace Federation became strong among pacifists in Washington, Chicago, Boston, and New York. Its small activist leadership, headed by Louis Lochner, attracted other social workers, antimilitarists, and many college students. Before the House Committee on Foreign Affairs February 22, representatives of college sections of the Federation testified in favor of a popular war referendum. Delegates from Columbia University, a center of pacifist activity, reported that their local poll indicated 64 percent in favor of an advisory referendum. Other students sought prestige as well as numbers by asserting that George Washington, whose birthday the country was then observing, would have approved a war referendum.[22]

The Federation had organized earlier peace demonstrations in Washington. At the time of its organization early in February, founders sent the following telegram throughout the country: "Emergency Peace Federation just organized. Planning great demonstration Washington Monday, February twelve. Headquarters Raleigh Hotel. Purpose mass meeting. Visit Congress. Can you go? Particularly desire many delegates authorized to speak for organizations demanding referendum before war declaration. Special train leaves New York midnight Sunday after mass meeting. Make every sacrifice to attend."[23] As a result, Federation delegates presented their views to Senator Stone's Foreign Relations Committee on February 12. They also met with Congressmen Oscar Callaway (Democrat, Tex.) and Warren Worth Bailey (Democrat, Pa.), both Bryan spokesmen who had already introduced war referendum resolutions in Congress. Led by Emily Greene Balch, Mrs. Henry Villard, Norman Thomas, and New York University Professor Harry Overstreet, the Emergency Peace Federation delegation then marched to the White House. There Secretary Joseph Tumulty received them in President

[22]U.S., Congress, House, 64th Cong., 2d sess., *Emergency Peace Federation:* Hearings, House of Representatives, Committee on Foreign Affairs, February 22, 1917, pp. 5–21. College sections were at Michigan, Illinois, Amherst, Harvard, George Washington, Vassar, Yale, Cornell, Brown, and Columbia.

[23]Emergency Peace Federation telegram, n.d., attached to "Report, Legislative Committee of Woman's Peace Party for 1917," Washington, 1917 (typescript), WPP Collection, SCPC. Lella Secor, who also tells of an early newspaper appeal for funds that brought the Federation $35,000 in one day, testifies that in the hectic days before intervention she "seldom slept more than four hours a night" ("The Ford Peace Ship and After," pp. 119, 122).

Wilson's office, where Thomas read a resolution asking for an advisory war referendum and a neutral conference.[24]

In addition to direct pressures upon Congress and the tactic of a local test referendum, the Emergency Peace Federation and other pacifist groups popularized the war referendum through public advertisements and mass meetings. A public rally in Washington, for example, ended the Federation's war referendum work on Lincoln's birthday. In comparison to the intellectual-dominated Committee for Democratic Control, whose peace work was typically illustrated by full-page newspaper and magazine advertisements challenging the interventionist views of the American Rights League, the Emergency Peace Federation demonstrated a broader appeal for war referendum support in its advertisements. Indicating another different tactic, Federation advertisements announced mass peace meetings, rather than organization views, as their primary means of popularizing the war referendum. The Federation was typical of the radically oriented peace workers' obsession with meetings. Groups like the American Union Against Militarism used advertisements to circulate test referendum forms to be mailed to congressmen. At the height of the crisis with Germany, the Union requested antiwar petitions to Congress and maintenance of armed neutrality. The antimilitarist emphasis upon war's threat to progressive goals at home continued in their assertion that "we can preserve Democracy in this country by staying out."[25]

Despite its radical leadership, the Emergency Peace Federation served as an effective clearing house for organized pacifism. Its effort to create more formidable pressure through an emphasis upon the war referendum even briefly produced remarkable cooperation among diverse peace groups. But this activity also illustrated the difficulties that peace workers had in attempting to speak as one voice during the crisis months of 1917.

[24]Dubin, "Collective Security," p. 351; *Public,* 20 (1917), 157; *Ohio State Journal,* Feb. 13, 1917; "Peace Demonstration in Washington, Lincoln's Birthday, 1917," Emergency Peace Federation Papers, SCPC. Marchand notes the Federation's promotion of a Joint High Commission with Germany but does not cite the war referendum as a unifying objective of the group (*American Peace Movement,* pp. 249–50). Randall, *Balch,* pp. 132–235, discusses her peace work to Apr. 6, 1917, but does not mention her advocacy of the war referendum. Frank L. Grubbs, Jr., *The Struggle for Labor Loyalty: Gompers, the A.F. of L. and the Pacifists, 1917–1920* (Durham, N.C., 1968), pp. 11–13, emphasizes the troubled origins of the Federation and its "pro-German taint," citing the later New York Lusk Committee Report on radicalism. He, too, fails to mention the war referendum plan.

[25]*New York Times,* Mar. 29, 1917. The American Rights League, which also used paid advertisements to present its views and announce public meetings, promised "Music by Sousa's Band" at a March interventionist rally (ibid., Mar. 19, 22, 23, 24, 1917).

In another attempt at unity, in which the Emergency Peace Federation participated, a National Pacifist Congress called by the American Peace Society was held in New York City February 22 and 23, 1917. Known as the Second Conference of Peaceworkers, this meeting saw groups like the Federation hail the war referendum as an emergency peace measure, an action that produced strong disagreement between conservative and radical peace forces. The search for consensus was indeed an ambitious undertaking, for among some twenty American peace groups represented were delegates from the American Peace Society, the Emergency Peace Federation, the Woman's Peace Party, the American Union Against Militarism, the German-American Peace Society, the Church Peace Union, and the Fellowship of Reconciliation. Other delegates represented the National Reform Association, the International Single Tax Commission, and the Federated Council of the Churches of Christ in America. State peace societies from New York, Pennsylvania, Connecticut, Massachusetts, New Hampshire, and Rhode Island also sent representatives, as did the Chicago Peace Society.[26]

Knowing that agreement on specific peace plans would be difficult, peace workers first had met in preconference planning sessions to iron out internal differences of opinion. There was no sentiment to form another organization, but the compulsion for meetings was obvious. At the outset the strength of radicals and their interest in the war referendum plan was shown in such preconference meetings. Radicals dominated a Cooper Union peace rally the night before they urged approval of the war referendum by the full Second Conference of Peaceworkers. Directed by college affiliates of the Emergency Peace Federation, the rally featured a speech by Columbia University Professor Henry R. Muzzey, who claimed that the "real fight is here at home for industrial justice and equal distribution of the riches of the country." Here again was the rub for radical peace workers. If the United States intervened, as the Cooper Union resolutions argued, *"the advancement of learning, culture, and of progressive legislation will be arrested."* Fears of liberals and radicals alike were once more made clear. Grasping for a last-minute salvation, they endorsed an advisory war referendum, a reform well fitted to the progressive belief in the individual man's inherent goodness. How could

---

[26]"Overruling Veteran Pacifists," *Survey,* 37 (1917), 646–47; 1917 folder, American Peace Society Papers, SCPC. The First Conference of Peaceworkers, held Oct. 26–27, 1916, and sponsored by the American Peace Society and the Church Peace Union, failed to achieve union (Marchand, *American Peace Movement,* p. 364).

any mortal reject a proposal based on such a concept of democracy, for did not "God move among men?"[27]

In a quieter gathering, also on February 21, the Woman's Peace Party made an effort to instruct its delegates to the Second Conference of Peaceworkers. Here some pacifist unrest over the war referendum was visible. During the planning session, Jane Addams, Mrs. Henry Villard, Lillian Wald, Emily Balch, and Mrs. William I. Hull debated the war referendum's merits. They were hopeful due to reports of activity by the American Union Against Militarism, for the referendum plan, and assurances that President Wilson desired "to obtain the opinion of the public." Yet Mrs. Hull, of the Pennsylvania branch of the Peace Party, reported her state organization divided on the war referendum. As Emergency Peace Federation Chairwoman, Mrs. Villard believed the proposal at least would give "publicity to the peace cause," whether practicable or not. The women agreed, after further debate, to support it in principle, although reserving a final consideration of the plan's practical worth until after a Party poll. Even so, the Party endorsed it the next day, during the Conference of Peaceworkers, and then actively sought legislation for an advisory referendum.[28]

As the crisis with Germany produced the nation's anxious wait for "overt acts," peace workers and interventionists often rubbed elbows, and occasionally locked horns. Rallies in Madison Square Garden, sponsored by both groups, were scheduled dangerously close together, for example, and the meeting of the Second Conference of Peaceworkers in New York's Biltmore Hotel was no exception. Among delegates to conferences of the World's Court League and the League to Enforce Peace were Hamilton Holt and Theodore Marburg. But the press took greater notice of the peace conference due to its drive for unity and the already well-known divisions among pacifists. They could and did unite on resolutions opposing conscription and espionage legislation. Older middle-class organizations, as always, endorsed arbitration and mediation.

[27]*New York Times,* Feb. 22, 1917 (emphasis mine).

[28]"The Special Conference of the Women's Peace Party February twenty-first, 1917," typescript of minutes and "Statement of Principles Formulated by a Conference of Members of the Executive Board and Representatives of Affiliated and Local Branches of the Women's Peace Party, February 21st, 1917," WPP Collection, SCPC. Degan, *Woman's Peace Party,* pp. 183–84, is wrong in recording this as the first party consideration of the war referendum plan. Marchand, *American Peace Movement,* pp. 219–21, discusses the generally disruptive issue of "radicalism," expressed by the New York rather than Pennsylvania and Massachusetts branches, but does not note the war referendum conflict within the party.

Some surprisingly even supported a conference resolution blaming President Wilson for the nation's past preparedness moves. It was, however, an American Union Against Militarism resolution that threatened, for a time, to split the congress. "Speaking from our faith in democracy as well as from our hope of peace," the resolution read: "We demand that in this as in all other crises, no matter how grave the provocation, the question of war and peace, most vital of all questions in the life of a nation, be submitted to the people by a national advisory referendum, before Congress declares war, or before any irrevocable step is taken toward war."[29] Certain leaders of the most conservative and largest group—the American Peace Society—"shied at the idea of popular judgment shaping national policy," at least in the form of an advisory war referendum. President George W. Kirchwey, although a former war referendum advocate when chairman of the American Neutral Conference Committee, and Secretary Arthur Deerin Call refused to endorse it. Kirchwey called it "needless, impracticable, and dangerous." Call echoed disapproval, believing the pacifists could differ on peace plans "until the crack of doom." But they were overruled by a voice vote endorsing the war referendum plan.[30]

To remove all element of doubt from its achievement, the Conference appointed a committee to formalize its peace proposals. Led by Swarthmore College Professor and Quaker internationalist William I. Hull, a member of the American Peace Society Executive Committee, this group included the war vote measure as one of "Eight Alternatives to War." The Conference also agreed to bring home their qualified unity on the war referendum plan by sending a delegation to President Wilson. Illustrating interest in the war referendum within the American Peace Society, in contrast to the positions of Kirchwey and Call, the White House delegation included Professor Hull, always influential in American pacifism.[31] With Hull were Emily Balch and Jane Addams, who together represented the largest and most determined preintervention peace groups in America—the American Union Against Militarism, the Woman's Peace Party, the Emergency Peace Federation, and the American Peace So-

[29]*New York Times,* Feb. 22, 23, 1917; American Union Against Militarism Executive Committee, "Statement Proposed at Joint Conference of Peace Societies, February 22, 23 (1917)," Amos Pinchot Papers; text quoted from copy in AUAM Records, SCPC.

[30]*New York Times,* Feb. 23, 24, 1917. Kirchwey's stand against the measure was surprising to the *Times* editors since the day before he seemed to favor a popular war decision. See his letter to the editors, Feb. 22, and editorial, Feb. 23, 1917.

[31]American Peace Society Papers, SCPC, includes the Committee's *Why Not War?,* listing the alternatives. See also Dubin, "Collective Security," pp. 354–55; *Public,* 20 (1917), 205.

ciety. In their February 28 meeting with President Wilson, however, they spoke for the recent Conference attempt at unity rather than their individual organizations.

Their alternatives to war included the agreed-upon proposals of a neutral conference and an advisory war referendum. The latter was presented to the president, according to Miss Addams, especially in the interest of labor. A former student of Wilson's, Professor Hull advocated continued neutrality, citing, on the face of it, convincing historical precedents. Actually, however, events had already dealt another blow to the pacifist campaign. Wilson told the pacifists of recent but still secret German machinations in Mexico—the Zimmermann Note, known to him for three days. No wonder the president's stern mood impressed Miss Addams and that he now felt adjudication with Germany impossible. Events again had overtaken the pacifists; apparently they were too late.[32]

In still another attempt to achieve pacifist unity, the Emergency Peace Federation organized an Unofficial Commission of liberals to devise ways for peace. Coming after public knowledge of the Zimmermann Note and during the critical March week of Wilson's decision for war, it represented one of organized pacifism's final grasps for peace.[33] As before, radical pacifists dominated this group. During the week of March 19 to 24, Miss Balch, Professor Hull, Mrs. Villard, Professor Overstreet, Louis Lochner, David Starr Jordan, and *Public* editor Stoughton Cooley met in New York City and drew up resolutions favoring a neutral conference, mediation by the United States, and an advisory referendum on war.[34] It was the same prescription for peace that pacifists had been making since 1915. But their appeals in 1917 were understandably more desperate.

At a public rally sponsored by the Commission to climax their week-long study, Rabbi Judah L. Magnes, one of few remaining radicals in the New York Peace Society, adequately summarized the peace workers' recent war referendum emphasis. He indicted munitions makers and the press, as many radicals then did, for favoring intervention. Claiming to

[32]Notter, *Foreign Policy of Wilson,* pp. 626–29; Addams, *Peace and Bread in Time of War,* pp. 63–64.

[33]Wilson acted Mar. 12 to arm American merchantmen, after the Senate filibuster against the Armed Ships Bill and during a subsequent special session of the Senate. The cabinet met Mar. 20 to advise Wilson on the final decision; the next day he called Congress for Apr. 2 (Notter, *Foreign Policy of Wilson,* pp. 633–34). See chapter 4 below for a more complete discussion of official and pacifist activities in late March.

[34]Emergency Peace Federation, *Alternatives to War: Findings of the Unofficial Commission Which Met at the Holland House, New York City, March 19–24, 1917* (New York, 1917), Emergency Peace Federation Papers, SCPC; *Public,* 20 (1917), 306.

speak for "the people," he further maintained that "if a declaration of war is to be made by this country, the people should first be asked to express their will. The President and the Congress must be petitioned that before declaring war they submit the question to an advisory referendum of all the people."[35] Besides Magnes, speakers who endorsed the war referendum were Stanford University Chancellor David Starr Jordan and New York radical Benjamin C. Marsh, who solicited prayers for Root's and Roosevelt's deaths! Two days earlier, Elihu Root and Theodore Roosevelt had been among speakers at an interventionist rally. Princeton President John Grier Hibben, in the interventionist public meeting sponsored by the American Rights League, had urged that America send an army to France and then join "the new republic of Russia" in common campaigns against Germany. Hibben at first had shocked his audience with the confession that as a pacifist, he believed in peace at any price. But his views were unmistakable after his remark that "the price at the present time is war."[36]

As such interventionist outcries became louder, drowning out the pacifists, there was less time for choice and, in addition, less chance for any referendum. Whereas the war party was certain that America was already at war, organized pacifism, led by the radicals, was just as persistent in its demands for peace and progress. Each continued its determined fight. On March 29, after an American Rights League advertisement urged Wilson to ask for a declaration of war, the Emergency Peace Federation purchased an entire page of the *New York Times*, appealing for an emergency fund of $200,000 to finance an immediate antiwar press campaign. Announcement of a peace delegation to Washington, to appeal for congressmen's votes against war, indicated their sense of crisis. Their campaign, directed especially to women, also continued to seek a conference of neutrals to determine possible bases of peace. "War Is Not Necessary" boldly declared another full-page advertisement on March 31. Among its alternatives to war was the advisory referendum.[37]

The Emergency Peace Federation served as an effective clearing house for organized pacifism. In spite of its ultimate failure to win America to

---

[35]Magnes, *The People Do Not Want War* published by the Emergency Peace Federation (New York, 1917) was a reprint of this Mar. 24 speech. It was also used as an advertisement by the Committee for Democratic Control; copies in Emergency Peace Federation Papers and Emergency Anti-War Committee (Chicago) Papers, SCPC.

[36]*New York Times* advertisements announcing the Emergency Peace Federation rally (on Mar. 24), Mar. 23, 24, 1917, the earlier American Rights League meeting, Mar. 19, 22, 1917, and reports of the two meetings, Mar. 23, 25, 1917.

[37]Ibid., Mar. 28, 29, 31, 1917.

nonintervention, its February and March activities illustrated, first, increased radical attention to the war referendum, and, second, greater cooperation among pacifist groups. There was less difference of opinion among them than expected. As it turned out, its nearly one hundred local federations, led by the New York headquarters, waged a significant but losing campaign for neutrality and peace. The Federation's activities—namely, mass meetings, pressures upon congressmen, paid advertisements, Washington peace demonstrations, and affiliate groups on college campuses—gave the war referendum plan an entirely new emphasis as a radical and purely emergency peace measure.

In addition to the Emergency Peace Federation and the Committee for Democratic Control, a third new organization embodied all aspects of recent interest in the war referendum proposal. The brief history of that new group, the Emergency Peace Committee of Washington, revealed, once more, emergency reliance upon the war referendum plan, legislative goals, and an internal pacifist search for unity. Furthermore, the work of this organization illustrated again William Jennings Bryan's activities in support of the plan.

After the break in diplomatic relations with Germany, Bryan believed he should remain in Washington to give congressmen "courage, and help and plan." War was so near that he felt his personal counsel was necessary to organize peace efforts.[38] Indeed, Bryan, before the February 3 break with Germany, as noted before, set the tone for pacifist activity; his New York speech had inspired the Emergency Peace Federation and its war referendum emphasis. From Washington the next day his "Statement to the American People" further encouraged pacifist unity around the war referendum as an alternative to war. He urged that Americans be kept off belligerent vessels and out of the danger zones in Europe. And before the Washington Anti-War League he repeated both peace proposals—strict neutrality, to the point of waiving American rights on the seas, and the advisory referendum on war.[39]

Bryan's Washington speech, just three days after the New York meeting, however, proved more significant. Invited by American Peace Society President Kirchwey and Wellesley Professor Emily Balch, pacifists and other interested individuals attended a peace meeting on February 5 at the Raleigh Hotel. The former secretary of state again called for concerted action to keep the country out of war. It was a call for unity around his alternatives to war. Declaring that Americans *should* seek peace at any price, he urged renunciation of neutral rights as an ethical

---

[38]Levine, *Bryan*, p. 86.
[39]*New York Times*, Feb. 4, 5, 1917.

obligation, a conference of neutral nations to mediate the war, and a referendum vote of men and women. At the conclusion of Bryan's address, the Emergency Peace Committee of Washington was formally organized to press for pacifist unity and an advisory referendum.[40]

For William Jennings Bryan the war referendum became during the emergency with Germany the best alternative to war. He considered it "the best way to defeat the war traffickers and the 'worshippers of the scimitar.' The people who must share the sufferings and sacrifices if war comes should be consulted as to whether war is necessary."[41] His example was not in vain. It influenced Jane Addams's view of the war referendum as "our best hope" for peace.[42] It encouraged popular demands for, and congressional action on, war referendum legislation. But the search for pacifist unity around the war referendum plan, made by the two new peace organizations which his speeches encouraged, best indicated Bryan's influence.

As in the case of the Emergency Peace Federation of New York, radicals dominated the Washington Emergency Peace Committee. Led by officers or members of a branch of the local Woman's Peace Party, the Washington group maintained close ties with the Party's legislative committee by locating its offices in the local Party headquarters. Other radical pacifists who also dominated the new organization, once more at the expense of American Peace Society participants, included representatives of the American Union Against Militarism.[43]

As the crisis for America seemed imminent after the Washington Committee's organization, the new body's program became clearer. The Washington ladies cooperated with the New York Emergency Peace Federation in a February 12 Capitol demonstration. But since none of the peace organizations were in a better physical position to direct war referendum pressures upon Congress, the Washington Committee's major efforts were for war referendum legislation. In all of its war referendum work, however, the Emergency Peace Committee of Washington stressed it as an emergency measure, a panacea to meet an

[40]Harriet P. Thomas, Emergency Peace Committee of Washington, *Report,* copy sent to Jane Addams, Feb. 10, 1917, WPP Collection, SCPC.

[41]William Jennings Bryan to Jane Addams, Feb. 13, 17, 1917, Emergency Anti-War Committee (Chicago) Papers, SCPC.

[42]"The Voice of the People for Peace," *Survey,* 37 (1917), 580.

[43]Harriet P. Thomas to Jane Addams, Feb. 10, 1917; form letter, on Woman's Peace Party letterhead, to members of the Party, from Lella Secor (secretary, American Neutral Conference Committee), Feb. 9, 1917, WPP Collection, SCPC. See also "The People's Referendum," *Four Lights: An Adventure in Internationalism* (New York), No. 3 (Feb. 24, 1917), back page.

international crisis that, the women believed, threatened domestic liberalism.

In addition to the emergency effort for an immediate advisory referendum, on the question of war with Germany certain war referendum partisans offered another alternative, thereby revealing inner conflicts over the use of force in diplomacy. Before the break with Germany many liberals had telegraphed President Wilson to use caution. Lillian Wald and Columbia historian Carleton J. H. Hayes were in this group, comprised chiefly of members of the American Union Against Militarism and the American Neutral Conference Committee. Published also in the *New York Times* as a paid advertisement, their appeal insisted that the president not allow America to be "dragooned into the war" by the belligerents' desperation. They believed that "eleventh-hour participation in a struggle for mastery" that was not our own would needlessly sacrifice American goals at home.[44]

Miss Wald also sent Wilson a Hayes memorandum soon after the break with Germany. Reiterating the earlier view that European belligerency did not begin or continue over any vital American interests, Hayes urged upon Wilson a policy of armed neutrality. He proposed "constructive action" by the United States, rejecting the extremes of passive talk of staying out and full-fledged American belligerency. He then cited two European precedents for his proposed American-led League of Armed Neutrals. In previous threats to the maritime supremacy of Great Britain, during both the American Revolution and the wars of the French Revolution and Napoleon, some European nations joined to enforce, by means of an armed neutrality, their common neutral rights.

Conscious of a similar threat to American neutral rights in 1917, Hayes urged Wilson to adopt a policy of restraint and armed neutrality. He argued, in addition, that America in 1798 broke relations with France and even fought limited naval engagements without a formal war declaration.

[44]This appeal, along with Bryan's speeches to peace rallies the next few days, set the tone for pacifist activities in February. Although often unknown to the public, Wilson's patient and continued search for peace throughout the winter of 1916–17, had included much of what pacifists called for during the emergency. For Wilson's response to demands for mediation, neutral conferences, and statements of peace terms, see Link, *Wilson,* V, 165–340, and Notter, *Foreign Policy of Wilson,* pp. 572–628. Included in the group telegraphing Wilson were Oswald Garrison Villard, Emily Balch, William I. Hull, George Peabody, Amos Pinchot, Lillian Wald, Crystal and Max Eastman, Paul Kellogg, and George W. Kirchwey. Telegram (as an advertisement), the article on pacifist reaction to German submarine warfare announcement, and the advertisement announcing Bryan's speech at the rally are in *New York Times,* Feb. 2, 1917.

A policy of armed neutrality in 1917, he maintained, should consist of a collective defense of neutral rights by European and especially South American nonbelligerents. Convoying merchantmen and even returning fire when attacked, along with constant diplomatic protests, could do much toward removing the submarine menace. Hayes believed that America could thereby avoid complete alliance with one or another of the European powers and, at the same time, preserve both the opportunity to champion neutral rights and safeguard America's legitimate interests.[45]

Professor Hayes's proposal was significant because, in the first place, it appeared publicly in liberal pacifism's official journal, the *Survey*. Furthermore, the Committee for Democratic Control, led by Chairman Amos Pinchot, quickly endorsed it alongside the war referendum plan. In articles and advertisements, the Committee used Hayes's views as fuel for its increasingly heated campaign against other intellectuals who were joining the war party. Pointing to America's troubles with France in 1798, the Committee caustically concluded arguments for a war referendum and armed neutrality with the judgment: "It is a pity we had no American Rights League then."[46] Finally, the Hayes memorandum was significant because it was as influential in Wilson's decision, by late February, to arm American merchantmen as other similar but earlier proposals.[47]

Endorsement of armed neutrality by certain war referendum partisans, therefore, demonstrated a marked, though qualified, adjustment of some peace workers' traditional views about using force in diplomacy. To be sure, not all were willing to concede any portion of their antimilitarist convictions. Among those who did, in addition to the New York Committee for Democratic Control, were Oswald Garrison Villard, editor of the *Nation,* and war referendum proponent Paul U. Kellogg. The Woman's Peace Party called upon the government to use the navy as a "police force" in the event of an "overt act," thus protecting neutral rights

[45]Hayes, "Which? War without a Purpose? or Armed Neutrality with a Purpose?" *Survey,* 37 (1917), 535–38. Copies of the memorandum reached Wilson Feb. 8 from both Miss Wald and Colonel House; Wilson sent it to Secretary Lansing on the ninth. It appeared publicly in the *Survey* as an article the next day. See Link, *Wilson,* V, 306–7; Baker, *Wilson,* VI, 472; U.S., Department of State, *Papers Relating to the Foreign Relations of the United States: The Lansing Papers 1914–1920* (Washington, D.C., 1939), I, 596.

[46]Antimilitarists often referred to the American Rights League, the leading interventionist group, as "the enemy." The Committee for Democratic Control reprinted Hayes's memorandum as "Which? Armed Neutrality or War?" (from the *Survey* and *New York Evening Post,* Feb. 10, 1917), Committee for Democratic Control Papers, SCPC, and as an advertisement, "1917—American Rights—1798," *New Republic,* 10 (1917), 82.

[47]Notter, *Foreign Policy of Wilson,* pp. 626–27. Between Feb. 8, when he read the memorandum, and his Feb. 26 address to Congress requesting an Armed Ships Bill, Wilson had readily recognized the favorable public response (Ernest R. May, *The World War and American Isolation, 1914–1917* [Cambridge, 1959], p. 428; Link, *Wilson,* V, 306–7, 340).

without a formal war declaration. This recourse, they urged, should not be taken without an advisory referendum of the people.[48]

Circulation of Professor Hayes's article among congressmen on February 13 highlighted pacifist interest in armed neutrality as an alternative to war. Letters from the Committee for Democratic Control stressed that armed neutrality would, in a sense, extend the Monroe Doctrine into the sea, for Latin American republics were expected to be early associates in any league of armed neutrals. Another proposed advantage, and one that led to pacifist faith in the war referendum as well, was that armed neutrality would not require sending large armies to Europe. America could both defend its rights in a limited naval war and, for the most part, maintain its traditional isolation.[49] Armed neutrality, like an advisory referendum on war, conformed to its proponents' limited-defense concepts, also typically illustrated by their claim that the country was in "no danger of invasion."[50] In mid-February, it is true, "overt acts" by Germany had not occurred, and since there was "virtually no articulate" popular drive then for intervention, the radical peace movement strengthened Wilson's own determination to exercise patience and restraint.[51] But he stopped short of the advisory referendum.

The earliest intensive interest in, and appeals for, the war referendum, made by what the *New York Times* called "violent and pragmatical pacifists," awakened opposition from only a small group, most of whom were themselves involved in the debate over America's choice. Opponents at first could do little more to counter proponents of a war referendum and armed neutrality than to charge them with "a coward's peace," a "bankruptcy of ideas," and an "irresponsibility of mind." Few saw the inconsistencies of the peace workers' views on using force in diplomacy because they, too, were uncertain of how much force would be needed or where it

[48]"A League of Armed Neutrals," *Nation,* 104 (1917), 178–79; Paul U. Kellogg, "The Fighting Issues: A Statement by the Editor of *The Survey*," *Survey,* 37 (1917), 576; Amos Pinchot, "Armed Neutrality," *Public,* 20 (1917), 154; "Statement of Principles of the Woman's Peace Party, February 21st, 1917," Executive Board Minutes, WPP Collection, SCPC.

The *Nation* endorsed Hayes's armed neutrality idea, and editor Villard associated with the war referendum groups, although his journal never commented on the referendum in February 1917.

[49]*New York Times,* Feb. 14, 1917. Further debate on the Committee's use of history to support its views appeared in the *New Republic,* 10 (1917), 105, 163–64. Pinchot continued to defend armed neutrality to the eve of intervention. See "For a 'Strongly Defensive Policy,' " reprinted as a Committee for Democratic Control advertisement in the *Chicago Tribune,* Mar. 30, 1917, and originally his letter to the editor, *New York Evening Post,* Mar. 24, copies in CDC Papers, SCPC.

[50]Typical assertion in the Committee's advertisement, "Referendum: A Letter to *The Public*," *Public,* 20 (1917), 168, copy in CDC Papers, SCPC.

[51]Link, *Wilson,* V, 307–8, 313.

should be applied. Interventionists only managed to invert the liberal pacifist's own argument that intervention would end domestic progressivism. War referendum adherents hoped, according to editors of the *New Republic,* merely "to divert attention from the threats of Germany to the illiberalism of those who wish to resist the threats."[52]

After March 1 and public knowledge of the Zimmermann Note, however, debates over war and peace took on greater significance. When war referendum proponents then argued that Americans were no more disposed to war than after the submarine war-zone decree, they gave notice that the war referendum had become first and foremost a peace-at-any-price measure. The interventionists, now a larger minority, could not agree with the viewpoint, asserted by the Committee for Democratic Control, that an advisory referendum or even armed neutrality could preserve American domestic reform. In addition, they certainly did not accept the Committee's belief that the Zimmermann Note indicated only Germany's "insane desperation." Release of this diplomatic dispatch had in reality caused still greater pressure for intervention. Yet peace advocates continued to assume that the country remained basically neutralist.[53]

As American liberals rallied in increasing numbers behind President Wilson, whose own decision for intervention slowly evolved in March,[54] alternatives like the advisory referendum or armed neutrality not only became impracticable but irrelevant. Even the limited-defense and limited-war concepts of the Committee for Democratic Control, indicated by its recent acceptance of armed neutrality, were no longer valid. Yet most war referendum proponents, including the minority that adopted armed neutrality, continued their efforts to avoid, or at least to postpone, America's use of unlimited force in diplomacy. Within the organized peace movement their untiring efforts had produced an unusual, though vulnerable, consensus on the measure. Their enthusiasm, however, had its greatest effects not within the peace movement itself but upon Congress.

[52]*New York Times,* Feb. 8, 14, 22, 1917, all editorials opposing the war referendum plan. "Taking the Referendum Seriously," *New Republic,* 10 (1917), 92, was also typical of eastern press opposition.

[53]Joy Young to Randolph Bourne, Feb. 28, 1917, Box 6, Bourne Papers. See also Committee for Democratic Control advertisement in *Chicago Daily Tribune,* Mar. 5, 1917, copy in CDC Papers, SCPC, and *New Republic,* 10 (1917), 145. Link, *Wilson,* V, 346, 354, comments on the impact of the Zimmermann Note.

[54]Wilson's decision for full belligerency came between the inauguration on Mar. 5 and a Mar. 20 cabinet session, after which he called Congress to meet on Apr. 2. Factors in his decision included Germany's sinking of four American ships Mar. 12 to 18, cabinet approval, the Russian Revolution, and his desire "to do right whether it is popular or not." See Link, *Wilson,* V, 390–431; May, *World War,* pp. 428–30; Notter, *Foreign Policy of Wilson,* pp. 631–40, and chapter 4.

CHAPTER III

Straw Votes and Congress

SEVERAL GALLUP POLLS revealed popular war referendum interest in the 1930s, but in pre–World War I days, with no such service available, what better demonstration of faith in a national advisory war referendum could be devised than to resort to the referendum method itself? Not a new scheme when the American Union Against Militarism conducted a post-card poll of the war referendum plan, test referendums in 1917 were also taken by the Woman's Peace Party, student groups of the Emergency Peace Federation, and even legislators. Furthermore, with Let the People Decide flashed across five local theater screens, Chicago peace organizations conducted polls on the peace plan.[1]

Even so, the American Union Against Militarism exceeded the success of previous efforts of this kind, both in the scope of its poll and in its impact upon Congress. After telegraphing messages in favor of an advisory referendum to Vice President Thomas Marshall and Speaker Champ Clark, the Union decided on two brief questions to appear on some 100,-000 postal cards: "I. Should we enter the war in order to uphold our legal right to go into the war zone? II. Do you believe that the people should be consulted by referendum—in any event short of invasion—before Congress declares war?"[2] The Union decision to conduct the poll, begun February 7, reflected both the crisis atmosphere following the break with Germany and two of the very questions being posed by William Jennings Bryan between February 2 and 5.

Union officials who approved this text and recognized Bryan as their unofficial leader, including Crystal Eastman, Lillian Wald, Paul Kellogg, Amos Pinchot, Oswald Garrison Villard, and Charles Hallinan, were among those also engaged in war referendum work in other groups. Affiliation with the American Union Against Militarism and its advisory postal referendum, therefore, was not their sole effort for peace or the

---

[1]The vote, 5 to 1 against American intervention, reflected the popularity of silent movies among women and the influence of peace-oriented movies like *The Battle Cry of Peace*. See Curti, *Peace or War*, p. 235, and "The Voice of the People for Peace," *Survey* 37 (1917), 579.

[2]Minutes, Executive Committee, Feb. 5, 14, 1917, AUAM Records, SCPC; *New York Times*, Feb. 8, 1917.

war referendum idea. They of course hoped for a negative response to the first question and positive sentiment on the referendum question. To assure those results, the sponsoring officials suggested how one should vote. An explanatory note, carried on the card, read: "A national *advisory* referendum is not unconstitutional and could be carried out by the census bureau, through the postmasters, in twenty five days."[3]

Within days after agreement on the postal referendum's text, Secretary Hallinan suggested an extension of the project. But limited finances prevented this and led the executive committee to request that Hallinan allow interested congressmen only one to two thousand cards per district. Such coordinated efforts between congressmen and sponsoring pacifist groups, although significant, were frequently hampered by a lack of resources. Even late in February 1917 two special contributions of $1,000 each finally paid expenses of the one hundred thousand or more postcards circulated in the test referendum.[4]

Physical as well as financial problems of this test referendum were large and called for every talent of organized pacifism. Miss Angell and Mr. Hallinan of the Union's Washington offices, however, were well qualified in public relations and lobbying techniques and served as able directors of the effort. At Union headquarters over fifty volunteer workers addressed thousands of postal cards from prepared lists of cooperating peace groups and congressional sponsors. Gradually those receiving the postal referendum cards returned them to the peace organizations or sent them directly to congressmen, as requested on the card. Not overlooking any available mass media techniques, the referendum promotion entailed newspaper advertisements, resolutions and petitions to Congress, letters to editors, and mass meetings.[5] Only the radio, used as the war referendum's primary means of publicity in the thirties, would have been of greater assistance to the peace workers.

Meanwhile, as the American Union Against Militarism coordinated the test referendum, it also organized peace rallies and cooperated in demonstrations with other groups. It helped form and actively supported the new emergency organizations with a war referendum emphasis in

[3]Minutes, American Union Against Militarism Executive Committee, Feb. 5, 1917, Amos Pinchot Papers.

[4]Ibid., Feb. 10, 20, 1917, AUAM Records, SCPC. Merle Curti, *Peace or War,* p. 249, explains the Carnegie Endowment's sympathy for the Allies and its effect upon the American Peace Society, which the foundation supported. Radical peace groups, which dominated the war referendum plan, never enjoyed strong financial support such as the Carnegie-backed middle-class groups had.

[5]Press notice, Feb. 8, 1917, CDC Papers, SCPC; Minutes, Executive Committee, Feb. 14, 1917, AUAM Records, SCPC.

Washington, Chicago, and New York. Amos Pinchot, in fact, encouraged the Union's own branches "to form emergency groups to promote the idea of a national referendum on war or peace." As a leading member of the Union, as well as a founder of the Committee for Democratic Control, Pinchot was a significant figure in this phase of radical peace work. In addition, the Union was an important associate of the Emergency Peace Federation in leading the Second Conference of Peaceworkers, February 22–23, to endorse the war referendum plan.[6]

Union leaders met approximately three to four times a week in February to coordinate work and receive reports on the postal referendum. Then, after some difficulty in confirming an appointment with President Wilson, the executive committee met in special session, February 27, to discuss matters to be presented the next day.[7] Agreeing to give emphasis to this phase of recent Union activity, they planned to tell the story of the test referendum, outline its results, and then endeavor to get the president "to declare in favor at least of the *principle* of a referendum on war and peace." In planning their White House statement, Union officials decided to present their traditional reasons for opposing "undemocratic legislation such as conscription or compulsory military training." But after some debate the executive committee agreed to omit their previously proposed League of Armed Neutrals.[8] Once more, organized peace workers were careful to plan every detail, limit their demands, and seek prior consensus among themselves.

The Union's delegation to the White House on February 28 included Paul Kellogg, Max Eastman, Lillian Wald, Charles Hallinan, and Amos Pinchot. Speaking for the group, Miss Wald reported 100,000 postal cards mailed out and replies that were overwhelmingly favorable to a national advisory referendum. The Union's poll, according to Miss Wald, reflected primarily public sentiment from five congressional districts in Pennsylvania, Colorado, Ohio, Missouri, and Texas. But she also reported antiwar sentiment revealed by some twenty-five other congressmen who had polled their districts in similar test referendums.[9]

[6] Minutes, Executive Committee, Feb. 14, 1917, AUAM Records, SCPC.

[7] Pinchot to Woodrow Wilson, Feb. 17, Pinchot to Tumulty, Feb. 23, 26 (telegram), Tumulty to Pinchot, Feb. 19, 26 (telegram), Amos Pinchot Papers.

[8] Minutes, Executive Committee, Feb. 27, 1917, AUAM Records, SCPC. See Marchand, *American Peace Movement,* p. 243–44, 248–49, concerning the Union's supportive relationship to Wilson and an earlier positive response by the president to their "frequent interviews."

[9] "Memorandum of Statement Made to President Wilson Regarding the Referendum on War," n.d., AUAM Records, SCPC. Copy also in Amos Pinchot Papers. No tabulation of referendum results was located in the official records of the Union, SCPC.

There is no indication that the Union's war referendum efforts directly influenced President Wilson any more than did similar pressure tactics by other groups. Their White House appointment came just after delegates from the Second Conference of Peaceworkers came away without any assurance of either a neutral conference or an advisory war referendum. As we have seen, Wilson had learned of the Zimmermann Telegram three days earlier. Furthermore, the Union delegation, and others, knew of Wilson's request, on February 26, for congressional endorsement of his decision to arm American merchant vessels.[10] Even so, the American Union Against Militarism remained active in behalf of their war referendum project, frequently claiming for the unofficial test referendum "a decidedly steadying effect on Congress."[11]

Historians frequently cite the Bartholdt embargo resolutions, the Gore-McLemore Resolutions, the Hensley clause of the 1916 Naval Appropriations Bill, and the Senate filibuster on Wilson's Armed Ships Bill as examples of congressional pacifism and neutralist thinking. Congress indeed had only "moved toward war by slow stages," not attempting, even after the break with Germany, "to hurry the President" into a final war decision. Despite interventionist sentiment of some cabinet members, such as Secretary of State Robert Lansing, President Wilson found it necessary, as a test of peace strength in Congress late in February, to request support in arming American merchant ships.[12] But among other examples of pacifist activity and strength, generally neglected by historians heretofore, were the nine new resolutions seeking a referendum on war. Although none became law, their introduction between February 9 and 23 indicated greater effectiveness by peace workers for such legislation than most historians have recognized.[13]

Within the organized peace movement, the Washington Emergency Peace Committee and its leading sponsor, the Woman's Peace Party, were among the most active groups continuing to encourage war referendum legislation in 1917. The Washington emergency committee

[10]Notter, *Foreign Policy of Wilson,* pp. 626–29; Addams, *Peace and Bread in Time of War,* pp. 63–64.

[11]Crystal Eastman to Members of the American Union Against Militarism, Mar. 1, 1917, Amos Pinchot Papers.

[12]Alice M. Morrissey McDiarmid, *The American Defense of Neutral Rights, 1914–1917* (Cambridge, 1939), pp. 115–17, 190; May, *World War,* pp. 422–23.

[13]Curti, *Bryan and World Peace,* p. 242; Levine, *Bryan,* p. 87; Link, *Wilson,* V, 306. John Milton Cooper recently did not cite interest in war referendum legislation among criteria used to discover "patterns of isolationist support." See "Statistical Descriptions of Congressional Voting on Preparedness and Foreign Policy, 1915–1917," Appendix, *Vanity of Power,* pp. 220–40.

prepared a "catalogue of members of Congress—based on their willing-ness to put the question of war to a referendum vote."[14] Early in Feb-ruary, after the break with Germany, the legislative committee of the Woman's Peace Party, including several wives of congressmen, even considered the possibility of hearings on Senator La Follette's 1916 pro-posal of an advisory referendum on war. Since the La Follette bill remained buried in the Census Committee, and after debate within the Emergency Peace Committee turned up other objections, the women re-jected it for a less elaborate version.[15]

La Follette's bill had applied to the existing electorate only, despite Mrs. La Follette's insistence on including women in the advisory vote. Reliance upon state petitions to originate the referendum in addition to its complicated machinery made it cumbersome and inapplicable to emergency needs. Even so, the Washington women's substitute measure, though avoiding complex origins and machinery, incorporated too many reforms. There could have been little real hope for the Emergency Peace Committee's revised draft resolution. An immediate advisory referendum vote of men and *women* above *eighteen* on the question of war with Germany was called for.[16]

With this new version of La Follette's advisory referendum in hand, a delegation of the Washington Emergency Peace Committee met on Feb-ruary 9 with Congressmen George Huddleston (Democrat, Ala.), Robert Crosser (Democrat, Ohio), and Warren Worth Bailey (Democrat, Pa.). After all three admitted the importance of introducing several referendum bills in Congress, the Washington ladies were confident of legislative assistance.[17] Yet on the very day of these interviews a more helpful legislative development, unrelated to the Washington Emergency Peace Committee, took place.

Oscar Callaway (Democrat, Tex.) introduced in the House, February 9, the first of nine war referendum resolutions presented during the

[14]Lella Secor to Members of Woman's Peace Party, Feb. 9, 1917, and Minutes, Special Meeting of Executive Board (Washington Branch), Feb. 7, 1917, WPP Collection, SCPC.

[15]Minutes, Legislative Committee, Feb. 8, 1917, WPP Collection, SCPC. This commit-tee, headed by Mrs. Ellen Maury Slayden, wife of Texas Democrat James L. Slayden, also included wives of Congressmen Edward Keating (Democrat, Colo.) and William Kent (Inde-pendent, Calif.). Slayden was president of the American Peace Society, Kent was something of a radical, and Keating was a labor spokesman.

[16]The Committee's decision, Feb. 8, against La Follette's bill and in favor of the substitute draft turned on objections made by J. David Thompson, director of the Library of Congress Legal Reference Bureau and advisor to the women's group. See Emergency Peace Commit-tee of Washington, *Report,* attached to Harriet P. Thomas to Jane Addams, Feb. 10, 1917, WPP Collection, SCPC.

[17]Ibid., p. 2.

month. House Resolution 492, introduced "by request" and referred to the Committee on Foreign Affairs, provided "that no declaration of war by Congress and no act of war by the executive branch of the Government of the United States of America shall be taken, except to suppress insurrection or repel invasion, as provided by the Constitution of the United States, until the question at issue shall be submitted to a referendum of the voters of the United States."[18]

After beginning his career in Congress in 1911, Callaway had gradually joined the peace minority in the House Naval Affairs Committee, supporting antipreparedness forces in 1916 by frequently speaking in radical fashion against war profits. At the same time, he emphasized a Populist type of faith in the people. One speech in the House directed against Congressman Augustus P. Gardner (Republican, Mass.) was so strong that it led to formation of a special committee to consider expunging certain of his remarks from the record.[19]

During debate on the Naval Appropriations Bill, less than a week before introduction of his war referendum resolution, the Texas Democrat and Naval Affairs Committee member called himself a "belligerent pacifist," ready to fight those who wanted to drive the country into war. While he believed there was no danger of invasion, he thought that our defense was adequate to repel any foe. Typical of some war referendum proponents in the thirties, Callaway also often associated munitions makers and an unneutral press with preparedness forces.[20] Callaway's interest in the war referendum, therefore, followed a radical pacifist record in the House and on the Naval Affairs Committee. His unsuccessful candidacy for renomination in 1916, furthermore, gave him greater affinity with Bryan, making their relationship even closer in such peace efforts as the war referendum cause.[21]

[18]Text from original draft of bill, House Resolution 492, 64th Cong., RG 233, NA.

[19]U.S., Congress, House of Representatives, *Special Committee Appointed to Report on Expunging from the Congressional Record Certain Language of Honorable Oscar Callaway in Reference to Honorable Augustus P. Gardner* (Washington, D.C., 1916). On this incident see Thomas Lloyd Miller, "Oscar Callaway and Preparedness," *West Texas Historical Association Yearbook,* 43 (1967), 80–93, who does not mention his efforts for the war referendum. Dewey W. Grantham, Jr., concluded that Callaway was an expert at plain talk and the art of denunciation in his study "Texas Congressional Leaders and the New Freedom, 1913–1917," *Southwestern Historical Quarterly,* 53 (1949), 47.

[20]*Cong. Rec.,* 64th Cong., 2d sess., pp. 2569–72 (Feb. 3, 1917) and Appendix, pp. 545–52.

[21]Mrs. Callaway, also active in peace work, joined Mrs. Slayden two days after the Callaway resolution was introduced in their own peace demonstration at Union Station. Their scroll read, "War or Peace? Why Not Try a Referendum?" Congressman Slayden had been in the anti-imperialist ranks earlier; he was a friend of Richard Bartholdt in arbi-

Callaway's resolution, unlike previous bills in several respects, served as the text for five of the nine February proposals. It was different from Congressman Bailey's 1916 provision for referendums on *any national policy,* including the war decision. Since Callaway provided for an immediate advisory referendum, it was apparently much like the revised draft offered to other congressmen that day by the Washington Emergency Peace Committee. Yet in addition to rejecting La Follette's complicated machinery, Callaway avoided the excessive hopes for voting reforms in his plan. There was no attempt to provide a vote for women or to lower the age requirement to eighteen, both of which were features of the Peace Committee draft.

No direct influence upon Callaway by any of the peace groups can be inferred from the record.[22] Since the Emergency Peace Committee of Washington, most active in seeking war referendum legislation, made contacts with Congressmen Bailey, Huddleston, or Crosser, and earlier, with Senator La Follette, the roots of Callaway's interests in the proposal must be found elsewhere. House rules do not allow congressmen to reveal persons requesting introduction of legislation, but there is little need to speculate in Callaway's case. His pacifist-radical background, record, and associations made his sponsorship of the resolution no great surprise. But the direct, individual influence of William Jennings Bryan explains his interest and the form his resolution took at this time.

Among Bryan's alternatives to war, offered both in recent speeches and a "Statement to the American People" on February 3, was the advisory referendum on war. From his immediate shock, at the time of the break with Germany, until the war declaration in April, Bryan's emphasis upon a referendum placed him in more than a casual relationship, attributed by some historians, to this phase of emergency peace activity. Admittedly, he "did not openly affiliate" with the new radical peace groups, though he was a financial contributor to the Emergency Peace Federation.[23] But less

---

tration work (through the Lake Mohonk Conferences and the Interparliamentary Union); and in 1917 he was a trustee of the Carnegie Endowment. Perhaps such diverse peace interests, more middle class than those of Callaway, caused him to avoid what must have been strong pressures from radical pacifism—through his wife—for a more direct support of the war referendum plan. See Slayden, *Washington Wife,* pp. 56, 72–78, 84.

[22]The committee's Feb. 10 *Report,* cited above (n. 16), noted only that the press reported Callaway's bill that day. In fact, the peace groups never fully credited Callaway with the legislative recognition of their pressures, giving it instead to Congressman Bailey.

[23]*New York Times,* Feb. 10, 1917; Curti, *Bryan and World Peace,* p. 244. Curti's study does not give Bryan full credit for Callaway's resolution, or any other, although it does mention that "several" war referendum resolutions were introduced (ibid., pp. 226, 242).

accurate is the view that "Bryan had no connection with any of the radical peace groups."[24] To the contrary, his speeches before such groups had given radicals a program and encouraged their domination of the search for pacifist consensus. Furthermore, he was still, next to President Wilson, the most powerful Democratic leader, and his emphasis upon the war referendum directly influenced legislative action on it.

Following addresses in New York and Washington on February 2 and 5, Bryan spent the next few days conferring with congressmen. He had done this frequently after his resignation, meeting chiefly with Senator La Follette and Congressmen Bailey, Callaway, and Huddleston.[25] In the course of his conferences with pacifist and neutralist spokesmen following the break with Germany, therefore, Bryan's new emphasis upon the advisory referendum did not go unnoticed. The Texas agrarian radical, Oscar Callaway, adopted it as his own, leading other Bryan spokesmen only by a matter of days.[26]

Upon hearing of the Callaway war referendum proposal, several senators believed it would not get far if it ever reached the Senate. One of five senators who had voted against Senator Stone's February 7 resolution, and thus opposed the break with Germany, planned to introduce a measure similar to Callaway's but never did.[27] Unidentified by the press, it may have been Senator La Follette, who continued to work for an advisory referendum on war even though his 1916 bill was tied up in committee. La Follette did not reintroduce his bill, but, desiring a roll-call vote on the issue, he planned to make the proposal an amendment on any appropriate bill.[28]

However radical a solution this proposal seemed to most liberals, the

---

[24]Link, *Wilson,* V, 306. This recent volume does not mention any of the war referendum resolutions except Callaway's, and it associates the Texas congressman with Bryan only as a "friend." Coletta, *Bryan,* Vol. III, does not mention the resolutions or Callaway, and Levine, *Bryan,* does not directly associate the resolutions with Bryan's interest in the war referendum plan.

[25]Typical occasions for such conferences had been the Senate rejection of the Gore resolution, which the former secretary of state had inspired, the *Sussex* crisis, and the break in diplomatic relations with Germany. See Levine, *Bryan,* pp. 45, 47, 85. Other Bryan spokesmen, who swore by him on earlier preparedness issues, included Congressmen James L. Slayden and Martin Dies (Tex.), Clyde Tavenner (Ill.), and Walter L. Hensley (Mo.). Tavenner had sponsored a 1916 war referendum resolution. See also Curti, *Bryan and World Peace,* p. 235.

[26]Before introduction of Callaway's resolution, there was a conference with his colleagues, possibly including Bryan. The conference certainly included Callaway's Naval Committee associates of a pacifist mind (*New York Times,* Feb. 10, 1917).

[27]Senator James K. Vardaman (Miss.), who was among these five, said that a war referendum resolution would be a waste of time. Later he held otherwise (ibid.).

[28]La Follette and La Follette, *La Follette,* I, 599.

Callaway measure encouraged the organized emergency peace movement and its chief counsel, William Jennings Bryan. In view of the large expression of public support for the principle set forth in Callaway's resolution, as well as the introduction of eight other such bills in the next two weeks, a recent judgment that "no one, least of all Bryan, really thought that Congress would adopt the war referendum resolution" is questionable.[29] Legislative aspects of radical pacifism's emphasis on this peace proposal indicated more than merely a bid for sensational publicity. Both Callaway and Bryan, for example, urged the principle of a popular vote on war as a real possibility. As in the past, such supporters of this idea expressed unusual faith that it could be tried and that through its implementation by Congress real peace, divorced from or limiting the use of force, would follow.

Bryan remained constant in his devotion to the war referendum plan, for it had much in common with his arbitration views; each offered a way to postpone, and possibly prevent, an ultimate clash of arms. As Bryan commented to a *New York Tribune* reporter on the diplomatic break with Germany, "It is no surrender of a right to postpone enforcement of it." To illustrate his point, he used the analogy of a drunken driver heading his car onto a sidewalk where another man walked, fully within his rights. "I would prefer," Bryan concluded, "to step aside and settle with him when he is sober." Immediate defense of rights in this case would only leave a widow to settle with the driver. Bryan was dedicated, according to another reporter, to work for a referendum to "thwart the President's policy as far as ever," especially if Wilson went to Congress for further powers during the emergency.[30]

No wonder that Callaway's war referendum resolution referred to executive actions in diplomacy; it made explicit what heretofore had been only implied by war referendum adherents. Many formerly had implied that the executive branch alone was responsible for taking the country down a "road to war," eventually coming to the point beyond which the nation could not go without war. Callaway, like Bryan, was concerned that "no act of war by the executive branch" be taken without a referendum.[31] The referendum proposal then and later often reflected a determination to diffuse responsibility for war in order to thwart or reduce executive control of foreign affairs.

Bryan's war referendum efforts continued in an open letter to Jane Ad-

[29]Link, *Wilson,* V, 306.

[30]"Efforts of American Pacifists to Avert War," *Literary Digest,* 54 (1917), 452–53; and Link, *Wilson,* V, 305.

[31]House Resolution 492 File, 64th Cong., RG 233, NA.

dams, published on February 17 in the *Commoner*. Anticipating his actual reaction later, he promised support for the government in the event of war, but as a peace leader he made a plea, once more, for letters, telegrams, and petitions to Washington. "If opposed to entering this war on either side, say so at once. If you favor a referendum on a declaration of war," he continued, "tell your representatives so and tell them immediately."[32] Although such views led some congressmen to associate Bryan with Royalists in the Revolution and Copperheads in the Civil War, he continued to speak for peace and the war referendum plan. He remained the hero of Congressmen Bailey and Huddleston and, in addition, the inspiration of radical pacifists in the Emergency Peace Federation, conferring with its leaders before their February 28 meeting with President Wilson.[33]

Among legislators approached by the Washington Emergency Peace Committee, the Woman's Peace Party legislative committee, or any other peace organization, Warren Worth Bailey appeared most interested. Although his policy referendum measure was locked in the Judiciary Committee and no longer was popular among peace workers, he promised in the meeting with the Washington women on February 9 to support a bill of their type if his constituency so desired. The emergency committee, therefore, prepared to mail American Union Against Militarism postal referendum cards to voters in three Pennsylvania congressional districts, including Bailey's, just at the time Callaway introduced his resolution. Unknown to them, Bailey also had already requested, in his early February correspondence and through his own Johnstown *Democrat,* expression of public sentiment on the war referendum.[34]

Bailey, like Callaway, enjoyed the close friendship of William Jennings Bryan. Both congressmen frequently defended Bryan on the House floor and supported the war referendum, at least in part, because of Bryan's example. In fact, Bailey had been Bryan's "chief spokesman in Congress during the peace crusade" of 1915–17.[35] Bailey and Callaway also had in

[32]Paxton Hibben, *The Peerless Leader: William Jennings Bryan* (New York, 1929), p. 355. Hibben, however, makes no reference to Bryan's ties with the war referendum congressmen. John Cuthbert Long, *Bryan: The Great Commoner* (New York, 1928), pp. 345–46, and Bryan and Bryan, *Memoirs,* pp. 429–49, do not mention his war referendum interests.

[33]This was the delegation, dominated by the Emergency Peace Federation, from the Second Conference of Peaceworkers, discussed above. See also Levine, *Bryan,* pp. 86–88.

[34]Emergency Peace Committee of Washington, *Report,* p. 3, attached to Thomas to Addams, Feb. 10, 1917, WPP Collection, SCPC; *Cong. Rec.,* 64th Cong., 2d sess., p. 3049 (Feb. 10, 1917) and Appendix, pp. 319–21.

[35]Levine, *Bryan,* p.. 45. After the *Sussex* crisis, Bryan met with Callaway and Bailey, among other Democrats, to plan pacifist-neutralist strategy (ibid., p. 47).

common the fact that they would not be back for the Sixty-fifth Congress; Democrat, former single-taxer, and newspaper publisher, Bailey had been defeated in 1916 in a normally Republican district which he had represented since 1913.

When Bailey, therefore, introduced House Resolution 495 on February 10, he not only shared Bryan's faith in the war referendum plan but indicated his obligation to Callaway by using his text. Bailey's sponsorship of the proposal reflected, in addition, his strong antipreparedness viewpoint, the pressures of Pennsylvania pacifists (including some German-Americans), and especially his belief that American intervention abroad would end reform at home. The influence of the Washington peace lobbyists, the Emergency Peace Committee, who approached him only the day before, however, was not as important as these other factors in encouraging his action.[36]

Bailey's close relationship to Bryan, resulting in the introduction of his war referendum bill, was further evidenced in an episode immediately after that action. Like Callaway's head-on clash with Augustus P. Gardner (Republican, Mass.) in 1916, Bailey's defense of Bryan on the House floor led to another emotion-filled encounter. Gardner suggested that Bryan's pacifism appealed to man's cowardice and spoke critically of pacifists and Socialists, who insisted on a national "political campaign on the question of peace or war," equating advocacy of a war referendum with being pro-German. The 1917 confrontation became so emotional that it led to a vote to strike from the record certain remarks in which Bailey accused Gardner of loyalty to Great Britain.[37]

Joining Bailey in this spirited defense of the peace movement and Bryan was Alabama Democrat George Huddleston, one of the legislators approached by the Washington ladies in the Emergency Peace Committee. A Bryan Democrat, Huddleston's refusal to sponsor their war referendum bill had thrust Bailey into the role of their most hopeful advocate in Congress. Writing to Bryan in mid-February, Huddleston indicated that peace sentiment in Congress was strong but also revealed his personal opposition to the war referendum resolutions. He reported the recent bills for a popular vote on war, for which, he added, "there seems to be some little sentiment." Yet he did not hope for "any favorable report" on them.[38]

He was an excellent judge of congressional attitudes, for none of the

---

[36]*Cong. Rec.,* 64th Cong., 2d sess., p. 3049 (Feb. 10, 1917); *New York Times,* Feb. 11, 1917; text of the Bailey resolution in WPP Collection, SCPC.

[37]Levine, *Bryan,* p. 86; *New York Times,* Feb. 18, 1917; *Cong. Rec.,* 64th Cong., 2d sess., p. 362 (Dec. 14, 1916) and Appendix, pp. 25–26; ibid., pp. 3356–58 (Feb. 15, 1917).

[38]George Huddleston to William Jennings Bryan, Feb. 13, 1917, Bryan Papers.

nine new war referendum resolutions got out of committee. Even so, sponsors of the measures continued their efforts to make the emergency peace campaign more effective by uniting around this peace plan. After some debate on the merits of the Bailey bill (pacifists usually attributed the new legislation to him rather than Callaway), the Washington branch of the Woman's Peace Party agreed to support it. Several "suffragists urged that women be included in the question of voting upon the war," but in view of the urgency they finally conceded this was not practicable.[39] There was no better indication of how reform groups had shifted attention from domestic progressivism to foreign affairs. Yet the suffragists abandoned this issue in the belief that peace afforded the only chance for further domestic reform. They had not rejected progressivism; rather they sought to apply progressive principles and goals in diplomacy.

The New York Emergency Peace Federation was also among the peace groups rallying behind the Bailey resolution. In spite of pacifist unity, however, the same Washington Emergency Peace Committee which first approached Bailey apparently was not entirely satisfied with the recent legislative interest shown the war referendum. This group took steps to ask the Rules Committee of the House to insert "a new rule making a referendum a necessary step in declaring war against a foreign government."[40] The Washington ladies overlooked nothing in their efforts to get an immediate advisory vote on war or peace.

In addition to Bailey, Civil War General Isaac R. Sherwood (Democrat, Ohio) used the Callaway text in a war referendum resolution introduced "by request" on February 10. His reputation in Congress as one of the most outspoken and aggressive pacifists resulted, in part, from his 1916 resolution seeking to apply the machinery of Bryan's arbitration treaties to the World War.[41] Frank Buchanan (Democrat, Ill.) also borrowed the text of his resolution from Callaway, who was a colleague on the House Naval Affairs Committee. Buchanan had tried without success in 1915 to commit the American Federation of Labor to a Bryan-type pacifism and was still among Bryan's followers in 1917, especially after his own defeat for reelection. A structural iron worker from Chicago, he revealed his debt to Bryan in House arguments that the executive branch was usurping the war-declaring powers of Congress. Buchanan's affinity with the Callaway-led peace minority in the Naval Committee was clear from arguments that America was adequately prepared and in no danger

[39]Minutes (Washington Branch), Feb. 11, 1917, WPP Collection, SCPC.

[40]Emergency Peace Committee of Washington, *Report,* p. 3, attached to Thomas to Addams, Feb. 10, 1917, WPP Collection, SCPC.

[41]*Cong. Rec.,* 64th Cong., 2d sess., p. 3049 (Feb. 10, 1917); *Ohio State Journal,* Feb. 13, Mar. 20, Apr. 27, 1917; Curti, *Bryan and World Peace,* p. 238.

of invasion.[42] The Illinois Congressman supported the war referendum because of his antipreparedness views, an affinity with Bryan, a belief that it would reflect labor's interest in peace, and the conviction that it might limit executive control of foreign affairs.

Congressman Walter L. Hensley (Democrat, Mo.) introduced on February 15 a fourth war referendum resolution based on Callaway's text. It followed his successful effort to add to the 1916 naval appropriations bill an amendment providing for an international disarmament-arbitration conference. He was another of Callaway's pacifist colleagues on the Naval Committee, and a friend of, and spokesman for, Bryan. Hensley's support of the war referendum reflected, therefore, his internationalist and antipreparedness views and his convictions that the war-declaring power must be democratized.[43]

Introduction of five new war referendum resolutions in less than a week, all using Callaway's text, led the House Committee on Foreign Affairs to grant a hearing on the parent resolution. After professional peace workers had solicited the loudest outcry in favor of an advisory referendum, the hearing apparently was only a superficial recognition of the war referendum's sudden strength, both in Congress and within the peace movement. It came just a week after Callaway's resolution and lasted only forty-five minutes. Callaway did not testify. Testimony by only half a dozen radicals indicated some support of the measure by migratory and unskilled labor, represented by the International Brotherhood Welfare Association, and interest by such reform groups as the Initiative and Referendum League and Single Tax Club.[44]

Witnesses stressed two themes already evident in the war referendum movement. Believing that munitions makers and the press were moving the country toward war, the pro-referendum voices declared they would not defend Americans from attack in war zones, being interested only in continental self-defense. In this the radical spokesmen were announcing the war referendum adherent's typical defense concept, one

[42]*Cong. Rec.,* 64th Cong., 2d sess., p. 3049 (Feb. 10, 1917), pp. 3431–34 (Feb. 16, 1917), and Appendix, pp. 884–88; Curti, *Bryan and World Peace,* p. 223–24. Copies of Sherwood's House Resolution 497 and Buchanan's House Resolution 495 are in WPP Collection, SCPC.

[43]Hensley's House Resolution 507 is in the folder on House Resolution 492, 64th Cong., RG 233, NA. It is a copy of Callaway's printed resolution, edited to read "H. Res. 507, Mr. Hensley." See also *Cong. Rec.,* 64th Cong., 2d sess., p. 3385 (Feb. 15, 1917); John Clark Crighton, *Missouri and the World War, 1914–1917: A Study in Public Opinion,* University of Missouri Studies Vol. 21 (Columbia, Mo., 1947), pp. 131, 167–68; and Curti, *Bryan and World Peace,* p. 235.

[44]U.S., Congress, House, 64th Cong., 2d sess., *Referendum on Declaration of War:* Hearings before the Committee on Foreign Affairs, House of Representatives, on House Resolution 492, February 17, 1917, pp. 1–18.

characterized by their conviction that some preparedness was necessary but that America's defense began near the shoreline. Promising to defend America "in the event of invasion" and making the war referendum inoperable in such an eventuality, they nevertheless based their faith in the plan on the premise that America would *not* be invaded. From this premise, they moved to the second theme. The only requirement, since there was no danger of invasion so long as the country maintained an "adequate" defense, was to restrict the Executive from going down "the road to war" without *direct* and *immediate* advice by the people. Several witnesses agreed that the secretary of state was too powerful, charging the State Department with moving the country to the very "brink of war." They then offered popular control, through a referendum on war, to check such independent action by the Executive.[45]

Absence of testimony from leading pro-referendum pacifist bodies was not unusual in view of their crediting legislative operations to Bailey. Furthermore, Callaway was in Chicago addressing an antiwar meeting sponsored by the Woman's Peace Party and its local emergency affiliate, the Chicago Emergency Anti-War Committee. Before the mass meeting on February 18 in the Coliseum, the Anti-War Committee appealed for public attendance and support in the German language press and through the churches, emphasizing as the expressed purpose of the pacifist rally "the demand for popular referendum before war is declared." With La Follette unable to speak, Callaway followed local radical minister Herbert S. Bigelow, denouncing in radical fashion the "league for war" made up of the metropolitan press, munitions makers, the military establishment, and capitalists. Indeed, a description of Callaway made by a Washington Woman's Peace Party official suited him well. Callaway, as promised, was a "stirring speaker" with "hot radical stuff."[46] During the 1916 preparedness debate, Bailey had commended Callaway in a similar vein, calling him "a powerful speaker, unique in his methods and absolutely convincing in his presentation. . . . I think in many ways he makes the strongest argument against the big army and big navy crowd

<hr>

[45] Ibid.

[46] Harriet Thomas to Mrs. Eleanor G. Karsten, Feb. 14, 1917, and form letter, Feb. 15, 1917, Emergency Anti-War Committee (Chicago) Papers, SCPC; and *New York Times,* Feb. 19, 1917; Link, *Wilson,* V, 305-6. Bryan endorsed this meeting, and his correspondence to Miss Addams, read at the rally, endorsed the war referendum as the "best way" to prevent intervention. Callaway's speech in favor of his referendum resolution, Bryan's testimony, and local enthusiasm for it led to full acceptance by the 12,000 citizens present as well as local sponsors (Bryan to Addams, Feb. 13, 17, 1917, and Grace Abbott and Fred A. Moore [for the Chicago Emergency Anti-War Committee] to Woodrow Wilson, Feb. 18, 1917, Emergency Anti-War Committee [Chicago] Papers, SCPC).

that I have heard. He is loaded to the muzzle with facts and drives them home with sledge hammer blows."[47] Despite Callaway's enthusiastic effort for the referendum in Chicago, however, the previous day's hearing proved only a sop to the referendum's supporters. The resolution was never reported out of committee.

Nevertheless, it did publicize efforts for an advisory referendum. The American Union Against Militarism's straw vote was in full operation, and an extensive petition campaign by other groups was in force. In one week before the hearing, the House Foreign Affairs Committee had received numerous petitions in favor of the war referendum. Some specifically endorsed the Callaway resolution, although the mass expression of support, for which Bryan and others had hoped, never materialized.[48]

Direct appeals to senators, on the other hand, failed to produce any marked increase in support for an advisory referendum. Not even John D. Works, Republican agrarian radical from California, could be persuaded to introduce a war referendum resolution. His mail was full of letters and petitions supporting his antiwar speeches, especially his views against further delegation of the war-making powers to the president.[49] Likewise, Robert La Follette, in spite of petitions to the contrary, never made good his threat to attach a war referendum rider to any appropriate bill.[50] Ohio Senator Warren G. Harding, when asked to support the House measures, answered most emphatically: "No, it is useless to urge that. I will resign my office before I will vote for such a proposition."[51] Yet Harding when president came close to endorsing the principle as part of his association of nations scheme proposed as a substitute for the League of Nations.

[47] Warren Worth Bailey to Daniel Kiefer, Apr. 29, 1916, Box 9, Bailey Papers.

[48] These petitions reveal marked support for the war referendum plan from Illinois Socialists, the North Dakota German-Hungarian Society, and pacifists in Boston and Baltimore. The frequent form of antiwar and pro-referendum views was, in addition to the formal petition, the American Union Against Militarism postal card. One contained the comment "Bryan and La Follette talk sense. Do thou likewise!" See U.S., Congress, House, 64th Cong., Foreign Affairs Committee, "Petitions: Referendum on the Question of Declaring War against the Central Powers," Feb. 1917, RG 233, NA, especially John B. Moore to James A. Gallivan (Democrat, Mass.), Feb. 13, 1917.

[49] *Cong. Rec.*, 64th Cong., 2d sess., pp. 3057–61 (Feb. 12, 1917), especially Dr. Charles Sumner Bacon to Senator Works, Feb. 8, 1917, p. 3057; ibid., pp. 2729–31, 2734–35 (Feb. 7, 1917).

[50] Daniel O'Connell (of the Anti-War Society of San Francisco) to Senator La Follette, Mar. 28, 1917, forwarding petitions (7,555 names) urging the referendum plan, U.S., Congress, Senate, 65th Cong., "Petitions Which Were Tabled; War Referendum" (File 65A–K10), RG 233, NA. O'Connell was west coast leader of Irish-Americans. See Edward Cuddy, "Irish-American Propagandists and American Neutrality, 1914–1917," *Mid-America,* 49, (1967), 271.

[51] *Ohio State Journal,* Feb. 13, 15, 1917.

Senator La Follette, however, continued indirectly to influence the emergency war referendum campaign; three referendum bills after the superficial hearing borrowed La Follette's 1916 text. On February 20, Congressmen Charles A. Lindbergh (Republican, Minn.) and 1900 Bryan-organizer and Populist James H. "Cyclone" Davis (Democrat, Tex.) introduced war referendum resolutions. Three days later General Isaac Sherwood, in a second effort for the war referendum, introduced another resolution, based this time on La Follette's text. Like the other emergency resolutions, and in keeping with Bryan's own change after the break with Germany, all three provided an immediate advisory referendum rather than a permanent reform through a constitutional amendment. In the absence of existing machinery to conduct the straw vote, Lindbergh, Davis, and Sherwood adopted La Follette's earlier suggestion to work through the Census Bureau. But like the other proposals, these too died in the Foreign Affairs Committee.[52]

A majority of the new war referendum resolutions introduced in February did not reflect, in their origin, German-American or other ethnic influences. They were products of organized pacifist interest, legislators' personal pacifism, and, especially, William Jennings Bryan's example. Once introduced, however, evidence of ethnic bases to antiwar attitudes existed, particularly in petitions presented to Congress and in the case of two of the war referendum resolutions. Introduced February 16, between the resolutions based on either Callaway's or La Follette's texts, Henry T. Helgeson's war referendum resolution stood alone. The North Dakota Republican devised his own text and did not receive the organized pacifist interest accorded Bailey and Callaway.

Yet Helgeson's arguments for the war referendum were common to other sponsors. In a speech before its introduction, he charged that a "controlled press" and profiteers were moving the country toward war, being joined by some congressmen who did not consider war's cost to the common people. His bill quoted General Sherman's "War is hell" dictum in its preface and then proceeded to order a national advisory referendum. In agreement with Bryan and Callaway in aim but different in language, it also provided "that (except in case of threatened invasion) the President shall take no action that may tend to involve the United

---

[52]*Cong. Rec.,* 64th Cong., 2d sess., p. 3734 (Feb. 20, 1917), p. 4064 (Feb. 23, 1917); copies of the Lindbergh and Sherwood bills, endorsed by the Woman's Peace Party, are in WPP Collection, SCPC. Of these sponsors, only Sherwood would be returning to the Sixty-fifth Congress. Lindbergh, one of only two Republicans among the eight sponsors of the nine February resolutions, and Davis were among the anti–big navy congressmen (*New York Times,* Feb. 15, 1917).

States in war, until the result of said Referendum shall be made known to Congress."[53] It clearly reflected a fear, common among war referendum proponents, that the president would take some action obligating the Congress to a war declaration during the coming congressional recess.

After the Washington hearings on the war referendum, numerous petitions presented to the House Foreign Affairs Committee continued to come from Helgeson's North Dakota. Small town papers there urged people to avoid being "farmed by a capitalist class" by demanding a referendum on war. Such activity definitely reflected German-American and Socialist views.[54] Fearing that strong German-American sentiment for the referendum would weaken their appeal, the Washington Emergency Peace Committee had already urged special efforts for the proposal in "non-German" states like Indiana, Massachusetts, Minnesota, and Maryland.[55]

Indeed there was remarkable German-American interest in the war referendum movement at this time, although interest centered primarily around only two war referendum resolutions. The first indication of ethnic pressures, shown in 1913, was in support for Congressman Richard Bartholdt's embargo and war referendum resolutions. Certainly his Missouri district contained a large German-American constituency, and, besides, he was himself a German immigrant. Interest in Hensley's 1917 war referendum proposal was also, in part, German-American.[56]

Early in February the National German-American Alliance also got behind the war referendum plan. This was the largest organized ethnic group in America at the time, numbering over two and one-half million members; since its organization in 1901, it was directed by Charles John Hexamer. On February 6 Hexamer telegraphed state presidents to hold

[53]Original bill in "House Joint Resolutions, Originals, Numbers 1–393, 64th Congress, 1915–1917," RG 233, NA; *Cong. Rec.,* 64th Cong., 2d sess., pp. 3454, 3466 (Feb. 16, 1917). Support for this bill came from Los Angeles, Boston, New York, and North Dakota (ibid., Appendix, pp. 590–93). A copy of the bill is also in WPP Collection, SCPC.

[54]See 64th Cong., Foreign Affairs Committee, "Petitions: Referendum on the Question of Declaring War against the Central Powers," Feb. 1917, RG 233, NA. Other German-American support came from Wisconsin, Nebraska, and New York (Robert P. Wilkins, "The Non-Ethnic Roots of North Dakota Isolationism," *Nebraska History,* 44 [1963], 205–21).

[55]Emergency Peace Committee of Washington, *Report,* p. 3, attached to Thomas to Addams, Feb. 10, 1917, WPP Collection, SCPC.

[56]Before any of the February resolutions appeared in Congress, the German-language Saint Louis daily *Westliche Post,* Feb. 6, endorsed a war referendum. See Crighton, *Missouri and the World War,* p. 167. The *Saint Louis Post-Dispatch* opposed the idea the next day (ibid., p. 168).

peace meetings and adopt resolutions asking Congress to "submit the question of declaring war to a referendum."[57] Believing that the people were opposed to war, the Alliance worked for the referendum until America's decision for intervention.

Socialists and German-Americans, however, were not the only elements of continuing referendum support. *Capper's Weekly,* of Topeka, Kansas, urged that the war decision "be referred to the nation itself," or if that were not possible, it should at least reflect a majority vote in Congress, rather than what Governor Arthur Capper felt to be a minority in the administration. Callaway continued to speak for his bill before such peace groups as the Massachusetts Emergency Peace Committee, assailing army, navy, and press. To the Emergency Peace Committee of Washington, no legislative measure seemed "to be so much discussed . . . as that of the referendum." Believing that democratic control of foreign affairs was assured, the Committee covered the capital daily through its own membership or volunteers of the local branch of the Woman's Peace Party.[58] Charles Hallinan continued also to operate the American Union Against Militarism's mail center in Washington, still confident that his efforts would "stiffen up the war referendum sentiment" and help peace workers and legislators achieve their advisory referendum on war.[59]

America had witnessed, following the rupture with Germany, a remarkable effort for consensus within the peace movement. In this many peace advocates and opponents of intervention offered the war referendum as a practical but eleventh-hour peace measure to postpone, or even avoid entirely, use of American forces in Europe. Following Bryan's faith and example, some rallied behind the effort by creating new, more radical peace organizations. Others, like Amos Pinchot and Randolph Bourne, stressed the war referendum plan in debates with other in-

[57]The Alliance was strongest in Pennsylvania, Wisconsin, Ohio, New York, Indiana, Illinois, and Iowa. Bartholdt was its congressional spokesman at first, but by 1917 it paid little attention to any congressman. See Clifton James Child, *The German-Americans in Politics, 1914–1917* (Madison, Wis., 1939), pp. 2–5, 13–14. 157. Toledo German-Americans called for a referendum on Feb. 4, sending their resolution to Wilson and the Ohio delegation. Philadelphia Socialists heard radical state legislator and labor leader James H. Maurer propose a general strike if the government refused a referendum. Finally, Milwaukee German-Americans, representing some ten thousand members of the Alliance, telegraphed Senator La Follette in March, upholding his antiwar views and his opposition to the Armed Ships Bill. See *New York Times,* Feb. 5, 1917, and Child, *German-Americans,* pp. 161–62.

[58]*Public,* 20 (1917), 281; *New York Times,* Feb. 26, 1917; *Ohio State Journal,* Feb. 26, 1917; and Emergency Peace Committee of Washington, *Report,* p. 3, attached to Thomas to Addams, Feb. 10, 1917, WPP Collection, SCPC.

[59]Hallinan Memorandum, n.d., American Union Against Militarism folder, WPP Collection, SCPC.

tellectuals and continued to urge that only peace would permit further domestic progressivism. The test referendum and every other available method were used to publicize efforts for the measure, and nine new war referendum resolutions, seeking an advisory vote of the people, were introduced in Congress.

That advocates did not achieve an advisory referendum suggests, on the surface, that efforts were a failure. But the war referendum activity at this time was significant for several reasons. It was a tireless campaign, finally dominated by radicals, which saw disparate peace organizations and individuals unite quite successfully behind their unofficial leader and recognized hero, William Jennings Bryan. It revealed within the heated debate over war and peace the plight of progressives when faced with the ultimate challenge—the use of force in international affairs. Finally, the result of all the furor for peace was a degree of congressional interest and popular support for the war referendum plan not generally recognized by historians and strong enough to exert an important influence on the nation's foreign policy for two decades.

CHAPTER IV

Intervention and Civil Liberties

DURING PRESIDENT WILSON'S decision-making period, when he moved from armed neutrality to full belligerency as the only option remaining, several leading war referendum advocates made eleventh-hour efforts to postpone the apparently inevitable resort to force. As straw votes continued to demonstrate opposition to intervention and support for an advisory referendum, William Jennings Bryan made a final appeal for peace in letters to every member of Congress.[1] He continued to advocate his two favorite peace plans: arbitration of differences with Germany by an international tribunal and an advisory referendum. "If you reach the conclusion," he wrote, "that nothing but war will satisfy the nation's honor, is it too much to ask that, by a referendum, you consult the wishes of those who must, in case of war, defend the nation's honor with their lives?"[2]

As a last desperate indication of antiwar strength, some fifteen hundred pacifist demonstrators led by the Emergency Peace Federation of New York converged on Washington as Congress opened. Local authorities denied them a hearing before either President Wilson or Vice President Marshall; after police repelled them from the State, War, and Navy Department buildings, they refused the pacifists a parade permit. Senator La Follette failed to get them formal authority for a Capitol demonstration, but they made an effort to await congressmen on the Capitol steps. Some even entered the Senate wing, where one youthful pacifist engaged in a brief physical encounter with Senator Lodge. They adjourned then to a nearby national guard armory after police dispersed them from the Capitol steps.[3]

The peace advocates, nevertheless, were hesitant, even in the end, to recognize defeat. Amos Pinchot received from John Dewey about this time a letter that probably best reflected the sentiment of interventionists

[1] "Report on the Post Card Referendum in Massachusetts," 1917 folder, Emergency Peace Committee of Massachusetts Files, SCPC; "Report of Work in the National Office of the Woman's Peace Party," Apr. 1, 1917, WPP Collection, SCPC.
[2] Bryan to members of Congress, Mar. 28, 1917, Bryan Papers.
[3] Minutes (Washington Branch), Apr. 2, 1917, WPP Collection, SCPC. The best secondary accounts of the demonstration and related incidents are in Walter Millis, *Road to War: America 1914–1917* (Boston, 1935), pp. 432–35, and Curti, *Peace or War*, pp. 252–53.

on the eve of Wilson's war message. As if to console opponent Pinchot in his losing cause, Dewey claimed that "the general attitude of our public mind is one of a sober intent to make the best of a bad job, a job it would much prefer not to get involved in, but a job that has to be done."[4] Yet in spite of such a realistic appraisal as this, articulate Americans on both sides of the debate, neither of which represented the silent masses, remained, according to Arthur S. Link, "divided up to the very end of American neutrality."[5] Certainly most war referendum advocates, led by William Jennings Bryan, were not yet ready to concede on the basis of Dewey's argument.

Bryan telegraphed Congressman Benjamin Clark Hilliard (Democrat, Col.) April 3, in answer to a request for advice on his upcoming war resolution vote. In his last 1917 appeal for peace by referendum, the former secretary of state said: "Believing in right of people to rule, even on question of war, I favor referendum as means of ascertaining public will. If referendum refused each representative must conscineiously [*sic*] try to find out for himself the wishes of his constituents and then obey them or resign."[6] He added that if his constituents wanted war, he, as their representative, would resign rather than share responsibility for America's intervention. Thus, once more Bryan had prescribed his peace formula to congressional spokesmen and, in terms of his March 28 appeal, to all congressmen.

His calls for referendum in February had led to nine new war referendum resolutions. His efforts then helped place this peace plan in the forefront of organized antimilitarism. Support of the war referendum plan was sufficient by April 1917 for many Americans to regard it as their last hope for staying out of the European war. Yet in spite of its demonstrated strength and last minute appeals to support it, the congressional debate on war entry did not reflect any final, well-organized effort on behalf of an advisory referendum. To be sure, last ditch appeals to congressmen were full of references to it, but there were also numerous appeals for war and conscription. And no additional resolutions in favor of a referendum appeared in Congress.

In fact, most congressmen who mentioned the war referendum during the debate did so in an effort to justify their opposition to the war resolution. During the April 4, 1917, Senate debate, James K. Vardaman (Democrat, Miss.) prefaced his nay vote with the opinion that a

[4]John Dewey to Amos Pinchot, Mar. 30, 1917, Amos Pinchot Papers.

[5]Link, *Wilson*, V, 419. Link maintains, but does not prove (because he gives a more complete treatment of interventionist sentiment) that peace sentiment was as strong as war pressures.

[6]Bryan to B. C. Hillard, Apr. 3, 1917, Bryan Papers.

referendum would record a "thunderous vote directing the President to find some other way than war." Senator George W. Norris (Republican, Neb.) agreed.[7] Senator La Follette, even at this late date, spoke in favor of a national advisory referendum similar to those conducted in his state of Wisconsin, the results of which he reported during the debate. But these and other appeals for a referendum by Senator A. J. Gronna of North Dakota and, in the House of Representatives, by newcomer Ernest Lundeen, whose Minneapolis constituents had opposed intervention by ten to one in a straw vote, were to no avail.[8] Test referendums, petitions, emotion-filled speeches, and newspaper advertisements were no longer effective. With mixed national emotions, American belligerency became a fact in the early morning hours of April 6, 1917.[9]

Immediate reaction to the congressional decision included efforts by some radicals to demonstrate just the degree to which the war vote was not a national decision. Their intense enthusiasm for the referendum approach to peace did not easily or quickly subside. From an attempt at least to limit the war to Europe, irreconcilable pacifists now prepared to limit America's participation in that war. The war referendum was no longer a way to keep America out of *this* war, but supporters insisted that American neutrality could have been maintained by use of the plan. Socialists, for example, met in Saint Louis following the war decision and passed this resolution: "The American people did not and do not want this war. They have not been consulted about the war and have not had part in declaring war."[10] The party had been among leading antiwar voices just

[7]*Cong. Rec.*, 65th Cong., 1st sess., pp. 200–261 (Apr. 4, 1917). Vardaman's antiwar stand reflected, in part, his fear of universal military training upon the South's white supremacy views. See Vardaman to William Jennings Bryan, Apr. 2, 1917, Bryan Papers, and Holmes, *James Kimble Vardaman,* p. 318. Norris later did not recall discussion of the war referendum during the war debate (*Fighting Liberal: The Autobiography of George W. Norris* [New York, 1945], pp. 188–201).

[8]*Cong. Rec.,* 65th Cong., 1st sess., p. 362 (Apr. 5, 1917).

[9]War referendum sponsors in the House and their votes on the war resolution were as follows: Church, Hensley, Lundeen, and Sherwood, who obviously had again changed his mind, voted Nay. Helgeson did not vote, and others were no longer in Congress: Bartholdt (retired), Bailey, Callaway, Davis of Texas, Lindbergh, and Buchanan of Illinois, who were defeated or not renominated in 1916. Later House sponsors voting against war in 1917 were James A. Frear (Republican, Wis.) and Clarence C. Dill (Democrat, Wash.). In the Senate, war referendum partisans La Follette, Vardaman, and Gronna voted Nay; later sponsor Thomas P. Gore (Democrat, Okla.) did not vote; Owen, also of Oklahoma, voted in favor of war (*Cong. Rec.,* 65th Cong., 1st sess., p. 261 [Apr. 4, 1917], pp. 412–13 [April 5, 1917]). Oswald Garrison Villard later suggested that a secret ballot in Congress would have shown "a large majority" against intervention and charged that the president had "usurped the war-making power" (*Fighting Years,* pp. 322–23).

[10]H. C. Peterson and Gilbert C. Fite, *Opponents of War: 1917–1918* (Madison, Wis., 1957), p. 9.

before the congressional vote, having urged in a telegram to Wilson that the matter "be put to a referendum vote of the adult citizens of the United States, both men and women."[11] Despite internal differences the war decision created among Socialists, the party and its members continued to express a lack of faith in the representative system of government and especially argued soon for a conscription referendum.

In contrast, and as he had indicated on several occasions since his resignation, William Jennings Bryan pledged to Americans generally and to President Wilson directly that he would render the services of a patriot.[12] Jane Addams, on the other hand, returned to Washington after the decision for war and protested before the Military Affairs Committee against conscription without a referendum of the people. She believed that conscription would threaten "the whole theory of self-government founded upon conscious participation and inner consent."[13] Her reaction was typical of many progressive pacifists, and she continued to manifest the same fears certain progressives had in opposing, first, preparedness and then full belligerency. After losing the first two battles, pacifists tried once more to limit war's impact on America, this time by advancing such schemes as a national referendum on military service.[14]

It is true that the most uncompromising peace workers, which included most war referendum partisans, represented a radical minority in the peace movement. Even before April 6 organized pacifism had experienced defections, some of which hinged on the war referendum plan. With American intervention, however, more and more peace groups and individual peace advocates agreed with Bryan and pledged loyalty to the American government's war effort. Among them, the Carnegie-backed organizations like the Church Peace Union and the World Peace Foundation joined Hamilton Holt's League to Enforce Peace, the American Peace Society, and the Carnegie Endowment in full support of Wilson and the war effort. George Creel's Committee on Public Information even used the Carnegie Endowment's offices. Finally, although several leaders of the Woman's Peace Party followed the example of Jane Addams and

[11]Socialist Party Emergency Committee to Wilson, rpt. in *American Socialist,* Apr. 7, 1917, National Office Files, Socialist Party of America Papers. See also Marchand, *American Peace Movement,* pp. 291–94.

[12]Levine, *Bryan,* pp. 90–92, attempts to answer Bryan's critics on the point of his sudden, but often previously announced, appearance as a "pacifist in arms." Levine concludes that he was not a nonresistant, that he was never blinded from devotion to duty by his vision for peace.

[13]Addams, *Peace and Bread in Time of War,* pp. 117, 119.

[14]Socialists were among this group. See plea for a popular referendum on military service, in John Spargo, "Committee on War and Militarism, Minority Report, 1917," p. 5, War and Peace File (1915–39), Socialist Party of America Papers.

refused to compromise their opposition to war, the organization itself did not condemn the war effort.[15]

As some peace workers directed their efforts to war-support activities or shifted attention to other social causes, others, including especially most of the war referendum proponents, stayed with the peace crusade. Radicalization continued as new sources of support were found and new leadership emerged. In the process interest in the referendum approach to peace remained high, and it became important in wartime civil liberties issues.

Two prominent voices for peace and progressivism who moved to protect civil liberties with new vigor were Saint Louis social worker Roger Nash Baldwin and Norman Thomas, a Presbyterian minister and also a social worker. Both had been active in the American Union Against Militarism earlier, but after March 1917 they became more active as part of its leftward trend. Showing special interest in civil liberties, they created within the Union a Bureau for Conscientious Objectors, and by April 6 Baldwin was in New York as an associate director of the Union.[16] As formulated by a Union committee headed by Oswald Garrison Villard soon after American intervention, the Union pledged primary emphasis upon "preservation of democratic institutions and civil liberties."[17] Specifically, Villard and Baldwin urged upon Wilson a plan of alternative service for conscientious objectors, who would work on farm camps to raise food for the army. Villard later recorded that this plan came to naught after apparent presidential approval and blamed Secretary of War Baker.[18] The radical pacifists continued to assert that war would end the American way of life, regarding militarism generally, and now conscription specifically, as repugnant to American ideals and democracy.

Other leaders in the Union, however, continued to stress past aims and opposed the new Thomas-Baldwin emphasis on civil liberties. Villard's committee thus reaffirmed the Union's traditional position in favor of a world peace organization, in statements of war aims by all belligerents, and in faith in "democratic control of our foreign affairs." The Union, in

---

[15]Curti, *Peace or War*, p. 255.

[16]Johnson, *Challenge to American Freedoms*, pp. 9–16; Marchand, *American Peace Movement*, pp. 252–54. Thomas, who had been more active in the Christian pacifist Fellowship of Reconciliation (FOR) for some time, intensified his antiwar activities through more radical organizations after intervention (Bernard K. Johnpoll, *Pacifist's Progress: Norman Thomas and the Decline of American Socialism* [Chicago, 1970], pp. 19–20). See also Chatfield, *For Peace and Justice*, pp. 37–41, on Thomas and FOR.

[17]"Policies," Statement of Mr. Villard's Committee on Policies and Programs, Apr. 13, 1917, AUAM Records, SCPC.

[18]Villard, *Fighting Years*, pp. 334–35.

fact, now carried that faith further than ever, advocating "submission to the people for a referendum vote of *any foreign policy*."[19] Villard later suggested that the "almost overnight establishment of the selective draft boards showed how quickly new machinery for taking a referendum" could be established.[20] The American Union Against Militarism, still under the same leadership, thus clearly reacted even more radically after failing to achieve its advisory referendum before intervention. Their faith in representative government had reached its nadir.

By the summer of 1917, the Union was on the verge of a split over its new emphasis, with Jane Addams, Paul Kellogg, and Lillian Wald certain the civil liberties issues would harm other goals of the Union.[21] Compromise was possible at first, with the renaming of Baldwin's inner organization the Civil Liberties Bureau, but by October 1917 the inevitable split in the American Union Against Militarism came. Chairman Lillian Wald resigned, Amos Pinchot headed the renamed American Union for a Democratic Peace, and Baldwin led his associates out of the Union to establish the independent American Civil Liberties Union.[22] With these internal changes in the Union Against Militarism, it became less active in peace work down to its official demise in 1922. Once more the peace movement's most serious problem—internal diversity of reform interests—had resulted in further organizational proliferation. But contrary to Roland Marchand's conclusion, that "influential participation" in the peace movement by social workers ended with the disintegration of the Union, continuity of interest and leadership was evident in a new, more radical peace organization—the People's Council of America.[23] Furthermore, this continuity was even indicated by continued

[19]"Policies," Statement of Mr. Villard's Committee on Policies and Programs, Apr. 13, 1917, AUAM Records, SCPC (emphasis mine). In 1964 Norman Thomas remarked that he would not favor putting the foreign policy of our country to a recurring referendum. When questioned about his own support of the war referendum plan in 1917, he thanked the writer for reminding him of it and added: "I would not oppose it today; I might even advocate a war referendum today; but I would not place main reliance on it in a nuclear age" (Interview, Norman Thomas, University of Georgia, Feb. 5, 1964).

[20]Villard, *Fighting Years,* p. 337.

[21]Kellogg and Wald threatened to resign over the emphasis given the Conscientious Objectors' Bureau (Crystal Eastman, Statement, Wald-Kellogg letters of Resignation, June 14, 1917, AUAM Records, SCPC).

[22]Miss Wald's Statement, Minutes, Sept. 13, 1917; ibid., Oct. 29, 1917; Oswald Garrison Villard to Crystal Eastman, Sept. 28, 1917, Lillian Wald to Miss Eastman, Sept. 27, 1917, Jane Addams to Miss Eastman, Sept. 28, 1917, all in AUAM Records, Civil Liberties Bureau folder, SCPC. The new name for the antimilitarists lasted only a few months. Johnson, *Challenge to American Freedoms,* pp. 19–24, and Marchand, *American Peace Movement,* pp. 254–58, comment on the Union's internal strife.

[23]Marchand, *American Peace Movement,* p. 258.

interest in the referendum approach to peace by some in the Union Against Militarism during its final troubled years.

Like organized antimilitarism before American entry into the war, the People's Council of America was a cross-section of radical pacifism, social progressivism, midwestern agrarianism, and socialism. It was another experiment in outward dissent and, to some extent, a focus for internal pacifist consensus. After America's war decision, the Emergency Peace Federation, the largest and most successful of preintervention radical groups, sponsored a peace rally at Madison Square Garden. On May 30–31, some fifteen thousand persons attended this First National Conference for Democracy and the Terms of Peace. They represented all of the major peace groups active before April 6, including the American Union Against Militarism, the sponsoring Emergency Peace Federation, the Woman's Peace Party, the American Socialist Party, and the Committee for Democratic Control. These groups still appealed primarily to antiwar radicals; but, as before, they exhibited more than a negative protest. They met to formulate a program to establish quickly permanent peace and promote industrial democracy.[24]

Important social radicals attending this meeting were Miss Rebecca Shelly and Miss Lella Secor, who late in 1914 had joined with others to create the American Neutral Conference Committee, from which most of America's radical pacifist groups could be traced. Both were members of the Ford Peace Ship venture and staff members of the Emergency Peace Federation, sponsor of the conference. Both had earlier supported the war referendum plan. Other war referendum advocates present—already familiar leaders within radical peace work—included Conference Chairman Rabbi Judah Magnes, Emily Greene Balch, Crystal and Max Eastman, Randolph Bourne, Amos Pinchot, David Starr Jordan, and Louis Lochner. Socialists Morris Hillquit, Norman Thomas, Eugene Debs, and Scott Nearing joined with many of these as the "organizing committee" of the People's Council of America, the new radical organization formed as a result of the May 30–31 Conference.[25]

---

[24]Emily Greene Balch, "History and Organization," June 8, 1940, PCA Papers, SCPC. See also *People's Council of America Bulletin,* 1, No. 1 (1917) (not paged until February 1918; cited hereafter as *PC Bulletin*). The best secondary account of the People's Council is in Frank Grubbs's history of wartime labor, *Struggle for Labor Loyalty.* Most writers emphasize the troubled short history of the organization. But see Chatfield, *For Peace and Justice,* pp. 27–29, 34–35, for brief notice of its support of the war referendum.

[25]Balch, "History and Organization," June 8, 1940, PCA Papers, SCPC; Grubbs, *Struggle for Labor Loyalty,* pp. 22–35. Max Eastman offers a description of several People's Council leaders in *Love and Revolution,* p. 49. Cantor, *Eastman,* does not mention his association with the People's Council.

The Council's program and aims, indeed, its ambitions, as formulated by the New York conference, revealed the new organization's political radicalism and socialist slant as well as its almost complete distrust of representative government. Miss Shelly, in fact, had made the call for a People's Council of America on May 31 on the premise that Congress did not represent the will of the people. Here lay the basis for the Council's central concern over "American Liberties" in wartime.[26]

The People's Council endorsed among its international objectives a world peace organization, a concrete statement of American war aims, an early peace based on no annexations or indemnities, and free development of nationalities. A radical, domestic "American Liberties" program, however, was the heart of People's Council. Conference resolutions protested the tampering with mails and the restriction of passports and pledged Council vigilance for freedoms of speech, press, assembly, and petition. The pacifists called for repeal of conscription legislation and passage of laws for direct democratic controls of foreign policy. They specifically urged that "no war should be declared nor system of conscription adopted without referendum of the people." Believing not only that the war decision had been unpopular but that it resulted from a "financial conspiracy," they advocated wartime conscription of wealth and a ceiling of $100,000 on annual individual incomes.[27] The Council's disillusionment with militant America was certain to challenge the tolerance of a war government. The result was a sometimes bitter clash between the two and suppression of civil liberties.

The rapid success of the People's Council—if its claim of almost two million members in forty-five local councils was accurate—did manifest significant popular disapproval of America's war entry.[28] Its success also

[26]*Report of the First American Conference for Democracy and Terms of Peace, May 30–31, 1917* (New York, 1917), p. 77, PCA Papers, SCPC. The full extent of its distrust of representative government was clear from a decision to restrict government employees from its leadership. In this way a "people's" organization would be assured (Minutes of Organizing Committee, June 28, 1917, ibid.) For treatment of the Council's origin and further documentation of Miss Shelly's distrust of representative government, as well as the organization's use of the Petrograd Soviet as a "model for domestic political reconstruction," see Marchand, *American Peace Movement,* pp. 307–9. Christopher Lasch regards the People's Council as "the most immediate and tangible manifestation in America of the impact of the Russian revolution" (*The American Liberals and the Russian Revolution* [New York, 1962], p. 40).

[27]"Resolutions," *Report, First American Conference for Democracy and Terms of Peace,* pp. 8–9; "American Liberties," n.d.; "Suggestions for Taxation Plank," n.d.; *PC Bulletin,* 1, No. 1 (1917); all in PCA Papers, SCPC.

[28]Grubbs, *Struggle for Labor Loyalty,* p. 23, maintains that the People's Council welcomed anyone "who wanted to obstruct the war effort."

demonstrated the gradual decline of the American Union Against Militarism, although the Union remained, under Amos Pinchot and then Oswald Garrison Villard, on the scene till 1922.[29] The People's Council's success caused rather a more complete destruction of the Emergency Peace Federation. Actually this preintervention group merely merged with the People's Council, transferring assets, equipment, files, leadership, and even office space to the new group. The Federation's executive committee authorized the merger in a final meeting on July 5. In existence only about six months, its radical pacifist voice had been loud and effective in producing the pre-April consensus on the advisory referendum plan. After initiating the conference that led to the People's Council, the Federation correctly evaluated its existence as "democratic as it was daring." "Instead of working as an isolated group of intellectuals aloof from the people," they believed their work had opened up "for the American people a channel through which they might express their sentiments on war and peace."[30]

Meanwhile, another preintervention peace group gradually declined as social radicals worked through the People's Council. Amos Pinchot, Crystal Eastman, and Randolph Bourne were among officials of the Committee for Democratic Control at the Council's birth. Although Pinchot believed that the Committee might serve pacifists better in wartime because of its name, the Committee for Democratic Control gradually disbanded in 1917. In June an effort to transfer its meager assets to the Woman's Peace Party failed. By August, however, the Committee's funds and list of 451 supporters went to advertising the Union Against Militarism's Civil Liberties Bureau.[31] Individual peace workers in this group thereafter found adequate opportunity for influence and peace leadership and continued advocacy of the referendum approach to peace, through the Council and their own individual endeavors.

The People's Council attracted trade unions, farmer's organizations, Socialist locals, and single-tax groups as well as earlier emergency peace

[29]See chapter 7. Among Union leaders apparently only Lillian Wald, John Haynes Holmes, Paul Kellogg, and Oswald Garrison Villard objected strongly to the People's Council (Marchand, *American Peace Movement*, pp. 304–5).

[30]"The Emergency Peace Federation to the People's Council," n.d., Emergency Peace Federation Papers, SCPC. Emily Greene Balch, "History and Organization," June 8, 1940; Minutes of Organizing Committee of People's Council, June 13, 1917, Appendix 1, PCA Papers, SCPC. Miss Secor regarded the change from the Emergency Peace Federation to the People's Council merely a "further reorganisation" (Lella Secor Florence, "Ford Peace Ship and After," pp. 119, 123).

[31]Pinchot, Miss Eastman, and Bourne were all active in the People's Council by then ("Committee Lists," n.d., PCA Papers, SCPC; Crystal Eastman to Amos Pinchot, June 21, 29, and August 15, 1917; Pinchot to Miss Eastman, June 23, 1917, Amos Pinchot Papers).

organizations. With such support it created a strong central office in New York, which published the *People's Council of America Bulletin* until August 1919 and maintained a Washington legislative bureau to keep a watchful eye on the domestic and war fronts. The Council's annual budget of $100,000 was administered by Executive Secretary Louis P. Lochner, another indication of continuity with preintervention peace work.[32]

The Council's real work, however, went on through local affiliates and regional conferences. To achieve goals set forth at its originating conference late in May, the Council prepared continuously for a September National Constituent Assembly, holding local conferences in Philadelphia, San Francisco, Salt Lake City, and Seattle. The peace movement thus continued to express its obsession with meetings. Regional preparatory conferences in July in Chicago and Los Angeles further prepared for the national "People's Parliament" in the fall. Since the Council's goals included direct democratic control of foreign policy and since it contained so many friends of the war referendum plan, these regional conferences featured endorsement of both war and conscription referendums.[33]

In fact, by September, when the "People's Parliament" convened, Council leadership and members included, in addition to those already mentioned, most preintervention war referendum partisans. Former Anti-Imperialist League Vice President David Starr Jordan, chancellor of Stanford University, went to Washington as Council lobbyist. Randolph Bourne and Max Eastman of the Committee for Democratic Control were active in the People's Council, especially on its literature committee. Bourne, former Congressman Oscar Callaway, and Socialist presidential candidate Allan Benson were also members of the important Democratic Control Committee. Progressive Frederic C. Howe joined the Council's leadership in mid-June. Although the war and conscription referendum proposals never dominated the Council's program or activities, these and other war referendum partisans gave the Council significant continuity with previous collective and individual hopes for an advisory referendum. Furthermore, advocacy of these "democratic con-

---

[32]"The Work of the People's Council from May to September [1917]," typescript news release, n.d.; Minutes of the Organizing Committee, June 8, 1917, pp. 1–6, PCA Papers, SCPC. Minutes of the previous four meetings are missing.

[33]"Resolutions," *Report of the Second American Conference for Democracy and Terms of Peace, July 7–8, 1917* (Chicago, 1917); *Report of the Third American Conference for Democracy and Terms of Peace, July 20, 1917* (Los Angeles, 1917), in American Conference for Democracy and Terms of Peace Files, SCPC.

trols," especially in wartime and in light of other radical Council aims, led to local, state, and federal action against it and its members.[34]

The People's Council considered one of its primary purposes accomplished before the September "People's Parliament" met. In adopting a revolutionary Russian statement of war aims and terms of peace, the People's Council advocated a peace based on no annexations, no indemnities, and free development of nationalities and reflected a similar Russian statement to Germany. When President Wilson, in a note to the Pope on August 29, seemed to endorse several similar principles, Max Eastman and others concluded that a part of the Council's program was completed.[35] The pacifist conference just two days later, nevertheless, had little to celebrate.

In the case of the People's Council, planning was necessary even to assure a meeting place. As early as July 12, in view of previous harassment of the organization, leaders discussed the use of tents in case public halls were not made available. Miss Shelley and Louis Lochner were, in fact, unable to arrange with local Minneapolis businessmen for a hall before the scheduled meeting. When a local rental agent suddenly refused them tents, Council leaders hurriedly raised $5,000 to purchase tents for a thirty-five-acre tract. Then Governor J. A. A. Burnquist denied the Council the right to assemble in the state. Support by Minneapolis Congressman Ernest Lundeen, who took this opportunity to endorse once more the war referendum, and sympathy expressed by the local mayor and Socialist chief of police were not enough. In the face of what Max Eastman called the "howling of the press and the official persecution by the Governor," who called all People's Council members and sympathizers traitors, they made plans to shift their meeting first to Fargo, North Dakota, and then to Hudson, Wisconsin. Finally Lochner and others agreed on Chicago.[36]

Largely due to this last minute conflict over a meeting place, only some two hundred delegates were present at the Chicago meeting. Sessions

[34]Minutes of Organizing Committee of People's Council of America, June 8, 13, 15, 1917; "Committee Lists," PCA Papers, SCPC. Eastman's the *Masses* and Socialist journals, *Pearson's Magazine* and *Appeal to Reason,* publicized the Council and solicited funds for it. Eastman tells of his "painful tension," torn between a sense of responsibility and feelings of futility, as well as his personal fears and loss of love by separation from his wife, during a speaking tour for the People's Council (*Love and Revolution,* pp. 49–57).

[35]*PC Bulletin,* 1, No. 4 (1917), PCA Papers, SCPC.

[36]Minutes of Organizing Committee, July 12, 1917, p. 3; *PC Bulletin,* 1, No. 4 (1917); Shelley to Members of People's Council, Aug. 28, 1917; Lochner to Members of Organizing Committee, Aug. 19, 1917; J. W. Fawcett to Lella Faye Secor, Aug. 30, 1917; Lochner to People's Council, Aug. 31, 1917; "The People's Council Convention," unsigned article by delegate, Sept., 1917, p. 1, PCA Papers, SCPC.

planned for six days barely lasted parts of two. Most of the pacifists' efforts were directed at internal organization amid a tense, emotional atmosphere. Local police brought the first session to an end, proving Chicago no more hospitable to the radicals than Minneapolis. Governor Frank Lowden finally ordered three companies of state troops to break up the meeting and took direct command of the Chicago police, over the head of a sympathetic mayor, William Hale Thompson.

When the latter allowed the Council to hold a second session, a clash between troops and pacifists was averted only because the pacifist meeting adjourned before troops arrived. Thompson was subsequently censured by the city council and the local chamber of commerce and was publicly hanged in effigy. Nevertheless, he entered the Illinois senate race late in September, only to be defeated on his "record" of anticonscription, his endorsement of free speech and assembly, and proposals of both war and conscription referendums.[37]

Before its forced adjournment, however, the convention led to two significant developments. An American Alliance for Labor and Democracy, called by Socialist John Spargo and American Federation of Labor head Samuel Gompers and financed by George Creel's Committee on Public Information, met while the People's Council held its meeting. President Wilson acknowledged support of him by the Alliance and in turn endorsed it. Indicating the traditional conservatism of the American labor movement, the Alliance claimed that it, not the People's Council, was a true spokesman for labor and tried hard to counter the Council's antiwar activity.[38]

The pacifists did manage to draw up and endorse committee reports on peace terms and civil liberties. War referendum sponsor Oscar Callaway was unable to address the convention as planned, but the proposal he favored easily found its way into the civil liberties report drawn up by Callaway, Bourne, and Benson. Another long-time friend of the war referendum, Cincinnati minister Herbert S. Bigelow, who as an Anti-Imperialist League vice president had urged a referendum on imperialism in 1899 and 1900, was also present and on the resolutions committee. Furthermore, Bigelow was a contributing editor of the liberal weekly the

[37] Material on First Constituent Assembly (1917), PCA Papers, SCPC; *Ohio State Journal,* Sept. 6, 26, 1917.

[38] *Ohio State Journal,* Sept. 6, 8, 1917. The best secondary account of the Alliance's fight with the People's Council is Grubbs, *Struggle for Labor Loyalty,* pp. 35–46, 58–64. Additional research by Grubbs has led to the conclusion that labor loyalty developed largely due to the increasingly closer relationship between the A.F. of L. and the League to Enforce Peace ("Organized Labor and the League to Enforce Peace," *Labor History,* 14 [1973], 247–58).

Public, which had led war referendum support among journals in February 1917.[39]

The difficulties of the People's Council of America in Chicago, typical of the pacifist dilemma in an emergency which demanded conformity, did not stand alone. Bigelow knew firsthand of attacks on pacifists during the war, for he suffered a severe beating by a Kentucky mob, due in part to his radical reputation as chairman of the Cincinnati People's Council. While in the normally neutralist Midwest and West to organize local councils, Scott Nearing encountered fines, arrest, and even suppression of his "Who Should Pay for the War?" speech, in which he urged conscription of wealth rather than war bond purchases. In San Francisco police raided Council offices and locked up its meeting hall. But such state and local opposition to the Council and its sympathizers was only the beginning. George Creel's Public Information Committee charged that the Council's members were traitors and claimed it was "fighting it to the death."[40]

Council experiences and gradual domination of the organization by Scott Nearing drew it closer to Roger Baldwin's Civil Liberties Bureau within the Union Against Militarism. Besides its views on the conscription of wealth, the Council's most controversial stand was its opposition to compulsory military service and advocacy of a conscription referendum. Both Nearing and Baldwin sought to protect conscientious objectors. In doing so, Nearing's 1918 broadside entitled "The Great Madness" and his Socialist condemnation of business in a series of "Open Letters to Profiteers," published in the *People's Council Bulletin,* led to his indictment under the Sedition and Espionage acts.[41]

Even before the Nearing trial, another civil liberties case made against two men and a woman—all Columbia University students—hinged on advocacy of a conscription referendum. They were members of the Socialist Collegiate Anti-Militarism League, and the two men refused to register under the Selective Service Act. Charged also with conspiracy to dis-

[39] *PC Bulletin,* 1, No. 5 (1917); 1, No. 6 (1917); Material on First Constituent Assembly; "Committee Lists," PCA Papers, SCPC.

[40] *PC Bulletin,* 1, No. 9 (1917); 1, No. 11 (1917); 1, No. 12 (1917); Nearing, "Who Should Pay for the War?" Miscellaneous People's Council Material; Executive Committee Minutes, Nov. 8, 1917, PCA Papers, SCPC. The best testimony of pacifist ordeals in wartime are in Addams, *Peace and Bread in Time of War,* pp. 132–51; Villard, *Fighting Years,* pp. 326–47; Eastman, *Love and Revolution,* pp. 22–57; Florence, "Ford Peace Ship and After," pp. 97–125. Chatfield, *For Peace and Justice,* pp. 42–87, is especially effective among secondary accounts.

[41] His acquittal in March 1919 was heralded as a victory for free speech and press (*PC Bulletin,* 1, No. 18 [1918], 4; 1, No. 19 [1918], 1, 4; 1, No. 20 [1918], 1; 1, No. 23 [1918], 4; 2, No. 3 [1919], 2, PCA Papers, SCPC).

tribute anticonscription literature, in which they urged a conscription referendum, the two received light sentences except for loss of citizenship.[42]

This was not the only civil liberties crisis at Columbia University, a hotbed of pacifism before American intervention. President Nicholas Murray Butler and Professor John Dewey were among the liberal majority, which had gradually exchanged pacifism for what others regarded as "war-liberalism." Professor James M. Cattell, whose son incidentally was one of the convicted students, and Professor Henry W. L. Dana, however, refused to heed Butler's warning against any type of pacifist "conspiracy." Regarding it a challenge to academic freedom and civil liberties, each continued his association in radical pacifism until dismissed from Columbia in October. Dana had worked closely with the American Neutral Conference Committee, the American Civil Liberties Union, the Collegiate Anti-Militarism League, and the People's Council; Cattell's academic sin, committed under a Columbia letterhead to three congressmen, was a plea for opposition to sending conscripts to Europe without a referendum. Butler learned of the Cattell incident from Congressman Raymond Bathrick (Democrat, Ohio), who saw the referendum suggestion as "seditious." Although the *New York Times* echoed charges of "treason," Butler's dismissal of Dana and Cattell led to Charles A. Beard's protest resignation and interest in the matter by the American Association of University Professors.[43]

Among defenders of the Columbia students and Professors Dana and Cattell was another People's Council associate, Randolph Bourne. His leadership of the intellectuals' debate over peace and war, conducted for a time in the *New Republic,* included advocacy of a national youth service—in education, social service, or cultural activities rather than military duty—and his endorsement of a war referendum through the Committee for Democratic Control. As we have seen, Bourne reacted to

[42]The students' tract "Will You Be Drafted?" maintained that conscription was abhorrent to true democracy and deplored the absence of a referendum on both the war resolution and universal military training. See the folder on the Cattell-Phillips-Parker Case, June 1917, Henry Wadsworth Longfellow Dana Papers, SCPC, and *New York Times,* June 1, 2, 19, 22, July 13, 1917. Actually, the *Times,* in publishing the document in question, gave the pacifists' ideas wider circulation than otherwise possible.

[43]Cattell's earlier conflicts with Butler included a suggestion that the President's house be converted into a faculty club! Complete accounts of Cattell's unsuccessful attempts, 1918–22, to get reinstated are in James M. Cattell Papers, LC. Dana's pacifism is discussed in the Dana Papers and American Neutral Conference Committee Papers, SCPC. See also *New York Times,* Sept. 13, Oct. 2, 3, 1917; and Richard Hofstadter and Walter P. Metzger, *The Development of Academic Freedom in the United States* (New York, 1955), pp. 498–501.

war in a typically radical-pacifist manner, believing that American progressive reform at home would cease with intervention. Thus after April 1917 his attacks on war and what he called "war-liberalism" culminated in a severe antistate pessimism.

Bourne praised the resignation of former teacher and friend Charles A. Beard and criticized the "irresponsible press" for its activities against the People's Council. A Columbia graduate himself, Bourne protested President Butler's attitude toward pacifism and, as a result, even urged state controls and faculty administration of universities. To Bourne, executive control of Columbia had made it a "corporation of learning," preventing development of ideas to challenge the status quo and leading to violations of academic freedom.[44] Similarly, his advocacy of a war referendum could, he believed, limit executive controls in diplomacy.

By mid-1917 Bourne's wartime rupture with John Dewey and the *New Republic* was completed. As Herbert Croly and Walter Lippmann turned down his contributions, his debate with other intellectuals shifted to the *Dial* and *Seven Arts,* both of which were radical organs of cultural nationalism. In the latter, especially, Bourne made his most lucid defense of peace and pragmatism, defying Dewey and other intellectuals who supported the war. Placing himself within the intellectual minority that did not accept the war decision, Bourne maintained that war could not be controlled for liberal purposes. His most famous essay, "The War and the Intellectuals," climaxed his debate with Dewey and made *Seven Arts* the leading antiwar journal of the period, almost landing its editor in prison. The journal normally attracted only a limited audience, but both the American Union Against Militarism and the Woman's Peace Party circulated reprints of Bourne's article.[45]

Randolph Bourne's most advanced support of the war referendum plan hinged on his ultimate and complete disillusion over war's relationship to the state. Regarding himself always as a "realistic" pacifist engaged in a

---

[44]Bourne, letter to the editor, *New Republic* 12 (1917), 328–29; idem, "The Idea of a University," *Dial,* 63 (1917), 509–10; John Spargo to Bourne, Aug. 29, 1917, and H. W. L. Dana to Alyse Gregory, June 30, 1948, Boxes 5 and 3, respectively, Bourne Papers. His defense of the Columbia students' anti-conscription–civil liberties case was in Bourne, "Conspirators," *Seven Arts,* 2 (1917), 528–30, and *New York Times,* June 2, 1917.

[45]John Dewey, "In a Time of National Hesitation," *Seven Arts,* 2 (1917), 3–7; Randolph Bourne, "The War and the Intellectuals," ibid., 2 (1917), 133–46; Charles Forcey, *The Crossroads of Liberalism: Croly, Weyl, Lippmann, and the Progressive Era, 1900–1925* (New York, 1961), pp. 281, 346; Louis Filler, *Randolph Bourne* (Washington, 1943), p. 117; James Oppenheim, "The Story of the Seven Arts," *American Mercury,* 20 (1930), 156–57. Crystal Eastman to Mrs. E. G. Karsten, Aug. 11, 1917, and American Union Against Militarism to Mrs. Karsten, July 28, 1917, WPP Collection, SCPC; Jane Addams to Bourne, June 30, 1917, Box 1, Bourne Papers.

search for alternatives to war, Bourne concluded, after America's intervention, that war ended the validity of pragmatism. In wartime he found no machinery for dissent in the rush for victory and conformity. Objectors could only submit or resist and be judged disloyal. To this leading intellectual critic before April, who feared war's effects on American reform impulses and intelligence, wartime experiences now confirmed his fears. Indeed, he even questioned whether an advisory referendum would have offered an effective alternative, since forces for war controlled warmaking machinery. Unconsciously, perhaps, Bourne struck at the central premise of war referendum partisans in his judgment that such an alternative was "supremely irrelevant to people who are willing to use war as an instrument in the working-out of national policy."[46]

Friends of the war referendum plan, for the most part, assumed that, if used, it would naturally demonstrate antiwar sentiment. To Bourne's associates in the earlier Committee for Democratic Control, which had previously adjusted its principles to accept "armed neutrality," Bourne's extreme pacifism later must have proved the inconsistency of their limited concession. When faced with the ultimate test which war presented to American reform impulses, Bourne and many like him rejected force in diplomacy.[47]

In Bourne's theoretical study of war and the state, unfinished at his untimely death in 1918, he expressed his most radical, almost Marxist, ideas. Stressing the theme that "war is the health of the State," as against the interest of the people organized culturally and socially, Bourne for the last time described how America's war decision came about and outlined its ill effects for American progressivism. First, he argued that it was the "country," organized as the state and through its agency the government, which made war.

It must never be forgotten that nations do not declare war on each other. . . .
There is no case known in modern times of the people being consulted in the initiation of a war. The present demand for democratic control of foreign policy indicates how completely, even in the most democratic of modern nations, foreign policy has been the secret private possession of the executive branch of the Government.

[46] Bourne, "Conscience and Intelligence in War," *Dial,* 63 (1917), 193–95; Bourne, "A War Diary," *Seven Arts,* 2 (1917), 537.

[47] Officials in the American Union Against Militarism also illustrated the pacifists' ultimate dilemma. When Charles T. Hallinan suggested purchase of an ambulance for the American war effort, radical publisher B. W. Huebsch expressed disgust: "If you can't make any headway against the war hysteria, then be silent, but don't go round trying to deceive people into thinking that you have changed your mind about it all" (Hallinan's statement to Executive Committee, Apr. 15, 1918, AUAM Records, SCPC).

Bourne suggested that American intervention came after the Executive's foreign policies brought the country to "the very brink of war"; thus even many thoughtful democrats believed an advisory referendum, at the time, was improper. Bourne maintained that others even argued "that a genuine referendum had taken place," in view of the "herd impulse" and conformity of mind that swept the country. He saw, however, only the confirmation of his previous fears; war resulted in a "derangement of values," "terrorization of opinion," and "regimentation of life." He was certain that in America there was too little democratic control of diplomacy. "Good democrats are wont to feel the crucial difference between a State in which the popular Parliament or Congress declares war, and the State in which an absolute monarch or ruling class declares war."[48] But for Bourne there was *no difference* between America's war decision and one reached by an absolute monarch. His loss of faith in representative government was complete.

Bourne also continued to attack former intellectuals who joined the wartime "herd mind." He regarded the *New Republic*'s leadership by 1918 as "obnoxious" and "middle aged," without any clear program of values. The war, with its "fatal backwash and backfire upon creative and democratic values at home," caused intellectuals to take "positive delight in throwing off the responsibilities of thought." Bourne's disillusion increased in proportion to attempts by liberals to "ride two horses at once." Dewey's defection was typical, he thought; for years Dewey had opposed conscription and then suddenly accepted it. No wonder Bourne expressed relief over the peace, near the end of his own life, and felt it was "like coming out of a nightmare."[49]

Despite the "Bourne legend," popular in the 1920s but now discounted, he was not hounded by the Justice Department, nor is it probable that Wilson ever heard of his foremost intellectual wartime critic.[50] Bourne's antiwar essays and his activities in several peace groups did not result in prosecutions.[51] Other Americans, notably some Socialist war referendum

---

[48]Quotes from Bourne, "Unfinished Fragment on the State (1918)," Box 7, Bourne Papers.

[49]Bourne to Van Wyck Brooks, Mar. 27, 1918, and Bourne to his mother, Nov. 21, 1918, Boxes 1 and 2, respectively, Bourne Papers. For a different treatment of Bourne's war activities, as "politically negative" and with "no interest in organizing an opposition," see Christopher Lasch, *The New Radicalism in America, 1889–1963: The Intellectual as a Social Type* (New York, 1965), pp. 81–82, 205–10. Bourne's opposition to the war was intensely personal, but it was also expressed through the Committee for Democratic Control and other peace organizations.

[50]Leuchtenburg, *Perils of Prosperity*, 46.

[51]On one occasion naval intelligence officers questioned him; they had interpreted his female acquaintance's beach front dancing as signals to an unidentified vessel offshore! Bourne did record the impression that his thoughts, out of touch with the times "except

partisans, however, were less fortunate in escaping direct government action.

As a part of the Post Office Department's vigilance, *Seven Arts,* the *People's Council Bulletin,* and Max Eastman's the *Masses* experienced difficulties such as late deliveries or complete suppression. The trouble former Georgia Populist Tom Watson had after advocating a conscription referendum, however, is less well-known. Through his newspaper and magazine, Watson severely criticized Wilson's policies, especially on conscription, and defended two Augusta, Georgia, Negroes who failed to register under the act. This defense and his anticonscription views led to two developments important for wartime civil liberties. First, his paper, the *Jeffersonian,* was withdrawn from the mails. Furthermore, his stand may have encouraged Georgia Senator Thomas Hardwick's introduction of a bill to prohibit sending conscripts abroad without their consent. Adversely reported by the Senate Military Affairs Committee,[52] the bill nevertheless pointed up again the limited-defense concepts of peace-by-referendum partisans.

Socialists, however, were among the most severely punished of wartime advocates of war or conscription referendums. Many Socialists found in the People's Council a comfortable home. Even Morris Hillquit, who had opposed party endorsement of the war referendum plan in 1915 and 1916, defended Socialists whom the government prosecuted for similar views in 1917 and 1918. He worked closely in the People's Council with former adversary Allan Benson. John Spargo, however, was no longer a member of the Socialist party, supported the war through the American Alliance for Labor and Democracy, and charged those in the Council with pro-German attitudes.[53] In the 1919 controversy over Victor Berger's seat in Congress, congressmen cited his advocacy of a war referendum in 1917 as the beginning of his disloyalty. The conviction of some twenty-seven

---

perhaps with the Bolsheviki," seemed to some unprintable (*New Republic*) and that his statements on public matters were "seditious" (Bourne to Everett Benjamin, Nov. 26, 1917, Box 2, Bourne Papers).

[52]See Thomas E. Watson, *Mr. Watson's Editorials on the War Issues* (Thomason, Ga., 1917); idem, *Will the U.S. Judiciary Permit, and the People Ratify, the Congressional Overthrow of Our Constitutional System of Government?* (Thomason, Ga., 1917). Ironically, the Senate committee cited former Augusta, Ga., Congressman William H. Fleming's arguments upholding constitutionality of conscription in its report against Hardwick's bill. Hardwick, backed by Watson, had defeated Fleming for reelection in 1906; Fleming, who headed the Augusta draft board in 1917, had advocated a referendum on imperialism in 1900. See U.S., Congress, Senate, 65th Cong., 1st sess., Senate Report Number 125, *Service of Persons Drafted into the Military Service of the United States,* pp. 11–15.

[53]John Spargo to Bourne, Aug. 29, 1917, Box 5, Bourne Papers; Grubbs, *Struggle for Labor Loyalty,* p. 40.

South Dakota farmers, furthermore, hinged in part on a petition to Governor Peter Norbeck for a war referendum; New Jersey Socialist Frederick Kraft, who urged war and conscription referendums, received a five-year sentence in the Atlanta Penitentiary. Another famous penitentiary resident at the time, Eugene Debs, could also trace part of his wartime difficulties to his objections to traditional methods of declaring war.[54]

Of course much activity for the war referendum or advocacy of a conscription referendum went unchallenged by state or federal officials. Senator Thomas P. Gore (Democrat, Okla.) suffered no criminal prosecution as a result of introducing a war referendum resolution late in August 1917.[55] Senator La Follette, likewise, was not jailed after urging a referendum on "aggressive war" before Professor Scott Nearing's Toledo, Ohio, "People's Church," and the Hearst papers carried editorial endorsement of the war referendum plan in mid-1917 without subsequent prosecution.[56] Nor was Congressman Clarence C. Dill (Democrat, Wash.) prosecuted for taking a local conscription referendum in Spokane.[57] Finally, those congressmen and senators who attended a People's Council meeting, held in the Senate Military Committee room in the Capitol, were not unduly harassed. Most of them, invited by presiding radical Louis Lochner, left after the antiwar speech began. Max Eastman first spoke of repealing the draft law and even advocated impeachment proceedings against Wilson. North Dakota Republican Chairman H. J. Lemke then praised the antiwar and referendum views of Senators La Follette and Gronna, who remained for the complete meeting.[58]

Most peace workers had dissatisfying wartime experiences; only in-

---

[54]*Cong. Rec.,* 66th Cong., 1st sess., pp. 8240–8247 (Nov. 10, 1919); Zechariah Chafee, Jr., *Free Speech in the United States* (Cambridge, 1941), pp. 51, 58–59; Peterson and Fite, *Opponents of War,* pp. 36, 46–47, 163, 251; 249 Fed. 919, Apr. 23, 1918; 247 US 520, June 10, 1918. Debs's 1918 statement before a Canton, Ohio, Socialist Convention, after which he was arrested, sounded much like some of Wilson's 1916 campaign remarks, except for its "class" implications. Debs said: "The master class has always declared the wars; the subject class has always fought the battles." See Ray Ginger, *Eugene V. Debs: A Biography* (New York, 1962), pp. 374–77.

[55]See chapter 5 for full discussion.

[56]*Ohio State Journal,* Sept. 24, 1917; *Atlanta Georgian and Sunday American,* July 1, 1917.

[57]Report of the Organizing Secretary, Week Ending July 19 (1917), Minutes of Organizing Committee, PCA Papers, SCPC.

[58]Congressman Edward Keating, pacifist and later editor of *Labor* and a war referendum advocate, also remained. Other speakers included war referendum proponents Daniel Kiefer, friend of Bryan and chairman of the National Single-Tax League, and his friend, Cincinnati Socialist minister Herbert S. Bigelow. Each was active in the People's Council at the time (*Ohio State Journal,* Aug. 10, 1917).

frequently, and then with doubtful validity, could they claim any practical success for their continuing efforts. After Wilson's January 1918 Fourteen Points speech, Louis Lochner proclaimed emphatically for most pacifists, "We knew we were right."[59] It is true that John Dewey, who never bothered to answer Randolph Bourne's pointed questions during the war, repudiated his championship of intervention in the 1930s.[60] Yet the armistice came, and for peace workers as well as others, it was a welcome respite. Irreconcilables in the peace movement, in Congress, and as individuals had continued to rely on a referendum approach to peace without success. Their persistence, and their attitudes toward defense and foreign policy, however, gave partisans of both the war and conscription referendums a significant place in organized pacifism and in the early twentieth-century history of civil liberties.

By mid-1918 the People's Council of America, which had been in the forefront of wartime support of the referendum approach to peace, operated under a deficit, and its publication appeared less often until the organization disbanded in 1919.[61] The American Union Against Militarism suffered a slow but sure death by 1922. But in the decades ahead many wartime proponents of the war referendum remained faithful, new support appeared in Congress, and a new liberal party endorsed the plan in 1924. If its friends exhibited unusually thick skins during the war, advocates of the referendum approach to peace showed no less commitment and enthusiasm following the armistice.

[59] *PC Bulletin*, 1, No. 13 (1918), PCA Papers, SCPC. For another similar pacifist claim of vindication, see ibid., 1, No. 24 (1918).

[60] Sidney Kaplan, "Social Engineers as Saviors: Effects of World War I on Some American Liberals," *Journal of the History of Ideas*, 17 (1956), 362.

[61] Marchand, *American Peace Movement*, 319–22.

CHAPTER V

The League, Normalcy, and the War Referendum Plan

THE POPULARITY AND persistence of the referendum approach to peace continued in the two decades following peace in Europe. Whereas it had taken the appearance of a national emergency measure during the war, especially among certain peace organizations and in Congress before American intervention, after the armistice supporters stressed its application and adoption internationally. The American peace movement, in contrast to earlier interest, did not concentrate on the war referendum idea during the next decade. At a time when liberalism was thought dead, however, several progressive Americans continued their interest in it. In doing so, they reflected the general postway disillusionment and participated in the ongoing American debate over the relation between peace and power.

Progressive Congressman Clarence C. Dill (Democrat, Wash.) first injected the war referendum peace plan into the debate over America's relationship to the League of Nations. Shortly after the armistice he introduced a war referendum resolution which, he believed, would complement President Wilson's proposed League and promote peace, if adopted internationally. It would put an end to "secret international agreements," a reflection of current demands, led by the president, for open diplomacy. Dill proposed a constitutional amendment that would provide for America an advisory referendum before any future congressional declaration of war. Success in America, he believed, would provide an example and encourage the rest of the world to follow.[1]

Dill also published an interesting but short-lived paper devoted to the "people's peace movement" in an effort to publicize his proposal. *Let the People Vote on War* was a significant pacifist journalistic endeavor; it signaled both Dill's faith in his cause after defeat for reelection in 1918 and his realistic appraisal of public indifference to matters of foreign affairs.[2]

Dill's resolution, like others, never got out of committee, but his efforts

---

[1] *Cong. Rec.,* 65th Cong., 3d sess., p. 838 (Dec. 23, 1918), pp. 1824–25 (Jan. 21, 1919); original text of House Joint Resolution 374 in "House of Representatives Joint Resolutions, 65th Congress 1917–1919, 1–445," LC.

[2] *Let the People Vote on War* (Washington, D.C.), March 15 to May 15, 1919. Defeated for reelection in 1918, Dill had left Congress Mar. 3, 1919. He had voted against the war declaration in 1917. Cooper, *Vanity of Power,* p. 207, cites the fact that 28 of 54 House opponents of the war declaration were reelected in 1918, whereas 14 were defeated.

were endorsed by the Nebraska State Grange and New York American Labor Party. He believed that the recent success of the prohibition amendment would be followed by adoption of his own proposed constitutional amendment. Yet the peace journal, which continued its propaganda for only five issues in the spring of 1919, failed to create grass roots interest. Local war referendum clubs, which Dill proposed, never materialized.[3] Contrary to his hopes, there was no national or international campaign for the war referendum plan. Like many war referendum partisans, Congressman Dill's efforts reflected a still widely held belief that wars were brought about by a minority of government officials, individuals who did not always have "the people" in mind. Men such as Dill and his friend William Jennings Bryan continued to seek the war referendum reform to counter the influence of what they often referred to as "the interests."

Other early postwar evidence of the persistence of the referendum approach to peace and its new internationalist emphasis was recorded during Senate debate on the commitment and responsibility to use force in Article 10 of the League of Nations Covenant. As Dill had hoped, several senators believed that the war referendum might become, with the dawn of peace following the armistice, an international experiment in democratic control and a means toward peace divorced from the use of force in diplomacy. It was no accident that it found friends in the Senate during debate on the League.

After President Wilson's appeal to the people to elect a Democratic Congress, Senator Robert La Follette became one of the earliest to assault the proposed League. Writing in his *Magazine* in December 1918, he urged that the Allies abolish conscription and refuse to declare war, except to repel invasion, without a referendum of the people. Only by attacking the causes of war in this way could an effective alternative to the League be created. Following publication of the Covenant in mid-February 1919, Georgia Senator Thomas Hardwick, among others, continued the attack on the League. Hardwick's enthusiasm for the New Freedom had soured during the war as Wilson assumed stronger executive powers. The Georgia senator was even numbered among those advocates of a conscription referendum. In retaliation for his defection Wilson brought direct pressure to block his reelection in 1918. By 1919, after his defeat, therefore, he became a leading opponent of the League.[4] Senator Hardwick's opposition, consistent with his wartime views, struck at the provi-

[3]*Let the People Vote on War,* 1, No. 1 (1919), 1, 4–5, 16; 1, No. 2 (1919), 17. There is no record of support by peace organizations for Dill's efforts.

[4]*La Follette's Magazine,* Dec. 1918; Denna Frank Fleming, *The United States and the League of Nations, 1918–1920* (New York, 1932), pp. 146–47; *Cong. Rec.,* 65th Cong., 3d sess., p. 4704 (Mar. 1, 1919).

sions that ultimately caused American rejection of League membership. He feared that United States participation in the League would cost America its traditional independence of action. It would necessitate sending "American boys from the farm and the factory and the foundry and the workshop and the bank" to participate in wars of no vital interest to America. Whereas the League ideal of achieving peace represented American hopes and traditions, Article 10, with its commitment of American *force* to achieve League ends, contradicted American traditions, according to Hardwick and many others.[5]

Some views expressed during both public and Senate debate on Article 10 in 1919 illustrated well America's traditional rejection of force in diplomacy. Renewed interest in the war referendum, especially in its presentation as an international peace reform, however, pointed up no less clearly the inherent contradiction between traditions and the League. Many "irreconcilables" and "reservationists" based their rejection of the League of Nations on the implied effects of Article 10 upon American constitutional provisions for war declarations. Senator Lodge, in fact, believed that the League's anticipated effect upon the congressional war-declaring powers summed up objections to Article 10.[6] Nebraska Senator Norris, although no defender of absolute freedom of action in foreign affairs, expressed similar doubts. He favored use of military, economic, and moral force to maintain peace and believed that disarmament, arbitration, and the war referendum were all necessary. Senator Borah believed that the League would produce peacetime conscription, a big navy, and higher taxes and would take from Congress its war-declaring power. La Follette, still the peace progressive interested in domestic reforms, once more offered the war referendum plan as a substitute for the League. With disarmament, the war referendum, and an end to conscription, he believed that the League's peace machinery would not be needed and Americans could turn their attentions to progressive legislation.[7]

[5] *Cong. Rec.*, 65th Cong., 3 sess., p. 4700 (Mar. 1, 1919); John Chalmers Vinson, *Referendum for Isolation: Defeat of Article Ten of the League of Nations Covenant* (Athens, Ga., 1961), p. 1. Hardwick subsequently served on the board of directors of the League for the Preservation of American Independence, an anti-League organization which was designed to prevent sending Americans into foreign wars without congressional consent. In Georgia alone forty-three anti-League meetings were sponsored by this group (Ralph Stone, *The Irreconcilables: The Fight against the League of Nations* [Lexington, Ky., 1970], pp. 78–80, 81).

[6] On the other hand, war referendum sponsor Senator Robert L. Owen supported the administration and did not feel that Article 10 represented any break in traditions. Rather, it put teeth into America's basic anti-imperialist views. See Vinson, *Referendum for Isolation*, pp. 89, 101, 103. On debate outside the Senate, see Stone, *Irreconcilables*, pp. 77–99.

[7] Stone, *Irreconcilables*, pp. 43, 85, 135. Norris, in *Fighting Liberal*, pp. 202–13, did not recall his support of the war referendum but did mention his opposition to secret diplomacy

Several days after Senator Hardwick's speech, and in contrast to his point of view, Senator Thomas P. Gore (Democrat, Okla.) inserted into the *Record* William Jennings Bryan's early reaction to the League. Although consistently a leader among those who relied upon the referendum approach to peace before April 1917, Bryan had fully supported the war effort and by 1919 supported Wilson's proposed League. One of his favorite peace plans, the one-year cooling-off period embodied in some thirty arbitration treaties negotiated while he was secretary of state, was "the chief cornerstone of the League." [8] Certainly Article 12 did incorporate the Bryan trademark—insistence on delay and caution in diplomacy. Its provision for a cooling-off period of thirty days offered no conflict with American traditions in foreign affairs. Yet in supporting the League for this reason, Bryan ironically missed the heart of the Covenant.

When the Sixty-sixth Congress began May 19, 1919, the League debate returned to the Senate. From then on attention centered upon strategy, Wilson's tour, amendments, and especially the Lodge Reservations, which implied the usual fear of loss of independent action. Although Senator Gore favored the Lodge Reservations, he also saw the League of Nations as an opportunity "to democratize war." On November 5, 1919, during the height of Senate debate on the Covenant, he addressed the Senate on his week-old proposal to expand the idea of a cooling-off period, provided by Article 12 of the Covenant, by international agreement on the advisory war referendum plan. One result of World War I, at least after American intervention, he believed, was to democratize the world. In the interest of what John Chal Vinson has called "cultural imperialism," or the projection of America's domestic traditions and techniques into international affairs, what proposal could be better than a war referendum, representing, as it did, both democratic control and reduction of force in diplomacy? [9]

---

and his use of *Foreign Affairs,* a publication of the British Union of Democratic Control, during the League debate.

[8] *Cong. Rec.,* 65th Cong., 3d sess., p. 4845 (Mar. 3, 1919); Levine, *Bryan,* pp. 136–37, 154–55; Coletta, *Bryan,* III, 90.

[9] Vinson, *Referendum for Isolation,* p. 20. Neither Vinson, nor W. Stull Holt, however, mentions efforts to insert war referendum plans into the League Covenant (*Treaties Defeated by the Senate* [Baltimore, 1933]). Thomas A. Bailey, who typifies the common emphasis upon the Lodge Reservations and neglect of "amendments" and other reservations, also does not treat interest in the war referendum during the debate (*Woodrow Wilson and the Great Betrayal* [Chicago, 1963]). Lloyd E. Ambrosius, who correctly faults several other writers for "emphasizing the negative, partisan, and isolationist role of the Republicans during the treaty fight," also does not mention efforts to obtain international acceptance of the war referendum plan. On the interest in a postwar guarantee of French security, see his "Wilson, the Republicans, and French Security after World War I," *Journal of American History,* 59 (1972), 341–52.

Senator Gore maintained that an international agreement for declarations of war only by referendum would be a corrective to the chief abuses of democracy remaining in the League Covenant. As proposed, the League of Nations failed to provide either direct choice of representatives or direct responsibility to the people, both essentials of democracy; yet its members would constantly be faced with war decisions under Article 10. The Oklahoma senator desired to add the advisory war referendum—"the best way to prevent and minimize war"—as an amendment to Article 12. "The voice of the people," he argued, "is the nearest approach to the voice of God." Gore hastened to explain that such a referendum in our country would only be advisory and hence not in conflict with our own Constitution. In the absence of such a provision in the Covenant, he felt that American adoption of the principle would make it acceptable internationally.[10]

The next day the Senate by a voice vote rejected Gore's amendment to the League Covenant. A request for reconsideration by a former war referendum advocate, Senator A. J. Gronna, led only to brief comments by himself and Senator James A. Reed (Democrat, Mo.). Their endorsement, however, was not enough to carry the amendment, for only thirteen other senators joined them in the final recorded vote.[11] This was only one of scores of amendments that met defeat by November 6, 1919. More than the others, this injection of the war referendum idea into the League debate pointed up again certain senators' interest in the relationship between congressional powers to declare war and automatic commitment of League members to the use of force in diplomacy as embedded in Article 10.

Senator Gore's interest in the war referendum plan was not entirely related to the League debate. On August 31, 1917, he had introduced a proposed constitutional amendment providing an advisory referendum on war. Furthermore, in contrast to earlier such proposals, it permitted the president to negotiate treaties in which contracting parties would agree not to: "declare or levy war against the other until the question of declaring or levying war shall have been submitted to the qualified electors of the country proposing the same and shall have been approved by a majority thereof." Such treaties, entered into with advice and consent of the Senate, would be binding until no longer observed in good faith by the signatory powers.[12] The only war referendum resolution introduced during

[10]*Cong. Rec.,* 66th Cong., 1st sess., p. 7953 (Nov. 5, 1919); the amendment was proposed Oct. 29, 1919 (ibid., p. 7663 [Oct. 29, 1919]). Billington, *Gore,* pp. 113–15, labels Gore's amendment "unrealistic." Stone, *Irreconcilables,* does not mention the Gore amendment.

[11]*Cong. Rec.,* 66th Cong., 1st sess., pp. 8011–13 (Nov. 6, 1919).

[12]Original typescript, Senate Joint Resolution 97, 65th Cong., 1st sess., Aug. 31, 1917, RG 233, NA. Also see Billington, *Gore,* p. 87.

the period of American participation in World War I, it anticipated Gore's proposed 1919 amendment to the League Covenant and sounded much like Bryan's ideas before American intervention. There is, however, no evidence that Bryan directly influenced Gore in 1917, although in 1919 he may have.

Encouraged by Chief Justice Walter Clark of North Carolina, Bryan claimed his cooling-off treaties were "the foundation upon which the League of Nations is built," but he was not entirely satisfied. In the *Commoner,* as well as through Gore in the Senate, he asked the president to consider adding to the Covenant an explicit "thirty treaties" plan and the war referendum plan. Bryan's interest in such revision of the Covenant and his later endorsement of Gore's effort to add the war referendum suggest that Gore was motivated primarily by his friend's example and influence.[13] After the defeat of Gore's amendment, Bryan continued to encourage him, still believing the United States should join the League, adopt the war referendum, and then offer it for international agreement through the American League delegate. As Gore reported to the Senate, January 22, 1920, Bryan believed that "a referendum on war would give greater assurance of peace than any other provision that could be made. With the advent of women into politics the argument in favor of a referendum gathers additional strength and probability of a peaceful solution of international difficulties increases."[14] Even after the Senate first rejected the League on November 19, 1919, both Gore and Bryan, therefore, remained interested in international adoption of the war referendum plan. Although Paolo Coletta maintains that Bryan's continued campaign for ratification of the Covenant, with reservations and amendments, may have been for the purpose of resuming "his old place of party mentor," there seems to have been genuine popular interest in the war referendum idea. Gore, for example, inserted into the record on January 30, 1920, evidence of support from the Oklahoma branch of the Farmer's Educational and Cooperative Union of America and the Oklahoma Democratic Convention. Bryan reported, also, that former Ambassador to Germany James W. Gerard had called for the war referendum in an address at the Jackson Day Dinner of January 8, 1920. Bryan spoke at the same gathering and proposed that the "next great reform" of the party be the endorsement of "the principle of the initiative

---

[13]Since Bryan's opposition to the League to Enforce Peace in 1916 had hinged, in part, on his belief that it would interfere with the constitutional power of Congress to declare war, his desire to add the war referendum plan to the Covenant was perhaps an attempt to correct a similar problem that many, including Gore, felt Article 10 created (Vinson, *Referendum for Isolation,* p. 19; *Commoner,* Feb. and May, 1919).

[14]*Cong. Rec.,* 66th Cong., 2d sess., p. 1865 (Jan. 22, 1920).

and referendum."[15] During that month his pleas among Democratic senators for compromise and his demands for immediate ratification of the
treaty were insistent and sincere, as was his interest in the war
referendum, for he was frustrated by the procedure which permitted a
majority in Congress to declare war and required a two-thirds vote of the
Senate to make peace.[16] For him, the war referendum plan was a
practical alternative.

Senator Robert La Follette also showed interest in securing international application of the war referendum idea through the League. After
the armistice he talked of possible international agreement on several
peace proposals that had proved unattainable as domestic reforms.
Proposed as three reservations to the League Covenant in November,
they all would have indirectly removed the heart of the Covenant. His
reservations included abolition of peacetime conscription, disarmament,
and international acceptance of an advisory war referendum. The last
proposal, although similar to Gore's amendment to the Covenant, took an
unusual twist; the United States promised *withdrawal from the League* if,
after five years from ratification, each League member had not agreed
"that in no case will it resort to war except to suppress an insurrection or
repel an actual invasion of its territory until an advisory vote of its people
had first been taken on the question of peace or war."[17] Like Senator
Gore, who along with a dozen other senators voted in favor of La
Follette's war referendum reservation, the Wisconsin progressive Republican challenged his colleagues to prove that America's recent
experience had been a war for democracy. If matters of policy, including
disarmament as well as declarations of war, were in the people's hands,
La Follette believed that peace would be inevitable.[18]

Senate rejection of the Gore and La Follette proposals and even defeat

---

[15]Coletta, *Bryan*, III, 94–97; John A. Simpson to Gore, Jan. 30, 1920, rpt. in *Cong. Rec.,*
66th Cong., 2d sess., pp. 2233–34 (Jan. 30, 1920); *Commoner*, Feb. 1920; *Cong. Rec.*, 66th
Cong., 2d sess., p. 1251 (Jan. 9, 1920), for reprint of Bryan's speech. For other comments on
the war referendum amendment to the Covenant, see Gore to "the sovereign people of
Oklahoma, Washington's Birthday," ibid., pp. 2240–41 (Jan. 30, 1920). At the time, Gore
was defending his wartime record in the Senate just before the Oklahoma Democratic
Convention met in February; he was defeated for reelection in the primary later. See Billington, *Gore*, pp. 120–26, for an account of "the campaign for his political life," which
followed the March 1920 vote on the League Covenant.

[16]Levine, *Bryan*, pp. 142–45, treats his compromise efforts but does not mention the war
referendum plan as a part thereof.

[17]*Cong. Rec.*, 66th Cong., 1st sess., p. 8750 (Nov. 18, 1919).

[18]Ibid., pp. 8749, 8751 (Nov. 18, 1919). See also Doan, *La Follettes*, pp. 94–97; La Follette
and La Follette, *La Follette*, II, 982. Stone, *Irreconcilables*, does not mention the La
Follette reservations.

of Article 10 and the League on November 19, 1919, and March 19, 1920, however, did not end American interest in international acceptance of the war referendum principle. Serious consideration was given to this means of extending popular control of foreign policy during the political campaign of 1920.

In view of interest in the war referendum by some farm organizations during the League debate, its endorsement by the new Farmer-Labor party in 1920 was no surprise. Its "100 per cent Americanism" platform plank called for restoration of civil liberties, repeal of espionage and sedition legislation, and national application of the initiative, referendum, and recall. "Democracy demands," the platform suggested, "that war may not be declared except in cases of actual military invasion, before referring the question to a direct vote of the people." A program of "open diplomacy," disarmament, and anti-imperialism would initiate an era of "no more kings and no more wars." [19]

A majority of Democrats in 1920, under Wilson's leadership, encouraged a "solemn referendum" on the administration's foreign-policy record in general. Bryan, on the other hand, offered a referendum principle in another form. As a member of the Committee on Platforms and Resolutions and in a later speech, "Peace and Prohibition," on the floor of the San Francisco Convention, Bryan unsuccessfully offered five platform changes. In order to make it "as easy to end a war as it is to declare war," he proposed an amendment to the Constitution to provide ratification of treaties by a majority vote of the Senate. Like Senator Gore earlier, he favored selection of League delegates by popular vote. Finally, Bryan believed that those delegates should be instructed "not to vote for war without specific instructions from Congress or from the people, given by referendum vote." [20] The last process, of course, would necessitate another constitutional amendment.

Never easily discouraged, Bryan did not end his plea for the war referendum plan after the Democrats rejected his platform suggestions. Following the Democratic defeat in November, he included among several proposed constitutional amendments, mentioned in the *Com-*

---

[19] Kirk H. Porter and Donald Bruce Johnson, comps., *National Party Platforms, 1840–1960* (Urbana, Ill., 1961), pp. 224–25.

[20] William Jennings Bryan, "Peace and Prohibition," speech delivered at the Democratic National Convention, San Francisco, July 2, 1920, Speech, Article, and Report File, Bryan Papers. See also Coletta, *Bryan,* III, 128–30, on the demonstration following what Bryan called his "mountain top" speech. Levine, *Bryan,* pp. 161–65, does not mention Bryan's favoring the war referendum at the 1920 convention, nor does Wesley M. Bagby, *The Road to Normalcy: The Presidential Campaign and Election of 1920* (Baltimore, 1962), pp. 76–78, 104–8.

moner as possible Democratic goals for 1924, the plan for a referendum on war.[21] It was no idle fancy to Bryan, for he also soon offered it to Republicans for immediate consideration.

Actually, New Freedom defector and recent Republican king-maker George Harvey already had made a similar suggestion. Former editor of the *North American Review* and at the time editor-publisher of *Harvey's Weekly,* he spoke to Warren G. Harding about international adoption of the war referendum idea during the celebrated Marion, Ohio, conferences between the president-elect and some of America's "best minds." The war referendum plan thereby became linked to Harding's ill-defined association of nations scheme, proposed during the campaign ostensibly to replace the League of Nations.

Harvey's three-day discussions centered around a proposal that, according to Republicans, dwarfed "all previous propositions designed to perpetuate peace and to democratize the world."[22] It was now time for Republicans to issue optimistic statements about utopian goals; Senator Harding's interest in the war referendum idea, now regarded by the press as basic to any American-sponsored association of nations, had changed significantly since his 1917 threat to resign from the Senate rather than endorse the principle. Harvey obviously had made an excellent case for the war referendum proposal.

By the time of Bryan's conference with Harding, therefore, the president-elect's new interest in international agreement on the war referendum, although unexplained, had created some sentiment in its behalf. Bryan testified to Harding that he still adhered to the idea of a national advisory referendum prior to war declarations. Pleased to learn of Harding's serious consideration of the proposal in conjunction with the association of nations, Bryan left Marion confident that his counsel once more had been influential.[23]

Indeed, Harding seemed interested at first. He credited the "big idea" to Harvey and Bryan and talked it over with several senators and foreign

[21]*Commoner,* Nov. 1920; Coletta, *Bryan,* III, 138; Levine, *Bryan,* p. 188.

[22]*New York Times,* Dec. 11, 14, 1920. Fleming, *United States and World Organization,* pp. 37, 41, mentions Harvey's visit with Harding but not their discussion of the war referendum plan.

[23]*New York Times,* Dec. 18, 1920. Bryan also received encouragement from a correspondent about this time. The dean of John Marshall Law School, Chicago, believed it was a good time to launch a movement for the war referendum plan; he thought it might produce "similar results in other countries" if the United States adopted it (Edward T. Lee to Bryan, Dec. 2, 1920, Bryan Papers). Neither Levine, *Bryan,* p. 189, nor Coletta, *Bryan,* III, 140–41, mentions Bryan's war referendum interest in connection with his trip to Marion.

affairs advisors, some of whom came to Marion. Among these advisors were Republican "irreconcilables" Hiram W. Johnson (Calif.), William E. Borah (Idaho), and Albert B. Fall (N.Mex.); Herbert Hoover and Elihu Root; and Missouri Democrat James A. Reed.[24] Most of these showed interest in the association of nations and even international agreement to the war referendum plan, but only Senator Fall, apart from Bryan and Harvey, clearly endorsed the latter idea. Senator Reed, who had favored adding Gore's referendum plan to the League Covenant, now objected that an aggressor might seize American territory before the results of such a referendum could be ascertained. Republican Senators Harry New (Ind.) and James W. Wadsworth, Jr. (N.Y.) also rejected the proposal. In view of such opposition, therefore, Harding abandoned further consideration of the war referendum plan, finally announcing his association of nations scheme without it.[25]

Harding's decision was partly in line with opposition to the plan by the pro-League *New York Times,* which editorially ridiculed Harding's Marion conferences, as well as his association of nations. The most caustic phrases, however, were reserved for the "sublime thought" previously offered, according to the editors, by Socialists and La Follette and now proposed by Harvey and Bryan. "It is humiliating," they wrote, "that the attention of the next President should have been devoted, even for a brief time, to puerilities like the proposal of a referendum before going to war and other matters of a like whimsical nature."[26]

Columbia University President Nicholas Murray Butler also offered opposition to the war referendum proposal. His differences with pacifists during the war had drawn him into conflict with several war referendum partisans, but in the less emotional peacetime atmosphere of 1920, his arguments against the idea of a national advisory decision on war were more significant. Friends of the idea, he believed, overlooked the basic "psychology of the crowd," which stressed that the public was more receptive to pressures than were chosen representatives. "The notion that wars are forced by Governments upon unwilling peoples," according to Butler, "has no foundation in fact." Resort to the war referendum would, furthermore, discredit representative government when it needed strength to endure a crisis.[27] Butler's opposition in these terms was the most thought-provoking attack on the war referendum idea. Indeed, most

[24]*New York Times,* Dec. 15, 16, 18, 1920.
[25]Ibid., Dec. 19, 20, 23, 1920.
[26]Ibid., Dec. 15, 20, 24, 1920.
[27]Ibid., Dec. 19, 1920.

of its supporters revealed a distrust for representative government and an advanced faith in more direct democracy. Their belief that the people, if given a chance, would vote for peace was unproved and of questionable validity.

Yet President Butler still had not struck the central premise held by war referendum partisans as accurately as did George Harvey, who continued to urge his proposal through editorials in *Harvey's Weekly*. He criticized the League of Nations, and now Harding's association of nations, for a basic lack of democracy; both placed controls in an "oligarchy of Great Powers." As much as Americans believed in representative government, he stated, "We must hold that in some few matters of transcendent importance the representatives should return their delegated power to the people, for action through a referendum." He offered, therefore, as an unprecedented exaltation of democracy and guarantee of world peace, that governments agree not to begin "aggressive wars" prior to sanction by plebiscite.

Harvey attempted, in fact, to answer some of Butler's objections to the plan by contrasting offensive and defensive war. The latter type, in which American security or territory was violated, would not require a referendum. In his insistence that the referendum plan would be a good beginning in the education of people to prefer the "rule of right to the rule of force," however, Harvey stated the fundamental premise of most war referendum partisans.[28] The choice for them was not really one of degrees of democracy; it was the basic problem of the use of force in diplomacy, a problem confronted in the debate over Article 10 and other foreign policy issues in which the public became interested during the interwar period.

Despite Harding's rejection of the war referendum plan as an international peace measure, legislative interest in it did not cease. During Harding's administration, seven new war referendum resolutions appeared in Congress, with all except one seeking international acceptance of the plan.

Senator Edwin F. Ladd (Republican, N.Dak.) borrowed Senator Gore's 1917 text for his own resolution, introduced July 25, 1921. He thus proposed not only American adoption of the peace plan but adherence by other nations through treaties with the United States. It would be a permanent reform achieved through constitutional amendment. When his 1921 resolution died in the Judiciary Committee, which was the usual fate of war referendum bills, Senator Ladd, a former chemistry professor and Nonpartisan League spokesman, introduced the Gore resolution text

[28]"For Democracy and Peace," *Harvey's Weekly,* 3, No. 52 (1920), 1–2; "Anti-Irenic Men of Straw," ibid., 4, No. 1 (1921), 5.

once more on December 6, 1923.[29] But, as before, only limited support of a local nature was furnished the Ladd resolution.[30]

Less than two weeks later Senator Clarence C. Dill (Wash.) introduced another such proposal. Actually it was the same text he had used as a congressman in 1918.[31] Congress was authorized, under the Dill amendment, to declare war without the assistance of an advisory referendum whenever United States territory or insular possessions were invaded or threatened with invasion by a foreign power. Insurrection or revolution within the United States also would disallow the referendum process. Dill again tried to distinguish between defensive and offensive wars. In the latter case, as in his 1918-19 effort, an advisory referendum of the people would be required. Furthermore, Congress under Senator Dill's proposed constitutional amendment could submit to referendum "such other questions . . . which are connected with a possible declaration of war, as may be provided for by any treaty with another nation."[32] The inference was clear; the people would serve as a possible check upon any executive agreement on the use of American force in diplomacy. The fear remained that America might lose its independence of action while cooperating with other nations to preserve peace.

Senator Dill's 1923 resolution died in the Judiciary Committee but lived on for a brief time in the House, where his text was used by Joseph S. Wolff (Democrat, Mo.) early in 1924.[33] All of these proposals continued the 1918-20 emphasis upon international agreement on the war referendum; all were in the form of a proposed constitutional amendment; and they reflected both Gore's and Dill's earlier efforts. Another proposed amendment seeking the war referendum was sought by Representative Edward Voight (Republican, Wis.) June 24, 1922. His

[29]Original texts of these proposals, Senate Joint Resolution 89, 67th Cong., 1st sess., n.d. (July 25, 1921), and Senate Joint Resolution 8, 68th Cong., 1st sess., Dec. 6, 1923, are in RG 46, NA. Ladd's vacant seat, occasioned in 1925 by his death, went to Gerald P. Nye primarily due to Nonpartisan League support. See Robert L. Morlan, *Political Prairie Fire: The Nonpartisan League, 1915-1922* (Minneapolis, 1955), which is primarily a study of the League's domestic interests.

[30]See Petition of Voters of the State of North Dakota Favoring Joint Resolution 89, Received by Judiciary Committee, 67th Cong., 1st Sess., Nov. 2, 1921, in Petitions and Memorials Referred to Committees, Committee on the Judiciary, RG 46, NA.

[31]Dill served in Congress, 1915-19, as a congressman, was defeated in 1918, and returned as a senator, 1923-35.

[32]*New York Times,* Dec. 19, 1923; copy of original typescript, Senate Joint Resolution 48, 68th Cong., 1st sess., Dec. 18, 1923, RG 46, NA.

[33]This resolution, too, died in committee. For text see House Joint Resolution 134, 68th Cong., 1st sess., Jan. 10, 1924, in "House of Representatives Joint Resolutions, 68th Congress 1923-1925, 1-385," LC.

resolution exempted from an advisory referendum, in the pattern previously established, any wars following invasion or threatened invasion. In
fact, Voight's proposal differed from earlier ones only in his requirement
that the referendum be conducted by governors of the states within a period of ten days.[34]

The most interesting war referendum resolutions before the 1924
political conventions, however, were two introduced by Mrs. Winifred
Mason Huck, Republican congresswoman from Chicago.[35] Introduced
January 16 and February 16, 1923, her war referendum proposals were
not in the form of proposed constitutional amendments but did attempt to
secure international agreement to the reform. The first resolution
directed President Harding to inform foreign powers that "the United
States will delegate to its people the sole power to declare war against any
nation that shall delegate the same power to its people." Such a war
referendum agreement was especially to be sought with nations enjoying
"a population of thirty-five million or over." She further provided that
votes by referendum, in any of the nations agreeing to the process, be
certified in sixty days; in the event of a national decision for war, "no
hostile act by either party or parties shall occur within one year."[36] This
was certainly a unique application of Bryan's tactics of delay and reci-
procity.

In her second resolution, February 16, 1923, Mrs. Huck proposed that
Congress authorize no financial or other concessions to "any country that
does not guarantee by law a plebiscite upon the question of the declaration of war."[37] Such would indeed have been an unusual sanction! Like
many Americans who were more successful in their efforts, the Illinois
congresswoman sought to impose American ideals for peace upon the rest
of the world.

Congresswoman Huck believed that centralization of power had been
the "proximate cause" of most wars.[38] But this did not entirely explain
her faith in diplomatic majoritarianism and support of the war
referendum plan. As a friend of peace and women's rights even before introduction of her two war referendum resolutions, she had addressed a
1922 Armistice Day meeting of the Women's International League for

[34]Copy of House Joint Resolution 356, June 24, 1922, in "House of Representatives, Joint
Resolutions, 67 Congress, 1921–1923, 1–466," LC. Chatfield mentions specifically the
Voight and Huck proposals (*For Peace and Justice,* p. 144).

[35]Mrs. Huck served only about four months in 1922–23, having been elected to fill a va-
cancy caused by the 1921 death of her father, William E. Mason.

[36]Copy of House Joint Resolution 423, Jan. 16, 1923, in "House of Representatives, Joint
Resolutions, 67 Congress, 1921–1923, 1–466," LC.

[37]Copy of House Joint Resolution 450, Feb. 16, 1923, ibid.

[38]*Cong. Rec.,* 67th Cong., 4th sess., p. 1828 (Jan. 16, 1923).

Peace and Freedom. This organization was the postwar descendant of the earlier Woman's Peace Party, which had supported the war referendum so consistently as an emergency measure. Presiding at the Chicago peace meeting was Jane Addams, president of the American section of the Women's International League for Peace and Freedom. Here, before a friendly audience, Mrs. Huck proposed both a war referendum amendment to the Constitution and compulsion of European nations to follow our example by refusing them credit.[39]

Mrs. Huck's peace work also had included participation in a march to the White House, December 10, to demand release of "war prisoners" still held under wartime sedition and espionage laws. She was by then only one of two women in Congress and readily announced the war referendum resolutions as her main goal. She also had addressed a New York Town Hall "No More War" meeting on December 21, 1922.[40] The favorable response of Miss Addams's group and others, therefore, must have encouraged Mrs. Huck's decision to introduce both proposals in January and February 1923.

Greater popular interest in the war referendum idea during the early twenties came in 1924, not in the form of congressional resolutions, but in party platforms. For the first time in history, two major parties placed this peace proposal in their platforms. For the Democrats, William Jennings Bryan was again the source of such endorsement, this time a key figure on the Committee on Platforms and Resolutions. His failure to achieve acceptance of the war referendum idea by Democrats and Republicans in 1920 had not diminished his faith in it. Early in 1921 his twenty-two point "National Legislative Program," anticipating the 1924 platform, had included a war referendum amendment to the Constitution.[41] By 1924 he was thus ready, once more, to champion what may indeed have been the "most pleasing of all" his reform interests.[42]

Bryan was chairman of the eleven-member subcommittee on resolutions, which began its work late on Tuesday, June 24, and for four days thereafter met daily until 6:00 A.M.[43] By the fifth day of the convention,

[39] *New York Times,* Nov. 12, 1922.

[40] Ibid., Dec. 11, 24, 1922, Feb. 13, 1923.

[41] Associated Press clipping, Feb. 16, 1921; Louis Post to Bryan, Feb. 18, 1921, Box 1, Louis F. Post Papers, LC. Assistant Secretary of Labor Post thought the idea "workable."

[42] Levine, *Bryan,* p. 308. Levine's judgment in this case is accurate, although surprising in view of the little attention he gives to Bryan's postwar efforts for the war referendum, and especially since he omits his 1920 work for it in the Democratic Convention. Curti, *Bryan and World Peace,* pp. 250–52, fails to mention Bryan's 1920 and 1924 work for the war referendum.

[43] Coletta, *Bryan,* III, 183, and David Burner, *The Politics of Provincialism: The Democratic Party in Transition, 1918–1932* (New York, 1968), pp. 103–41.

agreement existed on all points except planks dealing with the League of Nations and the Ku Klux Klan; in the process Bryan had secured acceptance of a war referendum plank. The Democrats continued to endorse international agreement on the peace plan but also added a new feature directly associating it with the more popular cause of disarmament. The platform read: "Our government should secure a joint agreement with all nations for world disarmament and also for a referendum on war, except in case of actual or threatened attack. Those who must furnish the blood and bear the burdens imposed by war should, whenever possible, be consulted before this supreme sacrifice is required of them."[44] Another Bryan plank called for a national referendum on joining the League.[45] In all, Bryan secured eight planks brought with him to the New York City convention, narrowly won the floor fight on the entire platform, and saw his brother, agrarian liberal Nebraska Governor Charles W. Bryan, nominated for vice president.[46]

Serving with Bryan on the Democrats' platform committee was war referendum advocate and former Oklahoma Senator Robert L. Owen. But inclusion of the referendum principle—in several forms—was entirely the work of Bryan and a reflection of sporadic, uncoordinated popular interest since 1920. His brother, Charles, associate with him in publishing the *Commoner,* had, as governor, led his state to memorialize Congress in favor of a war referendum amendment in 1923. Seven resolutions in Congress, 1921–24, also indicated interest in the measure. The Democrats in 1924, therefore, were certain that their change of mind on the war referendum issue would not be turned against them.[47]

This endorsement of the war referendum plan, however, was a surprising action for a party heretofore recorded among opposition to the plan. Perhaps agreement was possible only because Wilson's death left Bryan as the most familiar personality in the party and because other issues, especially attitudes toward the Klan and Prohibition, dominated the at-

[44] Porter and Johnson, *National Party Platforms,* p. 250.

[45] Ibid.; Levine, *Bryan,* p. 309; Coletta, *Bryan,* III, 184. Norman H. Davis, "American Foreign Policy: A Democratic View," *Foreign Affairs,* 3 (1924), 22–34, mentions the proposed referendum on League membership but not the war referendum plank. See also David Shannon, *Between the Wars: America, 1919–1941* (Boston, 1965), pp. 60–61.

[46] Coletta, *Bryan,* III, 184, 186, 191–92. Until the convention ended with his brother's nomination, Bryan felt he had failed, despite the victories on Prohibition (blocking Al Smith) and platform issues (e.g., K.K.K. and war referendum). William Allen White, *Politics: The Citizen's Business* (New York, 1924), p. 69, maintains that Bryan "dominated" the platform committee.

[47] Charles Bryan, *Governor Bryan Recommends that a Resolution Be Passed Memorializing Congress to Submit an Amendment to the Constitution Requiring a Referendum of the People before a Declaration of War, Unless the Country Is Invaded* (Lincoln, Neb., 1923); *Review of Reviews,* 70 (1924), 118, 137.

tention of delegates to the convention. More important, this action demonstrated quite simply the unusual popularity of peace plans in the 1920s. Most Americans, in spite of the Democratic showing in the 1924 election, agreed with the basic premise underlying the Democrats' endorsement of the war referendum; they believed that the search for peace, through plans which denied or at least limited the use of force in diplomacy, was just, realistic, and, above all, American.

Interest in the war referendum possibly would have been more formidable if liberal Democrats, represented by agrarian isolationists like the Bryans, had joined liberal Republicans in greater numbers in 1924 in their support for the Progressive party, revived under Robert La Follette and others. Old style progressivism, with its rural evangelical flavor, was slow to pass from the American political scene.[48] A remarkable effort to achieve a progressive coalition had been underway, in fact, since late in 1918. Involving Socialists, former Populists, single-taxers, labor leaders, former Bull Moosers, and Progressive-Republicans, a Committee of Forty-Eight worked in 1920, without success, for the nomination of Robert La Follette on a third-party ticket.[49] But as was often the experience of liberals seeking to act together in positive ways, the Committee of Forty-Eight failed to create a consensus among progressives.

By 1924, therefore, chances were slim for agreement on any program, much less one that included the war referendum plan. Progressivism's loss of leadership in the White House was then only one obvious reason for decline of the progressive movement.[50] Certainly, among war

[48] Arthur Link makes the major argument, once a dissenting one, that progressivism was far from dead, although admitting it was unable to coalesce in the 1920s. See "What Happened to the Progressive Movement in the 1920's?" *American Historical Review,* 64 (1959), 833–51; and Link, *American Epoch,* 3d ed. (New York, 1967), pp. 313–38, on "The Survival of Progressivism." Earlier, Kenneth C. MacKay, *The Progressive Movement of 1924* (New York, 1947), had argued that progressivism was alive and well under Robert La Follette and others who had been active in the earlier, prewar reform causes. In addition to MacKay on the third-party movement of the twenties, see James H. Shideler, "The La Follette Progressive Party Campaign of 1924," *Wisconsin Magazine of History,* 33 (1950), 444–57; idem, "The Disintegration of the Progressive Party Movement of 1924," *Historian,* 13 (1951), 189–201; and on Villard's role in the "quest for a liberal party," D. Joy Humes, *Oswald Garrison Villard, Liberal of the 1920's* (Syracuse, N.Y., 1960), pp. 133–53. For a brief comment on studies revealing reform continuity in the 1920s—both as "survivals" of past progressivism and "preludes" to New Deal reforms—see Burl Noggle, "The Twenties: A New Historiographical Frontier," *Journal of American History,* 53 (1966), 299–314. See Leuchtenburg, "Tired Radicals," in *Perils of Prosperity,* pp. 120–39, for an earlier explanation of "what killed progressivism?"

[49] Amos Pinchot was active in this effort. See his *History of the Progressive Party, 1912–1916* (New York, 1958), pp. 72–75.

[50] Since then historians have offered many reasons; see Herbert F. Margulies, "Recent Opinion on the Decline of the Progressive Movement," *Mid-America,* 45 (1963), 250–68.

referendum advocates the lessons of wartime efforts at union involving diverse reform personalities and interests were also remembered. Yet some cause for optimism existed. Bryan, for example, was still the recognized leader of the Democratic progressive minority and since 1919 had a legislative program emphasizing reform ready.[51] Furthermore, Progressive-Republicans held the balance of power in Congress after 1922, a result, in part, of work by Senator La Follette's 1921 People's Legislative Service in Washington. Its successor, the Conference for Progressive Political Action, began the next year. In both groups were several earlier war referendum advocates, including, in addition to La Follette, Amos Pinchot, Roger Baldwin, Norman Thomas, Jane Addams, and Oswald Garrison Villard.[52] These were not peace organizations but rather efforts to create progressive consensus; their attraction of liberal isolationists, however, demonstrated once more, this time in the so-called era of normalcy, the close relationship between progressivism and peace. In 1924 that affinity was heralded by a revitalized progressive movement whose program included the war referendum plan.

Senator La Follette, as noted, had supported the war referendum in 1916–17 and again as a reservation to the League Covenant in 1919. His next association with the idea came in 1922, when he and war referendum partisans Pinchot, Villard, Thomas, and Baldwin endorsed it as associates in the 1922 Conference for Progressive Political Action. Supported by this liberal coalition, La Follette won reelection to the Senate by his largest majority ever. His platform included support of the war referendum peace measure as well as reduced defense expenditures, direct election of federal judges, and a constitutional amendment to abolish child labor. Villard already was pushing La Follette for the presidency in 1924, and when the Republicans nominated Calvin Coolidge, as expected, the Wisconsin senator accepted the third-party challenge.[53]

In 1924 La Follette's efforts for the war referendum first included an unsuccessful attempt to get Republican party endorsement of it. The Wisconsin delegation carried its platform to the Republican convention,

[51]*Commoner,* Jan., May, 1919; Coletta, *Bryan,* III, 105–6, 151. Bryan was especially optimistic about the chances for Democratic progressivism in 1924 after the progressive Republican victories of 1922 (ibid., p. 156).

[52]Humes, *Villard,* p. 139; Norman Thomas hoped the Conference for Progressive Political Action would be the nucleus of an American labor party and led the Socialist party to endorse La Follette in 1924 (Johnpoll, *Thomas,* pp. 40–43).

[53]Doan, *La Follettes,* pp. 111–12; Richard Lewis Neuberger and Stephen Bertram Kahn, *Integrity: The Life of George W. Norris* (New York, 1937), p. 148; Shannon, *America, 1919–1941,* p. 59.

meeting in Cleveland, June 10. The platform proposed amendments to the Constitution to provide "direct nomination and election of the President, to extend the initiative and referendum to the Federal Government, and to insure a popular referendum for or against war except in cases of actual invasion." Wisconsin progressive Republicans also endorsed treaty agreements with all nations "to outlaw wars, abolish conscription, drastically reduce land, air and naval armaments, and guarantee public referendums on peace and war."[54] But such a peace program, attached to an equally progressive domestic program, was not acceptable to conservative rank-and-file Republicans. It was necessary, therefore, to form a third party.

When the Conference for Progressive Political Action met in Saint Louis in February 1924, a third party effort was not certain, but in case the Republicans rejected their program, a nominating convention was called for July. In preparation for that convention, which also hinged on whether the Democrats would nominate a liberal candidate, the Conference drafted among its resolutions in February several antiwar and anti-imperialist pronouncements. But the progressives failed to include a war referendum clause that had earlier been written into their approved program for action.[55] Following the Republican convention and during the Democratic convention, however, La Follette worked into the Progressive party's platform a clear endorsement of the "public referendum on peace and war." Meeting in Cleveland in July, the progressives chose the Wisconsin senator, as expected, and Montana Democrat Burton K. Wheeler to represent their liberal domestic goals and equally ambitious peace program. They hoped for success commensurate with that of Woodrow Wilson's 1916 race on peace and progressivism. Their peace proposals especially left little to the imagination; in addition to the war referendum, these included the legal outlawing of war, anti–war-profits legislation (another of La Follette's plans), and opposition to compulsory military service. Of some four hundred planks considered by the platform committee, the 1924 platform included over 40.[56]

[54]Robert M. La Follette to William Jennings Bryan, June 6, 1924, with a copy of the Wisconsin delegation's platform, Bryan Papers.

[55]*Report of the Proceedings of the Third Conference for Progressive Political Action,* Saint Louis, Mo., Feb. 11, 12, 1924, in Robert M. La Follette and Burton K. Wheeler Collection, LC.

[56]Porter and Johnson, *National Party Platforms,* 256; MacKay, *Progressive Movement of 1924,* pp. 143–44, 270–73; Shannon, *America, 1919–1941,* p. 61; and Villard, *Fighting Years,* pp. 502–6. Link, "What Happened to the Progressive Movement?" p. 841, mentions Progressive party endorsement of the war referendum as illustrative of old, meaningless

La Follette, however, did not at first stress foreign policy issues or peace plans. In a typical speech emphasizing domestic reforms, these matters came up at the end. He urged that victory in November would mean cooperation with liberal governments abroad "to outlaw war, to abolish conscription, to reduce to a purely defensive basis naval, aerial and land armaments, and to place in the hands of the people of every country the decision upon the declaration of war."[57] Later, in response to a suggestion of Oswald Garrison Villard, La Follette concentrated on foreign affairs for the first time in a Rochester, New York, speech, October 6, 1924. Believing that the last war was brought about by financiers and imperialists, he advocated democratic control of foreign policy through his entire peace program and especially the war referendum plan.[58] He continued this theme in Cincinnati on October 10, urging an end to secret diplomacy. Congress must be kept advised, and the Executive must "concede to it its constitutional share in the conduct of foreign relations." La Follette proposed an end to war profits, dollar diplomacy, and conscription; he favored a "pay-as-you-go policy" in the event of "defensive" wars, withdrawal of the marines from Haiti, Santo Domingo, and Central American states, self-government for the Philippines, and the war referendum plan.[59] A week later in Saint Louis he announced again that bankers and munitions makers had forced America into war. If elected, he would never favor war without an advisory referendum of the people; and in the event of war, he would lessen chances of profit by conscription of wealth.[60]

The Progressive party effort of 1924, however, was too broad to emphasize any single reform such as the war referendum plan. Yet the liberal editor of the *Nation,* who campaigned for the ticket in several midwestern and western states, reported "from La Follette workers that the most popular plank" in 1924 was the one advocating a war referendum.[61]

---

reforms of "little significance for the future." George E. Mowry regards the war referendum plank as one of two "most original parts of the platform" ("The Progressive Party, 1912 and 1924," in Arthur M. Schlesinger, Jr., ed., *History of U.S. Political Parties,* Vol. III, *1910–1945: From Square Deal to New Deal* (New York, 1973), p. 2568. On the La Follettes' own account of the conventions, nomination, and election, see *La Follette,* II, 1107–47.

[57]This speech, made Sept. 18, 1924, in New York City, is reprinted in David Burner, "Election of 1924," in Arthur M. Schlesinger, Jr., ed., *History of American Presidential Elections 1789–1968* (New York, 1971), pp. 2552–53.

[58]Press Release No. 2, Oct. 6, 1924, La Follette–Wheeler Collection.

[59]This speech is reprinted in Mowry, "Progressive Party," pp. 2666–68.

[60]Adler, *Isolationist Impulse,* p. 185.

[61]Villard was convinced that the Progressives would carry South Dakota, North Dakota, Montana, Washington, and Nebraska and reported strong support among Scandinavians, as

Also, Mrs. Wheeler, who toured the country for the ticket, stressed the war referendum plank.[62] Such emphasis by the progressive ticket was, no doubt, an indication of agrarian isolationist disillusionment or protest sentiment. Yet it also demonstrated the general popularity of any sort of peace proposal in the 1920s. The progressives, with what Selig Adler calls their "shotgun prescription for peace,"[63] indeed, had their share in 1924, not the least of which was the war referendum plan.

The progressive ticket of 1924, also a significant indication of reform continuity, nevertheless was a failure as an effort at progressive consensus. As a third-party movement it received wide support from the American Federation of Labor, socialists, and several progressive Republicans. La Follette polled almost five million popular votes, or nearly one-sixth of the total, the largest received by any third party in American history. Yet he carried only his own state of Wisconsin in the electoral college.[64] The Coolidge victory turned on many factors, including a sudden preelection rise in farm prices, which dulled La Follette's appeal to farmers, and the divisions among Democrats. Bryan's influence was great in 1924, but the Democratic party lacked leadership, a viable liberal program, and effective candidates. Bryan himself had opposed John W. Davis in the convention and even had considered fusion with La Follette's progressives. Like most liberal Democrats, however, he remained faithful to the two-party system[65] and perhaps in doing so, reduced La Follette's appeal. Not even their common cause of peace and reform goals, including the war referendum plan, brought them together. Endorsement of the war referendum idea by two political parties in 1924, nevertheless, was unique in the history of the peace plan and would be cited often by later partisans.

---

well as German-Americans, in rural districts. He also discovered high praise for La Follette's peace program and previous antiwar stand in New York. See Oswald Garrison Villard, "The Winning of the West," *Nation*, 119 (1924), 435.

[62] Burton K. Wheeler with Paul F. Healy, *Yankee from the West* (Garden City, N.Y., 1962), pp. 246–66, especially p. 257.

[63] Adler, *Isolationist Impulse*, p. 185. He includes under this description their advocacy of such "noncoercive plans" as outlawry, disarmament, and the referendum on war.

[64] Shannon, *America, 1919–1941*, pp. 62–63; Adler, *Isolationist Impulse*, pp. 171–72, 184–85; Richard Hofstadter, *The Age of Reform* (New York, 1955), p. 281; Michael Wreszin, *Oswald Garrison Villard: Pacifist at War* (Bloomington, Ind., 1965), pp. 162–68; Burner, "Election of 1924," pp. 2459–90. Mowry, "Progressive Party," p. 2569, considers the La Follette vote evidence "of the tenacity of the progressive impulse."

[65] Coletta, *Bryan*, III, 105, 180, 194–95.

CHAPTER VI

Peace without Commitments
The State Department and Popular Diplomacy

EFFORTS TO OBTAIN the war referendum reform during the interwar period accurately reflected two main themes in American diplomatic practice. However sporadic or lacking in coordination among its diverse supporting elements, proponents of a referendum on war were persistent, first, because of general pressures for popular control of foreign policy. Secondly, the war referendum plan represented as well as any of the other better-known interwar peace measures the preference of most Americans for diplomacy devoid of military force.

The American search for peace by various means, but chiefly in terms of these two themes, reflected the twin forces of hope and popular disillusionment over World War I. The result was a peculiarly legal approach to international problems. It was encouraged by, but not generally attributed to, similar aims and programs of the major twentieth-century peace organizations. Examples remembered and cited by historians include defeat of American membership in the League of Nations, support of disarmament, and advocacy of legal outlawry of war. In all of these efforts to achieve peace through law and by popular control of diplomacy, attempts at increased leadership in foreign affairs by Congress, chiefly the Senate, reflected both American traditions and public opinion.

Such an approach to peace featured many sincere efforts for a referendum on war. Most of its friends after the armistice and before 1925 sought international agreement to the reform. Even so, the war referendum is not remembered as typical of America's peace aims and traditions. Its persistence has not been noted or understood heretofore, partly because it never dominated public attention as the other peace plans did. Yet its failure to be adopted by 1925, or even by 1941, did not render it any less significant. It was symbolic of antimilitaristic traditions in America, and it expressed an advanced faith in public opinion in formulation of American foreign policy.

In 1922–23 the symbolic nature of the war referendum plan became evident, once more, in a development that, on the surface, suggested its first official endorsement by a European nation. Dr. Wilhelm Cuno, chancellor of the Weimar Republic, in December 1922 offered to Europeans a thirty-year peace and security pact based on the war referendum. It appeared that the idea born of the revolutionary thinking of philosopher-democrats Condorcet and Immanuel Kant had returned to its European home. Germany, one of the least experienced of the new democracies, was ready to agree that "France, Great Britain, Italy, and Germany solemnly agree among themselves and promise the Government of the United States, that they will not resort to war against each other for a period of one generation without being authorized to do so by a plebiscite of their own people."[1]

Despite the European philosophical origins of the war referendum idea, Europeans had never accepted it as had Americans. In London in 1870, after reading a paper, "A Parliament of Nations and International Arbitration," Senor Don Arturo de Marcoartu of Spain discussed his proposals and advocated an end to war declarations by heads of states. As an alternative he presented the idea of wars "declared by the people."[2] But such an appeal was unusual for Europeans, for in Europe diplomacy traditionally hinged on use of force and alliances.

It was Wilson's idealism and rhetoric that gave the greatest impetus to development of European democratic control in diplomacy. His demands for an end to secret diplomacy, establishment of representative governments, and expanded legislative controls of diplomacy, as well as his efforts for disarmament, thus encouraged postwar changes in Europe. These included greater committee influence in legislatures, declaration of war by legislatures only, and legislative ratification of treaties.

Several postwar constitutions in Europe extensively provided for initiative and referendum, although Estonia expressly excluded foreign affairs from the referendum. Switzerland amended its constitution, by referendum in 1921, to provide a referendum on treaties. The Swiss also had held a referendum on joining the League of Nations in May 1920. The Weimar Constitution of 1919 stipulated legislative committee influence in foreign affairs and provided that a petition by ten percent of the elec-

[1]Charles Evans Hughes's Memorandum, Dec. 15, 1922, and German Embassy to Department of State, Dec. 21, 1922, U.S., Department of State, *Papers Relating to the Foreign Relations of the United States, 1922* (Washington, D.C., 1938), II, 203–5. Few historians have noted the Cuno proposal of 1922, and none have presented the interpretation offered herein.

[2]*Sessional Transactions of the National Association for the Promotion of Social Science, 1870* (London, 1871), p. 169.

torate could force a referendum on defense issues. The general rise of re-
publicanism in postwar Europe and provision for democracy in foreign
affairs seemed to signal a new era.[3]

In 1914 British liberal pacifists had formed a significant pressure group
that did not reflect Wilsonian influence but yet sought popular control of
foreign policy. E. D. Morel, Charles Trevelyan, Ramsay MacDonald, and
Norman Angell organized the Union of Democratic Control soon after
World War I began. It actively campaigned for parliamentary controls
over foreign policy by means of greater deliberations and committee
influence in Parliament. Many of its members, in fact, were members of
Parliament. The Union fought secret diplomacy and any transfer of peoples from one nation to another without their consent. With the end of the
war England's Union of Democratic Control began to influence English
politics and drew the support of Bertrand Russell, J. A. Hobson, and
Arthur Ponsonby. Its journal, *Foreign Affairs,* supported the League of
Nations, disarmament, arbitration, and free trade.[4] Members of the
Union assumed that foreign policies of democratic states would improve
as a result of popular participation and control of government and from
the beginning urged that "adequate machinery for ensuring democratic
control of foreign policy . . . be created." Its objectives, which, as noted,
influenced the Woman's Peace Party before American intervention, anticipated most of Wilson's later Fourteen Points.[5]

Even so, English interest in the war referendum plan itself never materialized as in the United States, despite evidence that Oswald Garrison
Villard was in touch with English liberals in the Union of Democratic
Control and even reported to them that he favored a war referendum late
in 1914.[6] Closer examination of the 1922 Cuno proposal, however, reveals

[3]Howard Lee McBain and Lindsay Rogers, "Democrats and Diplomats," in *The New
Constitutions of Europe* (New York, 1922), pp. 136–53.

[4]Charles Trevelyan, *The Union of Democratic Control: Its History and Its Policy*
(London, 1919), pp. 1–4, Union of Democratic Control (England) Files, SCPC. Good accounts of this organization are Frances Neilson, "The British Union of Democratic Control," in George H. Blakeslee, ed., *The Problems and Lessons of the War* (New York, 1916),
pp. 223–43, and Marvin Swartz, *The Union of Democratic Control in British Politics during
the First World War* (London, 1971).

[5]Arno J. Mayer, *Political Origins of the New Diplomacy, 1917–1918* (New Haven, 1959),
pp. 45–49, 54–55; Wreszin, *Villard,* pp. 80–81.

[6]Wreszin, *Villard,* p. 82. The Union's *Foreign Affairs* carried several articles on the war
referendum idea and the Cuno proposal, but its editors hesitated to endorse it without first
securing other popular controls of diplomacy. See Hubert C. S. Colborne, "World
Referendum and War," *Foreign Affairs* (London), 4 (Aug. 1922), 40; "Referendum and
Wars," ibid., 4 (Jan. 1923), 132; and "The German Offer to Stop War by Referendum,"
ibid., 5 (July 1923), 14–15.

an interesting diplomatic episode involving Europe and the United States. While Europeans were striving to achieve economic stability in the face of postwar reconstruction and German reparations problems, Americans in 1922 were at the height of their own interwar search for peace plans. During this search Chancellor Cuno borrowed the war referendum plan, with strong American urging to do so, as a solution to European insecurity and economic problems. In contrast to European political and economic problems, America's postwar stability was indeed conducive to peace planning and Cuno's action.

American postwar peace planning reached a significant stage late in 1922 with the announcement of a contest sponsored by the American Foundation for Peace and publisher Edward Bok. By 1924, 22,165 plans had been submitted. In November 1922 Senator Robert La Follette ran on a platform advocating the war referendum and disarmament as the proper road to peace. Since 1921 he had been studying the relation of industrial war profits to America's 1917 intervention. Typical of America's search for peace devoid of force yet replete with popular control in diplomacy was Senator William E. Borah's consideration, at this time, of disarmament, outlawry of war, international economic conferences, and the war referendum. His disarmament resolution had led to the Washington Conference in 1921–22. He frequently asserted his lack of faith in the "old system of secret diplomacy" and his advanced faith in public opinion. Borah never introduced a war referendum resolution but often claimed that the "more nearly you can bring the business of declaring war to the judgment and control of the people, the more certain you are to have peace."[7] Such was the atmosphere in the United States at the time of the 1922 war referendum–security pact offer, ostensibly German in origin, made through Secretary of State Charles Evans Hughes.

Chancellor Wilhelm Cuno was former director of the Hamburg-American Line and headed a "business ministry" in Berlin from November 21, 1922, to August 13, 1923. The ministry was a coalition cabinet composed of politically nonpartisan ministers such as Foreign Minister von Rosenberg, former German minister to Copenhagen. It dedicated itself to fulfillment of the Treaty of Versailles, yet its inheritance of general economic instability and the rapid decline in value

---

[7]John Chalmers Vinson, *William E. Borah and the Outlawry of War* (Athens, Ga., 1957), pp. 48–71; Borah, article in *Baltimore Evening Sun,* July 7, 1921, and "Borah," the *Searchlight* (Washington), July 1921, p. 14, Senator Borah's Papers (Scrapbook), William E. Borah Papers (microfilm), LC.

of the mark heightened Cuno's difficulties and prevented regular reparations payments.[8]

By late 1922 Germany had made two requests for a moratorium on reparation payments following its first payment of $250 million of the total bill of $33 billion. But as the German mark continued to sink rapidly in value, the Weimar Republic again requested a total moratorium on November 14, 1922, and witnessed a fall of the Wirth ministry the next day.[9] French diplomats and especially Premier Poincaré, on the one hand, did not believe the German request was justified and demanded "guarantees" before granting any Allied agreement to a moratorium. Great Britain, on the other hand, felt its own economic restoration was closely tied to Germany's ability to purchase English commodities. Gradually, therefore, England came to believe that German economic stability should precede scheduled reparations payments. The result was a diplomatic battle among Allied powers, chiefly England and France, a European war scare, the German war referendum plan offer, and, ultimately, the French and Belgian decision to occupy the Ruhr, Germany's industrial arsenal.

The timing of the Cuno proposal, presented by German Ambassador Wiedfeldt to Secretary Hughes December 15, 1922, offered the first clue as to its probable origins. It appeared at a critical moment in the general economic disorder associated with the reparations problem. Since mid-1922 the Germans had encouraged American assistance in the matter, while England talked of cancellation of America's war debts and France insisted on security by fulfillment of German reparations payments. Wiedfeldt had met with Secretary Hughes on October 9 and insisted, once more, that no other power than the United States could command Europe's confidence and bring a solution. He specifically asked Hughes to insist on a "real peace" in Europe and immediate solution of the reparations question.[10]

[8]The American ambassador's report of the German change of government reflected the early influence of Hitler's Munich tirades: "The weakness of this kind of Government is the one point of attack by all reactionaries, as well as by millions of sane and sober German men and women who see Germany drifting rapidly toward a breakdown, and are eager for a strong Government." He added that a "dictator" is commonly discussed and mentioned a "young Austrian named Hitler" (Alanson B. Houghton to Charles Evans Hughes, Nov. 21, 1922, Box 4B, Charles Evans Hughes Papers, LC. See also Erich Eyck, *A History of the Weimar Republic* (Cambridge, 1962), I, 227–29, 341; Henry Ashby Turner, *Stresemann and the Politics of the Weimar Republic* (Princeton, 1963), pp. 103–10.

[9]*Times* (London), Nov. 15, 16, 1922.

[10]German Chargé Von Thermann to Acting Secretary of State, Aug. 22, 1922, and Hughes's Memorandum, Oct. 9, 1922, *For. Rel. U.S., 1922,* II, 160, 163–64, 204; Hughes, "The Dawes Plan," pp. 1–2, Hughes Papers (copy in possession of John Chalmers Vinson).

Actually Secretary Hughes was already at work on the reparations matter, for he believed European difficulties were primarily economic rather than political. In September talks with Myron T. Herrick, America's ambassador to France, Hughes discussed a plan for settlement based on a conference of eminent international financiers. As the plan was enlarged in his own mind, it took a form similar to that of an earlier committee of bankers, appointed by the Reparations Commission in April to consider the matter of foreign loans to enable German payment of reparations. Hughes conferred with Thomas W. Lamont of J. P. Morgan and Company about this plan on the very day of Wiedfeldt's appointment.

Morgan, at the time in Paris, saw Herrick concerning the plan the day after the latter's return to France, October 12. Also in this meeting was America's unofficial representative on the Reparations Commission, Roland William Boyden. Morgan, who had served on the earlier advisory group, offered his services again, and both Boyden and Herrick approved Hughes's plan. Poincaré's early reaction, however, was unfavorable. Even so, Hughes insisted that Herrick renew the suggestion and continued himself to mention it in talks with Germany's Ambassador Wiedfeldt.[11]

At the same time, the Reparations Commission was considering a new British plan of more realistic schedules for German payments and was looking toward a proposed Brussels conference on reparations. Great Britain favored complete relief from the treaty's financial requirements for at least two years, continued payments in kind, and international loans to Germany. Among American spokesmen in Europe who believed that Germany's collapse was imminent if the United States did not exert influence at once, Boyden and others agreed with England's view that the reparations solution hinged on adjustment of Allied debts. But on that point Secretary Hughes was adamant. He continued to urge his plan for settlement by international financiers but rejected discussions on the basis of either reduction or cancellation of debts; the latter was totally a matter for congressional attention.[12]

Herrick and Boyden cautioned Hughes about growing French impatience as well as serious German economic problems. Boyden did not believe France would accept any concessions to Germany, such as those contemplated by England, unless on the basis of "pledges of definite security" and even financial controls. In the absence of American influence for peace, security, and economic reconstruction, therefore, those on the

[11]Hughes, "Dawes Plan," p. 2, Hughes Papers. Correspondence between Hughes and Herrick, Oct. 9, 13, 1922, and Hughes's Memorandum, Oct. 23, 1922, *For. Rel. U.S., 1922,* II, 165, 170–71.

[12]Herrick to Hughes, Oct. 14, 1922, and Hughes to Herrick, Oct. 17, 1922, ibid., pp. 165–66, 168–70.

scene feared both Germany's economic collapse and direct French action.[13] Such reports to Hughes from France intensified his reliance on the conference plan as an economic solution; they furthermore encouraged him to watch for some plan to guarantee peace as well.

Recent reports from America's ambassador in Berlin also confirmed what Hughes had gathered in the dispatches from France and from Ambassador Wiedfeldt's frequent meetings with him. Alanson B. Houghton suggested late in August that Germany's problems had created a "tense and electrical situation" that could see the fall of the government. He urged, in light of that fact, that the United States make its influence felt "in some way in their behalf."[14] By late October, Houghton was ready to make his own suggestion as to the form of that American influence.

On the very day that Houghton was drafting his suggestions in Berlin, Hughes characteristically cautioned Wiedfeldt to keep their continued talks confidential. Hughes believed that publicity of his plan for an international advisory conference of financial experts would give rise to rumors and possible congressional opposition. He felt it necessary to sound out France first to see if the proposal would be favorably received. After Herrick reported that Poincaré, the same day, again took a noncommittal attitude toward Hughes's proposal, the secretary decided to present his reasons for it directly to Jusserand, the French minister. In that interview Hughes revealed how typically he represented America's approach to diplomacy. He confessed that neither statesmen nor their delegates responsible to foreign offices could solve the European economic problem. Governments involved were hindered by politics at home and could devise a solution only with the direct participation of an unofficial and nongovernmental advisory financial conference such as he proposed. Government financial action then could be based on *public opinion* and would "carry the highest weight" possible.[15]

In the midst of this quiet diplomacy in the interest of his financial conference plan, Hughes received Ambassador Houghton's report on German-European conditions and his personal suggestion of a solution. Houghton agreed with others who saw in Europe, and especially Germany, the immediate need of economic and political stability. He em-

---

[13]Herrick to Hughes, Oct. 14, 1922, ibid., pp. 167–68.

[14]Acting Secretary of State to Hughes, Aug. 28, 1922, and Houghton to Acting Secretary of State, Aug. 29, 1922, ibid., pp. 160–63. See also Houghton to Secretary of State, Aug. 24, 1922, Decimal File 862.00/1140, RG 59, NA. Houghton's frequent reports on German financial conditions are in DF 862.51.

[15]Hughes's Memorandum, Oct. 23, 1922, Herrick to Hughes, Oct. 23, 27, 1922, Hughes's Memorandum, Nov. 7, 1922, *For. Rel. U.S., 1922,* II, 170–71, 175, 177–80; and Hughes, "Dawes Plan," pp. 2–3, Hughes Papers.

phasized more than others, however, the "mirage of Bolshevism" that beckoned the people toward collapse.

Already the conditions are dangerous. Already the Bolshevist tide is beating against the barriers of European civilization. And if once those barriers go down, if the German people, in despair, believing that sympathy and help and understanding of their position are denied them, turn, for relief, to the East, the time is past. That tide will sweep resistlessly to the Atlantic.[16]

Houghton had been reporting on conditions in Germany for some time and had been commended by Secretary Hughes, who was "impressed by the soundness" of his judgment. Expressing further confidence in the ambassador, Hughes added, "I also desire to have directly and fully the benefit of your views and conclusions even in the most confidential matters."[17] While Hughes was on vacation, the Houghton reports continued to reach the State Department, where William Phillips again noted the thoroughness of reports on German conditions.[18] Late in September, in another such report, Houghton wrote that the German economy was experiencing "a sort of quiet bleeding to death," which, he predicted, would result in new alignments and a "movement toward the Right."[19] Such confidence in his reports on German conditions, coupled with Houghton's own sense of urgency, gave his later suggestions an authoritative tone that made them more credible.

In late October, Houghton advised immediate action by the United States to save Germany and Europe. His proposal was twofold, seeking to calm Germany internally and to furnish France the security guarantees necessary before settlement of the reparations problem could be effected. He did not believe, however, that Europe's settlement could come without debt relief. A former congressman from New York, Ambassador Houghton was well aware that Americans would not readily allow *unconditional* remission of Allied debts. Anyway, such action would bring only temporary relief of Europe's insecurity. To prevent the "inevitable" war and to provide Americans evidence of Europe's commitment to peace, he thus proposed to Hughes that America encourage a fifty-year peace pledge by England, France, Italy, and Germany. Believing peace to be de-

---

[16]Houghton to Hughes, Oct. 23, 1922, *For. Rel. U.S., 1922,* II, 171–75.

[17]Hughes to Houghton, Aug. 23, 1922, Box 26, Hughes Papers. Similar praise is in Hughes to Houghton, Sept. 11, 1922, ibid., and William R. Castle to Houghton, July 13, 1922, William R. Castle Papers, Herbert Hoover Presidential Library, West Branch, Iowa.

[18]William Phillips to Houghton, Sept. 21, 1922, Box 26, Hughes Papers. See also Houghton's reports on "Reparations" (DF 462.00R29), the "Cuno Cabinet" (DF 862.002), and "German Political Affairs" (DF 862.00), RG 59, NA.

[19]Houghton to Hughes, Sept. 22, 1922, Box 4B, Hughes Papers.

pendent upon "the will of the peoples most concerned," he urged that the question be squarely put to them. Houghton, furthermore, saw governments, in the recent past, as unsuccessful in avoiding war; thus he proposed that America

say to the plain people of England and France and Italy and Germany, that if, first they will by a plebiscite, agree not to make war on one another for fifty years; if, second, they will make it part of their fundamental law that such a war cannot thereafter be declared except by their affirmative vote; and if, third, there shall be a substantial disarmament,—the American people, believing that peace, humanly speaking would then be assured, will remit and cancel the debt.[20]

No more ambitious or comprehensive peace plan was suggested in 1922. Houghton sought to involve the United States in responsibility for European peace and security through a proposal that would have touched off debate in every capital. Actually, Houghton's proposal to use debt cancellation as a club was a familiar one at the time. In exchange for partial cancellation or deferred interest payments, other Americans had suggested Allied reduction of reparations, balanced budgets, stabilized currencies, liberal trade policies, and disarmament.[21] If made public, therefore, some aspects of Houghton's proposal would have been appealing, especially to men like Senators La Follette and Borah and William Jennings Bryan. Chicago lawyer Salmon O. Levinson hoped at this time to use debt cancellation as an inducement for international acceptance of his scheme to outlaw war. Borah considered ways to obtain public support for using debts as a "bargaining tool" to achieve further disarmament and abolition of military aircraft.[22] But since the Houghton proposal also would have created formidable political debate and opposition in America, especially just before the 1922 fall elections, Hughes's decision on it certainly must have weighed heavily on his mind.

[20]Houghton to Hughes, Oct. 23, 1922, *For. Rel. U.S., 1922,* II, 173. Edward Joseph Berbusse, "Diplomatic Relations between the United States and Weimar Germany: 1919–1929," Diss. Georgetown 1951, p. 227, mentions the Houghton proposal only in a note. Merlo Pusey, *Charles Evans Hughes* (New York, 1951), II, 579–93, does not mention the Houghton proposal, nor does a recent study of President Harding (Andrew Sinclair, *The Available Man* [New York, 1965]). Dexter Perkins, "The Department of State and American Public Opinion," in Gordon A. Craig and Felix Gilbert, eds., *The Diplomats, 1919–1939* (Princeton, 1953), p. 305, notes Hughes's rejection of Houghton's proposal but does not relate this to the later Cuno offer.

[21]Melvyn Leffler, "The Origins of Republican War Debt Policy, 1921–1923: A Case Study in the Applicability of the Open Door Interpretation," *Journal of American History,* 59 (1972), 588. Cancellation was the school debate topic in the fall of 1922. See Julia E. Johnsen, comp., "Cancellation of the Allied Debt," *Reference Shelf,* 1, No. 1 (1922).

[22]Vinson, *Borah,* p. 70; Robert James Maddox, *William E. Borah and American Foreign Policy* (Baton Rouge, La., 1969), pp. 126–31.

By this time Congress had already retained control over war debts and "effectively tied the hands of the executive."[23] Like the earlier Wilson administration, President Harding at first showed no interest in requests for cancellation. Yet gradually the Republican administration came to see the European debt situation differently, if not more clearly. Commerce Secretary Herbert Hoover led the president, Secretary Hughes, and Treasury Secretary Andrew W. Mellon toward a more flexible position by which, if Congress approved, the Treasury Department would deal with debtor nations individually on matters of funding and repayment. The result of such proposed legislation, however, was passage of a restrictive debt funding bill, February 9, 1922, by which a Debt Funding Commission was created. As a product of its first efforts, Hoover, Mellon, and Hughes, all members of the Commission, realized by the fall of 1922 that restrictions in the legislation would have to be bypassed to conclude any debt agreements.[24]

This judgment, based on political realities as well as experience under the law, brought stronger behind-the-scenes efforts, especially by Hughes, during the rapid deterioration of Europe's finances. Pressures also increased at home and abroad for American action.[25] Yet while historians have recently recognized the interest indicated by some American proposals, none have noted the Houghton proposal of October 23, 1922, its rejection by Hughes, and the secretary's subsequent revival of the plan in December.[26]

The ambassador's memorandum did not reach the State Department until November 11. At the time several American diplomats were in Berlin during a Reparations Commission meeting. Thus, in addition to earlier counsels on European conditions, Hughes had the advice of Boyden and William R. Castle, Jr., chief of the Division of Western European Affairs, on the very proposal under consideration. After reading

[23]Leffler, "Origins of Republican War Debt Policy," p. 592.

[24]Robert K. Murray, *The Harding Era* (Minneapolis, 1969), pp. 361–63. On passage of debt legislation, see also Leffler, "Origins of Republican War Debt Policy," pp. 592–95; Benjamin D. Rhodes, "Reassesing 'Uncle Shylock': The United States and the French War Debt, 1917–1929," *Journal of American History,* 55 (1969), 791–92; and Harold G. Moulton and Leo Pasvolsky, *War Debts and World Prosperity* (New York, 1932), pp. 71–80.

[25]Leffler, "Origins of Republican War Debt Policy," p. 596; Joan Hoff Wilson, *American Business and Foreign Policy, 1920–1933* (Lexington, Ky., 1971), pp. 123–56.

[26]Melvyn Leffler discusses, for example, Hughes's efforts to create "an international committee of businessmen to determine Germany's capacity to pay reparations" but not his revival of the war referendum–security pact proposal of Houghton. See "Origins of Republican War Debt Policy," pp. 586, 596–98. See also Murray, *Harding Era,* pp. 360–65; and Carl P. Parrini, *Heir to Empire, United States Economic Diplomacy, 1916–1923* (Pittsburgh, 1969), pp. 256–57.

Houghton's letter to Hughes, Castle assured the secretary of state that the people of Europe would support the plan. He was especially certain that the Ambassador to England, George Harvey, would endorse Houghton's views. Castle's personal reaction was also favorable to the proposal. He believed that debt cancellation "with such provisos as Mr. Houghton has included" would be "the only way" of beating the Democrats to "a great moral issue," to which he thought the American people usually responded.

It would get wide publicity, Castle continued, and would begin the education of the people, which was necessary before any congressional action. Castle could not have appealed to Hughes any more effectively. The diplomat suggested that the ideal method of proclaiming America's intention would be through a Washington economic conference, preceded, as in the case of the previous disarmament conference there, by a public opinion prepared to support the administration. Castle's most important advice, especially in determining the apparent actual origin of the later Cuno proposal, ended his dispatch: "it seems to me preliminary education is so necessary, and . . . *The first move might usefully be made here.*"[27]

The origin of Houghton's proposal remains a question. Yet there may be a clue in the association in 1922 between the ambassador and Oswald Garrison Villard, editor of the *Nation*. After a visit to Germany in the spring and summer, Villard wrote a series on conditions there, describing the country much like Houghton's own descriptions in dispatches to Secretary Hughes.[28] Houghton read the articles and then responded: "I have had in mind the last dozen years that you were somewhat of an extremist. But I want to say that your statements regarding Germany are not only scrupulously fair, but are even understated in fact, and that your presentation is so restrained and so without emotion that I wonder at it."[29] Earlier Villard had expressed alarm concerning what he regarded as uncurbed French militarism, suggesting that war debts should be "used as a lever" to force concessions. In the previous year he had urged the same cancellation plan to force a just peace settlement.[30] Lacking more direct evidence to the contrary, it is conceivable that Houghton's

[27]Castle to Hughes, Oct. 24, 1922, *For. Rel. U.S., 1922,* II, 176–77 (my emphasis). Castle, who regarded Houghton at the "very top" among his "good friends," carried on an extensive correspondence with the American minister to Berlin (Castle to Houghton, Dec. 2, 1922, Castle Papers).

[28]*Nation,* 115 (1922), 61–64, 87–88, 116–18, 144–45.

[29]Houghton to Villard, Aug. 11, Dec. 22, 1922, and Villard to Houghton, Dec. 12, 1922, Oswald Garrison Villard Papers, Harvard University Library, Cambridge, Mass. See also Wreszin, *Villard,* p. 158.

[30]*Nation,* 114 (1922), 181 and 112 (1921), 282.

knowledge of this and other suggestions about debt cancellation, in addition to his greater respect for Villard resulting from the 1922 articles on Germany, produced the plan which he presented to Secretary Hughes.

It is certain that Houghton presented a proposal similar to the one in his October 23 memorandum at a meeting of America's Central European diplomats in Berlin October 19. In the first session he read a letter to the State Department in which, after describing Germany's political and economic situation, he set forth the possibility of European plebiscites in exchange for American cancellation of debts. The peoples of Europe would be asked to disarm and promise fifty years of peace to obtain debt relief. Houghton, according to Major-General Henry T. Allen, commander of American forces in Germany, "did not ask that this be approved, but merely that all present give it careful consideration."[31] Those present included Castle and American ministers Hugh Gibson (Poland), Albert Washburn (Austria), Joseph Grew (Switzerland), and Theodore Bretano (Hungary).[32]

When the Houghton and Castle recommendations reached Hughes November 11, he had already received Boyden's comments on the debt cancellation and war referendum proposal. Boyden reported discussing it "many times" and confirmed, once more, the ambassador's diagnosis of Germany's despondency and suffering. He foresaw a serious "social disturbance" and cautioned against inaction toward solution of Germany's problems. Boyden, however, did not support Houghton's proposed use of debt cancellation to bring peace to Europe. Aware of Hughes's previous opposition to associating the debts with reparations, Boyden advocated continued concentration on the reparations problem and advised the administration, "either itself or through Houghton," against putting out even informally the total suggestion that he proposed.[33]

The congressional elections of 1922 in the United States were just over when Hughes reached his decision regarding the Houghton proposal. After talking with President Harding, he refused Houghton's request to make the proposal public in a Thanksgiving Day address. Harding au-

[31] Henry T. Allen, *My Rhineland Journal* (Boston, 1923), p. 452.

[32] Ibid., p. 450. See also Joseph C. Grew, *Turbulent Era: A Diplomatic Record of Forty Years, 1904–1945,* ed. Walter Johnson (Boston, 1952), I, 471–74, entry dated Oct. 20. Grew records primarily his report to the conference on Switzerland's role in the economic problems facing Central Europe. Waldo H. Heinrichs, Jr., does not mention this meeting in his study of Grew, who was then more concerned with the Lausanne Conference on Near Eastern Affairs (*American Ambassador: Joseph C. Grew and the Development of the United States Diplomatic Tradition* [Boston, 1966]).

[33] Boyden to Hughes, Nov. 9, 1922, *For. Rel. U.S., 1922,* II, 180.

thorized only a general statement that the American government wished "to be helpful" should European nations curtail armaments and try "to transform the present conditions of enmity and chaos into those of peace and order." Hughes carefully repeated his oft-cited argument that only Congress could remit debts but, significantly, recorded no opinion on the proposed referendum–security pact.[34] Hughes, like Borah in this respect, liked to study an idea carefully and prepare for its reception; thus he filed these features of Houghton's proposal away for future reference.

Hughes still believed that the reparations question and the French attitude were the keys to settlement in Europe. In this respect Ambassador Herrick in Paris and Hughes in Washington continued to work quietly for the advisory financial conference, although there were fewer dispatches on this subject in November. Late in the month there was talk that French patience had ended and that Poincaré was considering seizure of certain German assets in the Ruhr district should the Brussels Conference fail.[35] In view of the imminent crisis and approaching conference, therefore, Hughes was prompted to revive the Houghton proposal.

The outline of events from this time until Hughes's generous offer, December 15, to assist in the Cuno proposal as intermediary between Germany and France can only be suggested. Hughes rejected, of course, any further open participation in the matter by Ambassador Houghton; he might cloud negotiations with his fear of Bolshevism. Furthermore, Houghton's involvement might lead to publicity and controversy in America over his insistence on debt cancellation as a club to assure European adoption of the referendum–security pact. But, more important, and in typical Hughes fashion, he did not want it to appear to be an American peace plan. This would offend France, who continued to smart over differences with the United States at Hughes's Washington Disarmament Conference. Likewise, Poincaré at the time was still quite cool to Hughes's projected international conference of financial advisors as the proper settlement on reparations.

To avoid controversy at home and troubles with France, therefore, any referendum-security offer during Allied discussions on reparations would necessarily have to come from Germany. By early December, when French impatience was more noticeable, Hughes especially believed that Germany needed to offer France some assurance of peace. Why not have Germany use the substance of Houghton's proposal in hopes of placating France long enough to gain acceptance of the plan of an economic

---

[34]Hughes to Houghton, Nov. 14, 1922, ibid., pp. 181–82.
[35]Correspondence between Hughes and Herrick, Nov. 17, 29, 1922, ibid., 182–85.

conference? Had not Castle suggested a preliminary educational effort in Germany? And Boyden, like Hughes himself, had not criticized the referendum idea. Finally, Hughes also had previously injected his own economic conference proposal with a shot of "popular control."

The official American view—that inter-Allied debts could not be considered in reparations discussions—made inapplicable only part of the Houghton proposal. But Hughes saw no reason to scrap the war referendum–security pact section. Since his thinking in this matter escaped the contemporary record, as well as historical accounts since then, the exact date of his decision to revive Houghton's suggestion can only be surmised. Two events are important in concluding that the decision probably came before December 8 or immediately after December 11, 1922. On the first date President Harding predicted an impending peace move during his annual address to Congress. He suggested that it might take the form of the Washington Conference Four Power Treaty, attempting to abolish the possibility of war for Atlantic powers as the previous pact did for Pacific nations.[36] Could this have been the culmination of Hughes's plans for an economic conference on reparations? After adequate diplomatic feelers, could such a conference also consider matters of security and peace?

The day following Harding's speech Allied premiers met in London for the conference on reparations originally planned for Brussels. Amid rumors that Dr. Cuno would ask for a third moratorium and that Poincaré had decided on occupation of the Ruhr, the future of the Entente was indeed doubtful. The unexplained presence of Ambassador Houghton in London heightened speculation; few believed him when reportedly he told the press he had come "to get pants."[37]

Since America was not officially represented, however, news of Harding's address did not apparently offer much hope. The conference ended in a deadlock after two days of discussions that generally only confirmed earlier rumors. The premiers agreed to meet January 2 in Paris after hearing Cuno's request for *pourpalers* on the basis of a continued moratorium and two international loans. Poincaré, as expected, said Germany could be motivated to pay only by fear of Allied seizures in the Ruhr.[38]

If Hughes's decision on revival and revision of Houghton's plan had not been made before Harding's address to Congress, it was made soon after

[36]*New York Times,* Dec. 9, 1922.

[37]Ibid., Dec. 5, 8, 9, 10, 1922; Horace Green, "An Unloquacious Ambassador," *New York Times Magazine,* Nov. 4, 1923, p. 10.

[38]*Times* (London), Dec. 8, 9, 11, 12, 1922. See Germany's official report of France's alleged intention to occupy the Ruhr in Hughes's Memorandum, Dec. 12, 1922, *For. Rel. U.S., 1922,* II, 186–87.

the Allies' London deadlock. Time for compromise was running out as Hughes continued quiet negotiations with France concerning his economic conference plan. In separate and equally quiet negotiations he also prepared to receive the Cuno referendum–security pledge proposal based on Houghton's earlier plan. But he could no longer prevent some speculation as to America's activity.

On December 14 Washington was reported far from inactive in the reparations crisis and was hopeful of a concrete American proposal by the January 2 Paris conference. Harding's address to Congress was hailed, also, as a "sincere gesture" in that direction.[39] The press probably was not aware how close to the truth it had come. On December 12 the cabinet devoted its session to the reparations crisis. Hughes met with French Ambassador Jusserand December 14 to present again his plan for an international bankers conference and to protest any contemplated French occupation of the Ruhr as a threat to the "*future peace of the world.*" He concluded his lengthy conference by proposing that *France take the initiative* in offering a settlement based on his plan of an economic conference. The great prestige of Premier Poincaré would change world opinion in France's favor, he thought. Besides, there was no "pot of gold" for the French in the Ruhr.[40]

Four days passed before French Ambassador Jusserand and Secretary Hughes met again. By then they talked about Poincaré's continued rejection of the secretary's plan of an economic conference. But at this interview Germany's offer of a security pact based on the war referendum plan was also made to France for the first time. Secretary Hughes was desperate over the situation; since December 1 he had almost completely directed efforts for the first proposal through contacts in Washington. But the real sign of his concern over the mounting European crisis was his revival of the Houghton proposal and then the manner in which he directed Cuno's subsequent offer of December 15.

Hughes worked to get the French to propose an advisory economic conference and, at the same time, presented the Cuno proposal to the French as entirely a German idea. In both cases he typically sought to prepare quietly and in advance before making any formal offer or commitment by the United States. One American proposal he made appear to be French in origin; and the other, Houghton's idea, he succeeded in presenting as German. In such a way he could avoid any European or

[39]*Times* (London), Dec. 14, 1922.
[40]Hughes's Memorandum, Dec. 14, 1922, *For. Rel. U.S., 1922*, II, 187–92 (my emphasis). See also Hughes, "Dawes Plan," pp. 3–6, Hughes Papers.

congressional charge of American diplomatic meddling or any criticism for State Department encroachment on congressional prerogatives such as the debt question. In this episode, the secretary of state was, as usual, on top of the situation.

As presented on December 15 by Ambassador Wiedfeldt to Secretary Hughes, Germany was prepared to join the other three powers interested in the Rhine and involved in the reparations problem in a thirty-year peace pledge based on the war referendum idea. France, Great Britain, Italy, and Germany would "solemnly agree among themselves and promise the Government of the United States, that they will not resort to war against each other for a period of one generation without being authorized to do so by a plebiscite of their own people."[41] The United States would only serve as a "trustee" to see that the arrangement was carried out.

Secretary Hughes's satisfaction with the plan was so obvious as to indicate it was a revival of Houghton's October proposal. Besides, *Hughes asked Wiedfeldt* if Germany desired him to ascertain informally whether such a proposal would be acceptable to the other powers. In view of the crisis and Hughes's normal way of operating, it was not surprising that the Cuno proposal quickly was incorporated into the secretary's own plan for an economic conference and became part of an effort to mediate the German-French crisis. It had all the elements of a personal attempt at compromise. Hughes did not use diplomats in Europe in this matter, choosing rather to work in Washington without publicity and as intermediary between the German and French ambassadors. *His* memorandums are the only sources which recorded this effort until a news leak late in December. No wonder he said after the December 15 interview with Wiedfeldt: "It was gratifying to note the desire of the German Government to remove the apprehension of war."[42]

Just after the Hughes-Wiedfeldt interview, speculation mounted in London over an imminent "change in American policy toward Europe." But the "change" did not turn on that undisclosed meeting. Following earlier reports of Washington's far from inactive attitude toward the European reparations problem, London now reported that Ambassador Harvey had been summoned to Washington, that there was interest in a greater American initiative within Harding's cabinet, and that Pierpont

[41]Hughes's Memorandum, Dec. 15, 1922, and German Embassy to Department of State, Dec. 21, 1922, *For. Rel. U.S., 1922,* II, 203–5.

[42]Hughes's Memorandum, Dec. 18, 1922, ibid., p. 204. Hughes did not work through Harvey in negotiating with the British for the Washington Conference.

Morgan had met with Harding and Hughes. The supposed "change," sources predicted, would take the form of new loans to Germany or an "Atlantic Pact" such as Harding had mentioned in his address to Congress.[43]

As usual, there was some truth in the reports. Ambassadors Harvey and Houghton still conferred in London, the latter having been away from his Berlin post since before the London conference. Harvey, the State Department announced, was coming to the United States on his own request. Secretary Hughes, to be sure, was more active than was known to the public. Indeed, Morgan had met with him on December 15 and probably knew of Hughes's talk that day with the German ambassador. Morgan continued to support the plan of an economic conference, although his denial of plans for new loans to Germany relieved speculation along that line. In the end London assured the world that the United States position of isolation toward Europe would not change.[44] The validity of the report, of course, depended on what was meant by "isolation."

There continued to be no speculation, however, over Hughes's quiet diplomacy in behalf of the German security pact. Knowing of France's great apprehensions toward Germany, Hughes transmitted the proposal, in the name of Ambassador Wiedfeldt, December 18, to French Ambassador Jusserand. This was the earliest French notice of what were now Hughes's twin proposals to stabilize conditions in Europe—a security pact based on the war referendum idea and his own economic conference plan. Jusserand's first reaction to the new proposal was not favorable, but he agreed to convey the "German offer" to Poincaré. Hughes still was noncommittal as to how active America's role as peace guarantor would be but pointed out to the French diplomat that the war referendum–peace pledge "would encourage the people in the maintenance of peace and the desire for peace."[45] On the surface, all that was needed for further discussions, apparently, was French interest in the measure.

Hughes must have been satisfied in his role as intermediary. The same day he conferred with the English ambassador and heard insistent pleas for American mediation, desired by Prime Minister Bonar Law. The British and American governments agreed that direct, independent action of France in the Ruhr must be prevented. The prime minister even suggested that an American representative be present at the January 2 Paris conference. Hughes, nevertheless, chose not to inform the ambassador of

[43]*Times* (London), Dec. 16, 1922.
[44]Ibid., Dec. 18, 19, 1922; *New York Times,* Dec. 18, 1922; J. P. Morgan to Hughes, Dec. 22, 1922, *For. Rel. U.S., 1922,* II, 196–97.
[45]Hughes's Memorandum, Dec. 18, 1922, *For. Rel. U.S., 1922,* II, 204–5.

either the economic conference plan or the security pact offered informally to France. Characteristically, he insisted on quiet diplomacy,
avoiding any commitment by America until groundwork assured prior
agreement and success. While he did not desire "to make any public
statement" on the Ruhr matter, he felt it "very important" that
American views be presented not in "London or Berlin or anywhere else
but at Washington."[46]

As must have been expected by seasoned diplomats, Jusserand
reported to Secretary Hughes, December 21, 1922, that Poincaré had rejected both the economic conference plan and the latest offer as well.
Poincaré, who never seemed favorable to it in the first place, still wanted
to put off talks on the former plan until after the January 2 Paris
conference. As for the security pact and war referendum offer, Poincaré
said it would necessitate a difficult, if not impossible, effort to amend the
French Constitution. Besides, he did not believe the Germans could be relied upon. If a war policy was in their plans, they could get the people to so
vote.[47] Poincaré certainly must have believed it would also work that way
for France. However, he refused the security pact, for fear that France's
freedom of action in the Ruhr would be checked in the immediate future.
How could he agree even to consider such a pact and continue a threatening attitude toward the Ruhr in hopes of forcing Germany's hand on
reparations?

Poincaré's rejection of the Cuno offer further hinged on America's
undefined role in the matter. When Jusserand asked whether the United
States would guarantee the proposed treaty, Hughes admitted that
American participation as guarantor could not then be relied upon. Yet
he continued to stress, at least before the ambassador, that the
agreement "not to engage in war without their people endorsing such action . . . would be an important step toward the maintenance of peace."
Jusserand agreed to confer further with Poincaré but stressed that
France would be more likely to amend its Constitution in order to incorporate the war referendum idea if the United States could be relied upon
more substantially in the matter. Hughes answered only that America
would be "entitled to complain if the promise were broken." America's
inclusion in the offer, he said, was only to give the proposed pact "added
solemnity and weight."[48]

To have promised more would have probably revealed Hughes's hand;
it suited his purposes best for the peace pact always to appear to have

[46]Ibid., pp. 192–95.
[47]Hughes's Memorandum, Dec. 21, 1922, ibid., pp. 195–96, 206.
[48]Ibid., pp. 206–7.

originated in Germany. After all, was it not offered to relieve French apprehensions and to demonstrate Germany's peaceful intentions during a continued moratorium? Secretary Hughes thus encouraged French acceptance of the new offer and, at the same time, withheld any definite American commitment. Ironically, however, America's noncommittal attitude may have allowed Poincaré to shift responsibility for French rejection of it upon the United States.

Faced with French rejection and increasing American public demands "that the United States ought to do something" to prevent France's anticipated drastic action, Hughes nevertheless continued to work for both a conference inquiry by economic experts and the war referendum–security pact.[49] He met with Ambassador Wiedfeldt on December 22 but did not report Poincaré's initial rejection of the peace pact. They conferred again on the United States relationship in the offer, the secretary of state making it clear, once more, that it would be improbable for America "to assume any responsibility in the matter."[50] He still hoped for French recognition of Germany's pacific intentions, through the security pact offer, and saw no need of a firm American commitment to its principles or of American military force to guarantee the pact. Hughes sought at the time only a limited objective—postponement of the Ruhr crisis. But his hopes were soon destroyed.

On December 26 Jusserand reported for a second time that Poincaré had rejected the two plans. Actually Hughes already had begun to feel that his plan for an economic conference to recommend a settlement of the reparations problems should be made public. Time for compromise solutions was running out, the January Paris conference was approaching, and, besides, there had been a news leak. Correspondents had long tried to anticipate America's role and even confronted the State Department on December 19 with rumored plans to mediate in the reparations crisis. A spokesman replied only that the question in that form was "too broad." But London sources in Washington reported the next day that America had encouraged French acceptance of an inquiry of experts, including Americans.[51]

The apparent American news leak was augmented soon by information from Paris concerning the suggested peace pact. During the Hughes-Jusserand interview on December 26, the secretary of state attributed this second news leak to the French Foreign Office. That morning he had

[49]Hughes, "Dawes Plan," p. 6, Hughes Papers.

[50]Hughes's Memorandum, Dec. 22, 1922, *For. Rel. U.S., 1922,* II, 208.

[51]Hughes's Memorandum, Dec. 26, 1922, ibid., pp. 197–98, 208–9; Hughes, "Dawes Plan," p. 7, Hughes Papers; *Times* (London), Dec. 20, 21, 1922.

denied to ,the press any knowledge of a "proposal of the American Government for a four-power treaty" in which Great Britain, Germany, France, and Italy would guarantee the boundaries of Germany for thirty years. As he later told Jusserand, however, Hughes believed that reference to "the American proposal," Poincaré's rejection, and the thirty-year feature definitely indicated a leak.[52]

Hughes's quiet diplomacy now was forced into failure. The news leak on his economic conference idea and another consideration prompted his decision, December 27, to make public, as soon as possible, part of his recent negotiations. On December 26 the Reparations Commission declared Germany in default in timber payments. This heightened the inevitable crisis, which Hughes felt would come at the January 2 Paris conference.[53] Indeed, the peace pact news leak came at a critical time for Hughes and compromise.

Likewise, the man who inspired the peace pact felt matters had reached a critical state at about the time of the news leak. Ambassador Houghton, in Berlin, wrote Oswald Garrison Villard December 27 concerning the need of stability in Germany. He thought that the Cuno government was doing well, but Houghton still feared that Germany would turn to Russia in the event of economic collapse. He repeated privately to Villard his October fears transmitted to Secretary Hughes. Germany, he thought, was the "dam which holds back Bolshevism." If the United States did not do its part, he felt the Red menace would likely sweep to the shores of the Atlantic.[54] Understandably, Hughes could not have allowed Houghton a public role in the Cuno matter.

In view of the news leaks, his belief that crisis was inevitable, and French intransigence, Hughes now felt that the peace offer also should now be made public, although he would not do so without permission of both France and Germany. He assured the German ambassador on December 28 that the leak was not from Washington, for only President Harding, ambassador to France Myron T. Herrick, Undersecretary William Phillips, and William R. Castle, Jr., chief of the Western Eu-

---

[52]Hughes's Memorandum, Dec. 26, 1922, *For. Rel. U.S., 1922,* II, 208–9; *New York Times,* Dec. 27, 1922.

[53]Herrick to Hughes, Dec. 26, 1922, *For. Rel. U.S., 1922,* II, 198–99; Hughes, "Dawes Plan," p. 7, Hughes Papers; *Times* (London), Dec. 27, 1922.

[54]Houghton to Villard, Dec. 27, 1922, Villard Papers. Earlier the ambassador accepted the blame for Hughes's official coolness toward his peace plan but suggested to Castle that the administration support the plan without taking responsibility. "What you need is not a positive statement of belief, but a statement of inquiry, asking if America would act in a certain way if Europe acted in a certain way,—in other words, merely putting the question, not answering it" (Houghton to Castle, Dec. 2, 1922, Castle Papers).

ropean Division, knew of it. Having twice requested Jusserand to press the offer upon Poincaré, Hughes reported to Wiedfeldt, for the first time, the adverse French response.[55] It was regrettable that the Germans already had learned through the news leak of French rejection.

No longer concerned about offending France, Hughes's efforts for a conference of economic experts now came into the open. In an address before the American Historical Association in New Haven, December 29, he presented publicly for the first time his concern over Europe's impending crisis. He concentrated in this address on his plan for an advisory conference of financial experts. But he remained silent as to his unsuccessful efforts to win French acceptance of the plan.[56]

Hughes now only hoped that public knowledge of what he had believed to be a workable preventive for the crisis might yet create a public opinion favorable to settlement at the Paris conference. Chancellor Cuno, in a Hamburg speech December 31, announced adverse French response to the nonwar pact in a similar attempt to influence public opinion after the news leak. Never did he reveal the true origins of Germany's adoption of the plan, and at the time Cuno did not even divulge America's role in the recent negotiations with France. This led to early speculation that the "neutral power" involved had been either Holland or Switzerland.[57] Such was the qualified success of Hughes's private negotiations.

As the Allied Ministers Conference on Reparations opened in Paris, therefore, Secretary Hughes's two possible alternatives to French occupation of the Ruhr had been revealed. A Paris story on the eve of the conference confirmed that the intermediary in the Cuno matter had been Hughes. This was also officially announced in both Paris and Washington, January 2, but the secretary of state refused comment on either Germany's sincerity or certain statements by Poincaré.

The European press reported quite accurately that French rejection had turned on several facts. First, as a League member, France already had given notice of its own pacific intent. Furthermore, Poincaré believed

[55]Hughes's Memorandum, Dec. 28, 1922, *For. Rel. U.S., 1922,* II, 209–10. For Houghton's critical reaction to Poincaré's rejection of the peace plan, see Houghton to Castle, Jan. 17 and Mar. 12, 1923, Castle Papers.

[56]Acting Secretary of State to Herrick, *For. Rel. U.S., 1922,* II, 199–202; Hughes, "Dawes Plan," pp. 7–10, Hughes Papers. Frank H. Simonds, *American Foreign Policy in the Post-War Years* (Baltimore, 1935), pp. 45–52, and Murray, *Harding Era,* p. 365, are typical of treatment of Hughes's involvement in the Ruhr crisis entirely in terms of the New Haven speech and its significance in the later Dawes Plan, each implying that Hughes had done nothing to forestall the crisis. Adler, *Isolationist Impulse,* p. 144, refers to this speech as an example of Hughes's "open and frank diplomacy," but overlooks his quiet, private efforts before the news leak.

[57]*New York Times,* Jan. 1, 1923.

the referendum plan impracticable and dangerous; it would only enable Germany to mobilize its veterans for war more quickly and effectively, he thought. Now with its decision to invade the Ruhr almost certain, France simply regarded the security pact offer as an example of German "trick diplomacy" or what Poincaré saw as a political maneuver.[58]

What appeared on the face of it to be a German proposal suddenly assumed international attention. Hughes's efforts to placate Poincaré had failed. The secretary's hope that France would readily accept one or another of two suggested ways to avoid independent and direct action against Germany, and against most world opinion, simply was not fulfilled. Indeed, it was not realistic. How could France accept two alternatives that sought postponement of action when the immediate use of force conformed, in the eyes of Poincaré, to French interests, traditions, and even rights under the treaty? Likewise, Hughes's leadership in offering as alternatives both the economic conference and war referendum–security pact conformed to American interests and traditions. Each alternative sought to avoid American commitment and to prevent or postpone the use of force in diplomacy. That was just the reason France could not accept either one at the time, and, as such, marked one of a long series of disagreements on the basic issue of security, which was to frustrate Franco-American diplomacy for some time.

The efforts of Secretary Hughes in this instance failed, but not before he personally endorsed the war referendum idea contained in the proposed security pact and presented this typically American approach to peace to five major world powers. An editorial in the *New York Times*, in a caustic attack on the idea, compared Chancellor Cuno with Bryan, La Follette, and other "American happy thought improvisers of everlasting peace." Although the editors regarded the German offer awkwardly made and thought it an ostentatious bid for praise by a former enemy, they nevertheless chastised the French for refusing at least to test Germany's sincerity by further discussions.[59] Little did the editors realize how directly Secretary of State Hughes had been behind the matter!

In another independent effort at compromise, Cuno, like Secretary Hughes, quietly tried to revive the idea of a security pact on the eve of the Paris meeting. Unknown to Washington or the press, Cuno stressed Germany's sincerity in private talks with England's Ambassador Edgar D'Abernon. Cuno confirmed again Germany's willingness to adopt the

---

[58]Ibid., Jan. 2, 3, 1923; *Times* (London), Jan. 2, 1923; Hughes to Herrick, Jan. 2, 1923, *For. Rel. U.S., 1922*, II, 211; and John W. Wheeler-Bennett and Frederic E. Langermann, *Information on the Problem of Security (1917–1926)* (London, 1927), pp. 56–57. The last source is another which does not relate the Cuno offer to Houghton's earlier proposal.

[59]*New York Times*, Jan. 3, 1923.

referendum plan, which, he said, was inserted "to strengthen the security of peace." Since governments and parliaments were transitory, he believed that peoples should be made guarantors of the proposed treaty. Cuno also defended his elastic time period—a "generation"—as only a suggested effective period for the proposed agreement. He was willing to consider either a longer or shorter period. Finally, he even offered to delete the war referendum plan if the interested powers saw it as a weak feature.[60] This was about the time when Cuno also made the German offer public in a Hamburg speech, cited above. According to Ambassador Houghton, this speech evoked general approval of the plan by the German people, but it was regarded by diplomats as merely a "naive" effort of businessmen "to interfere in statecraft." Houghton, in the same report to the secretary, noted that Foreign Minister Rosenberg had told him about Germany's willingness to let *France* set the time limit for the security pact.[61]

Whether concessions were offered quietly through diplomatic channels or publicly, however, compromise was no longer possible. The French remained firm, the Allied premiers failed to agree at Paris, and finally French and Belgian troops invaded the Ruhr on January 11.[62] England's Prime Minister Bonar Law did not, of course, approve of the Ruhr occupation, but he also thought nothing could have been gained by discussion of the "German proposals" after Poincaré's flat disapproval. Ambassador D'Abernon agreed with other observers that Poincaré's rejection hinged on objection to the thirty-year time limit, the referendum feature, and, finally, the lack of guarantees by both Great Britain and the United States. This lack, in view of Cuno's late offers to negotiate, was obviously the most important. The English diplomat believed that Poincaré wanted assurances that, in the event of war, France would receive "support of the American and British military, naval, and aerial forces."[63] Certainly no such guarantee would have been forthcoming from the United States.

Even after the Ruhr occupation, Cuno's proposal was endorsed by D'Abernon, although he feared that the qualified condition in the form of a referendum on war may have been a mistake at the time. He hastened to add, however, that Cuno's proposal was endorsed as a "Peace Pact" by all German parties and thus represented, he thought, a united Germany. "The question is whether the child brought into the world by Hughes, and

[60]Viscount Edgar V. D'Abernon, *The Diary of an Ambassador* (Garden City, N.Y., 1929–30), II, 165–66; *New York Times*, Jan. 8, 1923.

[61]Houghton to Hughes, Jan. 3, 1923, Box 4B, Hughes Papers.

[62]*New York Times*, Jan. 11, 1923.

[63]D'Abernon, *Diary*, II, 164, 166.

smothered by Poincaré," D'Abernon continued, "can be brought to life again; possibly some prophet Elisha may be found."[64]

Little did the English ambassador realize how accurate were both his reporting and prediction. Many Elishas would appear on behalf of the war referendum plan, nearly all of them in the United States. Yet even Gustav Stresemann, who followed Chancellor Cuno after the failure of Cuno's disastrous passive resistance policy during the Ruhr occupation, revived the Cuno proposal in 1923 and 1925. Calling it an effort to establish "God's peace on the Rhine," he often cited it as his model for the Locarno Treaties.[65] Although France had rejected the idea in 1922–23 and the war referendum plan was dropped from the 1925 security treaties, the Houghton-Hughes-Cuno proposal was a high-water mark for the war referendum movement in the twenties. At no other time in its history did the proposal have the official sanction of the executive branch and figure in its actual plans for policymaking. Finally, more international attention was given the war referendum plan at this time than before or since.

[64]Ibid., pp. 167, 168; see especially his entry for Jan. 18, 1923.

[65]Ambassador Houghton reports on his and British Ambassador D'Abernon's roles in revival of the Cuno proposal, without the war referendum feature, in Houghton to Hughes, Jan. 12, 1925, Box 75, Hughes Papers. Further comment on Houghton's role is in C. A. Macartney et al., *Survey of International Affairs: 1925* (London, 1927–28), II, 17–20, 62. See also Hans Wehberg, *The Outlawry of War* (Washington, D.C., 1931), p. 33; *Gustav Stresemann: His Diaries, Letters, and Papers,* ed. Eric Sutton (London, 1935–40), I, 29, II, 59, 64, 74; Henry L. Bretton, *Stresemann and the Revision of Versailles* (Stanford, Calif., 1953), pp. 57, 88–89. Studies which briefly note the Cuno proposal in connection with Locarno include Royal J. Schmidt, *Versailles and the Ruhr: Seedbed of World War II* (The Hague, 1968), p. 174; Edward Hallett Carr, *International Relations between the Two World Wars* (London, 1947), p. 93; John R. P. McKenzie, *Weimar Germany, 1918–1933* (London, 1971), p. 175; and Jon Jacobson, *Locarno Diplomacy: Germany and the West, 1925–1929* (Princeton, 1972), p. 12.

CHAPTER VII

Peace, Politicians, and the Referendum

THE AMERICAN PEOPLE and Congress, as well as most Europeans, shared in the 1920s and 1930s one general aim: peace.[1] There was more talking and planning for peace than ever before, and a mere listing of American and European peace groups would be exhausting. Yet, and typically so, the American people and their representatives in Congress never could agree on any one peace plan. There was enough agreement officially to achieve limited naval disarmament in 1922 and adopt the Kellogg-Briand Pact in 1928, in which the major nations of the world renounced the use of war to settle international problems. The United States, on the other hand, remained out of the League of Nations and the World Court.

In America the most persistent peace proposal was the war referendum, given support sporadically by private individuals and limited interest by peace groups. Additionally, from 1925 to 1935 seventeen resolutions for a war referendum amendment to the Constitution appeared in Congress. As never before, in this and other ways, this reform entered upon better times in the early 1930s, when it became associated with anti–war-profits sentiment, finding eventually a genuine friend in Senator Gerald P. Nye; the twin prescription of a war referendum and anti–war-profits legislation became even more popular as revisionist historians turned war guilt from the Central Powers to the Allies. Private friends of the plan, including Ambassador Houghton, made interesting changes in its details and mechanics. As always, it meant many things to different people; yet it remained for most of them a peace plan incorporating increased popular control and less reliance on force in diplomacy.

William E. Borah, for example, still saw the appeal of a referendum on war in his attempts to guarantee greater influence for the Senate and public opinion in foreign affairs. As noted, this was a major goal in the

[1]On the background of the peace movement in the 1920s and 1930s, see Robert H. Ferrell, *Peace in Their Time: The Origins of the Kellogg-Briand Pact* (New Haven, 1952), especially the chapters "The Search for Peace: The Advocates," pp. 13–30, and "The Search for Peace: The Diplomats," pp. 39–51. Ferrell's "The Peace Movement," in DeConde, ed., *Isolation and Security,* pp. 82–106, is an excellent general essay, and Adler, *Isolationist Impulse,* pp. 115–28, is also helpful. Most valuable is Chatfield's *For Peace and Justice,* pp. 91–344. Less helpful for this period are Curti, *Peace or War,* pp. 262–300, and Arthur Beales, *The History of Peace* (New York, 1931). Devere Allen, *The Fight for Peace* (New York, 1930), is full of information but is unorganized.

1920s and especially in the 1930s. Public disillusionment with diplomats and a subsequent drive to "establish popular control of foreign policy," or "socialized diplomacy," was an important characteristic of the period.[2]

Senator Borah had failed to introduce a war referendum resolution when requested to do so in 1921. In 1923, as he became more directly interested in the plan to outlaw war, he continued to state that the people should control questions of war or peace. Borah believed that fewer than a score of men brought on World War I and frequently cited former President Wilson on the theme that no nation or peoples were responsible for the war.[3]

By 1925, when Borah's interests also included opposition to American participation in the League-sponsored World Court, the Idaho senator, now chairman of the Senate Foreign Relations Committee, clearly stated the basic appeal of the war referendum idea. "The mainstay of society," he said, "is public opinion, the organized moral forces and the intelligence of the people." As evidence of his rejection of force, he offered the war referendum to University of Michigan students. He stated that ten men in the League had power to declare war for the world. In opposing the League and World Court, therefore, Borah proposed positive alternatives in the outlawry of war, recognition of Russia, and a constitutional amendment to provide "that no war should be declared save on the vote of the people." Again in 1927 Senator Borah talked about guaranteeing open, or popular, diplomacy in these terms. "No war should be begun," he stated, "except in absolute defense, until the question has been submitted to those who are to do the fighting."[4] Had the senator not been preoccupied with the movement to outlaw war and other peace plans during the 1920s, certainly he would have introduced such a constitutional amendment. His interest in it continued even into the 1930s.

[2]John Chalmers Vinson, "Charles Evans Hughes," in Norman A. Graebner, ed., *An Uncertain Tradition: American Secretaries of State in the Twentieth Century* (New York, 1961), 128–29, and certain other of his works previously cited; Ferrell, *Peace in Their Time,* p. 14; and Adler, *Isolationist Impulse,* p. 114. As Professor Vinson has suggested, this theme may have reflected more than popular disillusionment over the war or a revolt against executive prerogatives. Since the theme was so strong in the new role of the Senate in foreign affairs, the fact that this body was now popularly elected may have been involved. See also Gabriel A. Almond, *The American People and Foreign Policy* (New York, 1950), and Dexter Perkins, "The Department of State and American Public Opinion," in Craig and Gilbert, *Diplomats: 1919–1939.*

[3]Borah, "Outlawry of War," *New York Times,* Apr. 1, 1923; typescript, press release of a Saint Louis speech, May 18, 1923, Borah Papers.

[4]Boston *Post,* May 12, 1925, *New York Times,* May 19, 1925, Washington *Herald,* May 23, 1925, all in Borah Papers. The University of Michigan address was entitled "Peace and the Peace Problem." His 1927 support is taken from Vinson, *Borah,* p. 120. Maddox, *Borah,* does not point out any of his sporadic interest in the war referendum plan during the 1920s.

Additional individual support came within the peace movement with endorsement of the war referendum plan during the Bok Peace Contest. This attempt to influence foreign policy through public opinion, as previously noted, came independent of, but coincident to, efforts for the war referendum plan by such men as Senator La Follette, Secretary of State Charles Evans Hughes and endorsement by Democrats and Progressives in 1924. Publisher Edward W. Bok sought to popularize peace by the offer of $100,000 to the person who proposed the best workable peace plan. He established the American Foundation to administer the contest, which by 1925 had encouraged submission of 22,165 plans. Among these were several serious proposals for the war referendum.

Of the total number submitted, only some eight thousand were deemed "ordered and orderly plans"; the remainder were "ineligible," not because they exceeded the 5,000-word limit but because they had "undeveloped phrases" or showed lack of thought or impracticability. The last class included, according to the Policy Committee in charge, prescriptions for peace on the basis of the Golden Rule. Other ineligible plans proposed "community peace sings," a committee of one thousand in every nation to "think peace," an international "league of hypnotists" to drive war from the thinking of rulers, and the plan of a popular referendum on war in which those voting yes would go to the front lines. In the more serious plans, men advocated removal of war profits and determination, in some way, of legal responsibility for war. Most of the plans wanted to outlaw war by international agreement, and one-third of them used that popular phrase. Finally, even the serious proposals presented the view that the common people would think more sanely than rulers; thus some entries advocated a direct vote of the people on "whether or not the battle is to be fought." Usually the war referendum supporters prescribed at the same time the taking of "profit out of war."[5]

Among those who submitted war referendum peace plans in the Bok contest were William Jennings Bryan, former Vice President Thomas R. Marshall, and retired Rear Admiral Samuel McGowan. Significantly, all of these men had served in the Wilson administration before or at the time of American intervention in World War I. Bryan's entry, no surprise in light of his record in the Wilson cabinet or his favoring a war referendum since 1915, seemed a fitting climax to his search for peace. As noted, he got Democratic endorsement of it in the platform of 1924. Then

[5] Esther Everett Lape, *Ways to Peace: Twenty Plans Selected from the Most Representative of Those Submitted to the American Peace Award . . .* (New York, 1924), pp. 4, 5–7, 30; Ferrell, *Peace in Their Time,* pp. 24–25. The American Foundation Files, SCPC, do not contain much manuscript material or a file on the plans submitted.

he submitted it to the Bok committee, just before his death the next year. To avoid publicity, he did not submit it under his name. Yet when it did not win, he forwarded it to President Calvin Coolidge and Secretary of State Frank B. Kellogg.[6] Former Vice President Marshall's contest plan for a war referendum was more surprising in view of his wartime stand against the radical pacifists who advocated it. Like Bryan, he also died in 1925, after spending his last four years in retirement engaged in a personal search for world peace. In July 1923 Marshall proposed that the United States encourage international agreement to the war referendum through changes in organic laws of each nation.[7]

The details of Marshall's Bok entry are interesting. Like many peace plans of the interwar period, his war referendum plan was infused with a typical appeal to the rule of law. Civilized nations of the world would, first, change their organic laws to provide for no war without a referendum of men and women over eighteen years of age. This legislation also would provide a sixty-day cooling off period after announcement of the referendum's results. Furthermore, all men and women in the armed forces of these nations would be sworn not to leave the "territorial land or water of the country" until after the referendum. Anyone who gave or obeyed such an order, in contempt of a referendum decision for peace, would be subject to international prosecution as a war criminal. All of this would be in force after "the Great Powers and two-thirds of all the nations" agreed to it. Because of the appeal to international law, Marshall's plan also provided an international criminal court. Each nation would have a judge, and the court would have authority to draft rules governing enforcement of the referendum procedure and the "international crime of making war" without popular authority. He believed that trial and execution of those found guilty by this court would have a "great moral effect" and encourage peace.[8]

Such was one of the most interesting Bok contest plans. Marshall had achieved a remarkable synthesis of America's peace preferences. He combined a smattering of internationalism, guarantees of independence of action, international law, popular control, and sanctions of moral force and public opinion. The result, at the moment, was front page attention. But opponents of such a road to peace regarded his plan "fatuous and foolish," challenging Marshall to stick to his more practical propaganda

[6]Curti, *Bryan and World Peace*, p. 252; Levine, *Bryan*, p. 205, fails to mention the war referendum idea contained in Bryan's Bok entry; Coletta, *Bryan*, III, does not mention his Bok entry.

[7]Charles Marion Thomas, *Thomas Riley Marshall: Hoosier Statesman* (Oxford, Ohio, 1939), pp. 252–53.

[8]*New York Times*, July 12, 1923.

for a good five-cent cigar. Marshall, who had been described in 1915 as second only to Bryan in his pacifism, now confessed that he had previously spoken to several senators (undisclosed) during the American debate on the League of Nations concerning the referendum peace plan.[9]

Franklin Roosevelt at this time also drafted a peace plan, a substitute for the League, which later was important in his attitudes toward the United Nations. But since Mrs. Roosevelt helped organize the Bok Award, he did not submit it. His former paymaster general of the navy, retired Rear Admiral Samuel McGowan, however, did send in a peace plan, one which endorsed the war referendum idea.[10] Admiral McGowan's war referendum plan differed from former Vice President Marshall's in several respects. At first notice, it is difficult even to ascertain whether his advocacy of popular control of the war decision derived from pacifism. McGowan attempted to make war unlikely, or if it were found necessary, at least efficient and characterized by national unity. He proposed an amendment to the Constitution which would allow male and female citizens over age seventeen to vote on war. Each citizen who voted in favor of war in such a referendum would thereby also obligate himself "to enlist for the duration of the war" in either military or industrial service. If the referendum carried in favor of war, all who opposed the majority decision, or who had not voted, would likewise be drafted for service. As a man certainly familiar with mobilization experiences, McGowan, furthermore, suggested that those who voted for war be first assigned to combat duty, either on the war front or on fighting ships. The last to serve in such areas would be those who voted against war. Typical of the thinking at the time and in the interest of greater efficiency during a war effort, McGowan also wanted wartime private and corporate profits in excess of 6 percent to be turned over to the government.[11]

The Admiral revised this earlier draft and resubmitted another late in 1923. He retained the war profits and conscription features of his earlier proposed war referendum amendment, but he indicated in the second draft that the referendum would not apply in case of attacks or invasion.

[9] Ibid., July 21, 1923; Thomas, *Marshall,* pp. 176, 253.

[10] During World War I, when Roosevelt was assistant secretary of the navy, Admiral McGowan was responsible for the Navy Department's Bureau of Supplies and Accounts and was paymaster general. After retirement in 1920 he participated in Red Cross relief work in Greece, was South Carolina highway commissioner in the mid-twenties, and lived in New York, Washington, D.C., Philadelphia, and Laurens, S.C., before his death in 1934. See Samuel McGowan Papers, Duke University Library, Durham, N.C.

[11] McGowan, "How War May Be Prevented," enclosed with McGowan to Edward Bok, July 31, 1923, and McGowan to Mrs. Elizabeth W. Ball, Aug. 2, 1923, McGowan Papers.

It also would be advisory in some cases and specifically violated the secret ballot in providing that each voter sign his ballot. If a majority of votes held for peace, Congress could not even consider war. McGowan hoped that other nations might follow America's example in this and thereby "make future world peace almost certain."[12]

Admiral McGowan testified to an unusual faith in the people and the majority principle. He believed that his proposal in its final form was simple and sound enough to make war virtually impossible. It would be, he thought, especially appealing to women, and most war referendum partisans never overlooked the relatively recent female vote. After talking it over with several senators, he received some editorial endorsement in South Carolina.[13] His inclusion of universal conscription of both a military and industrial nature made his proposed amendment unique. Such was a testimony to popular confusion over how to achieve grass roots influence and direction of foreign policy. Like many Americans, however, Admiral McGowan was convinced that he had a workable idea and continued, even after announcement of the Bok prize winner, to urge his plan.

As a climax to the Bok Peace Contest, the American Foundation conducted a national referendum on the winning prize. The result, announced in 1925, showed a strong interest in peace, to be sure, but it also disclosed cracks in the peace campaign, the contest failing to create the unity or popular influence in diplomacy, as intended. Other peace contests, however, were no more successful in following the example set by Bok. Local essay contests abounded in colleges in the 1920s and usually contained references to the war referendum plan. In North Carolina, a winning essay in 1925 suggested that since people of the state had decided by referendum to build a port terminal, they should be granted a referendum on war.[14] This peace plan, in fact, was a college debate topic in 1925–26, as well as later in the 1930s.[15]

Contests were not the only evidence, however, of continuing pacifist interest in the war referendum plan in the 1920s. Among earlier radical

[12]Typescript, "A Practicable Means by Which the United States Can Take Its Place and Do Its Share toward Preserving World Peace," enclosed with McGowan to Mrs. Elizabeth W. Ball, Oct. 21, 1923, ibid.

[13]McGowan to Mrs. Elizabeth W. Ball, Feb. 17, 1924, ibid. Editors of the *Greenville* (S.C.) *News,* Feb. 13, 1924, favored adoption of the McGowan idea and urged that "those who vote for war be the first upon the field of battle."

[14]Kenneth E. Neese, "Peace through Referendum," *Messenger of Peace* (Richmond, Ind.), 50 (1925), 402–4. This won a peace essay contest at Guilford College, N.C. Files of this journal, published by the Peace Association of Friends in America, are in SCPC.

[15]Edith M. Phelps, ed., *University Debaters' Annual* (New York, 1926), pp. 237–81; Egbert R. Nichols, ed., *Intercollegiate Debates,* 8 (New York, 1927), 357–87.

peace organizations that led in endorsement of the war referendum, only several had survived the World War. Some intellectuals, social workers, and youthful radicals in groups like the People's Council of America (extinct by 1920) found themselves later within progressivism, and by the mid-1930s in such peace organizations as the American League Against War and Fascism. La Follette's People's Legislative Service was not primarily devoted to peace, although one of its earliest editorials contained views strikingly similar to its founder's concepts. *"If those who make wars were compelled to fight them,"* the *People's Business* reported, *"we would soon see the dawn of universal peace."* Among La Follette backers in 1924, this group never advocated the war referendum but thought that front line trenches should include diplomats, international bankers, jingoistic editors, prowar congressmen, and munitions makers![16] It was a favorite theme: "the people" did not want war, and, if given a chance, would not vote for war.

One of the most successful wartime peace groups, the American Union Against Militarism, gradually curtailed its meetings and activities by 1922. From the armistice until mid-1921 it came under the direction of liberal pacifist Oswald Garrison Villard, editor of the *Nation*. But the Union suffered without money or a cause to champion, and the American Civil Liberties Union, which grew from within the antimilitarists, gained strength. An interesting but unsuccessful attempt to revitalize the organization in 1919, however, turned on discussion of renewing agitation for a national referendum on war. Such action would serve, according to sponsor Mary White Ovington, "as a real democratic check against war and imperialism." The executive committee discussed the matter but took no action.[17] Interest by this pioneer social worker, who was chairman of the board of the National Association for the Advancement of Colored People, indicated, once more, the close relationship between progressive reformers and the referendum plan.

As the Union's leadership found service in other reform causes and its staff transferred to such new groups as the People's Legislative Service, it suspended activities early in 1922. Although the Union denied a merger with Frederick J. Libby's newly organized National Council for Prevention of War, its executive secretary became director of Libby's Speaker's Bureau. The American Union Against Militarism, a victim of reformist strife and proliferation typical within organized pacifism, gave

[16] *People's Business* (Washington, D.C.), 1, No. 2 (1926), 1 (emphasis by the editor, People's Legislative Service Director, Basil M. Manly). Copy in La Follette–Wheeler Collection.

[17] Minutes, Executive Committee, July 29, 1919, and Mary White Ovington to Henry R. Mussey, Apr. 26, 1921, AUAM Records, SCPC.

way to another new, and ultimately stronger, group to prevent "duplication of effort." Libby's organization became the most successful peace group of the interwar period, involved in such peace causes as disarmament, outlawing war, the World Court, and, in the 1930s, the war referendum.[18]

The lack of organized pacifist interest in the war referendum plan in the 1920s was offset, as noted, by several individuals who furnished interesting private support. Another such person was Thomas Hall Shastid, a Duluth opthalmologist, peace enthusiast, and scholar who claimed to have supported the war referendum plan since 1895. By the mid-1920s, with his own study of war-declaring practices completed, he offered a detailed presentation of his "war-check vote" in addresses, the press, and in correspondence to congressmen.[19]

Shastid's proposed amendment to the Constitution provided, first, that *if Congress voted for war,* the people by referendum would be given an opportunity to "check" Congress. Yet the people could not override a congressional vote *against* war. Such a plan, he believed, would prevent "extraterritorial wars" or aggression by the United States abroad. He thus excluded from his "war-check" plan any use of the referendum in the event of attacks or invasion of the United States.

Inherent in his amendment was a limited-defense concept that was typical of many war referendum partisans. Shastid claimed that his plan was designed to prevent most wars but to win those that could not be avoided. In an interesting precedent for later appeals for deterrence and limited war, he urged a defense establishment strong enough to protect America against the next two strongest powers combined.

Shastid also proposed in a second constitutional amendment a "Loan and Gift Check Vote," in which the people would vote on foreign economic aid. He popularized the two constitutional amendments in five books between 1926 and 1937, in countless speeches, and through articles in the Duluth *Free Press*. Furthermore, he organized and directed three war referendum peace societies: Give the People Their Own War Power,

[18]Henry R. Mussey to Oswald Garrison Villard, Mar. 10, 1921; Villard to Belle Rankin, Jan. 20, 1922; Villard to Gibson Gardner, Feb. 3, 1922; Belle Rankin to Villard, Feb. 8, 1922; Minutes, Executive Committee, Jan. 20, 24, 1922, ibid. Libby, a Quaker minister, was more interested during the twenties in peace plans other than the war referendum, although he did report political interest in it in 1924. See National Council for Prevention of War *Bulletin,* 3, No. 8 (1924), 3, (hereafter cited as NCPW *Bulletin*) and Libby's *To End War: The Story of the National Council for Prevention of War* (Nyack, N.Y., 1969).

[19]Shastid held Master's and Law degrees from Michigan, was a Presbyterian and a Republican, and translated medical works from German, French, Latin, and Greek (Thomas Hall Shastid, *My Second Life* [Ann Arbor, Mich., 1944]).

Incorporated; War Check Vote, Incorporated (149 members in 1931); and the International War Vote Exchange.[20]

A no less untiring and better-known private supporter of the war referendum plan in the late 1920s was diplomat Alanson B. Houghton. A roundfaced, short, plump man, not the typical ambassador in appearance, he was regarded as one of America's best interwar diplomats. He was a Harvard- and European-trained businessman-diplomat and former congressman from New York, serving under Presidents Harding and Coolidge as ambassador to Germany and then Great Britain, 1922 to 1929.[21] With his move to the Court of St. James in 1925, Ambassador Houghton often publicly addressed himself to the problem that so dominated the decade—America's role in the search for peace. His May 4, 1925, address as the new American ambassador to England encouraged Senator Borah to praise his theme of peace as "an adventure in faith." Ambassador Houghton in 1928 chastised his friend Oswald Garrison Villard for "underestimating the value" of the Kellogg-Briand Pact "to the plain people."[22] On the war referendum plan, however, the two Americans were in complete agreement.

Before making an address in mid-1927, Houghton did not request State Department approval of his topic or acceptance of his views, as he had done in 1922. No longer was the peace problem so closely related to economic collapse in Europe. This time, therefore, his proposal of international agreement to the war referendum plan, in the form of a one-hundred-year peace pledge not to wage war without a referendum, became known as the "Houghton proposal." Speaking personally rather than officially, he challenged the world, before an audience of Harvard University graduates, to a "new experiment in democratic control." Durable peace, he maintained, could not be based upon force.[23] No better summary of the central arguments for the war referendum plan had been offered.

[20]Shastid, "The War Check Vote," *World Tomorrow,* 12 (1929), 120–22; Shastid, *Second Life,* pp. 829–37, 1137–56; Shastid, *How to Stop War-Time Profiteering,* 2d ed. (Ann Arbor, Mich., 1937), pp. 37, 130. His other war referendum books include *The Only Way* (Duluth, Minn., 1926), *Give the People Their Own War Power* (Ann Arbor, Mich., 1927), and *Just One Check on War* (n.p., 1928). He was the author of over thirty novels, medical treatises, and peace books (Allen, *Fight for Peace,* pp. 229–30).

[21]Green, "Unloquacious Ambassador," p. 10; Beckles Willson, *America's Ambassadors to England* (London, 1928), pp. 469–85.

[22]"Houghton Speaks for America," NCPW *Bulletin,* 4, No. 5 (1925), 5; Houghton to Villard, June 9, 1928, Villard Papers. See also Wreszin, *Villard,* pp. 169–83, for the editor's support of the Borah-Levinson type of outlawry and his vehement opposition to the World Court.

[23]*Cong. Rec.,* 70th Cong., 1st sess., pp. 1046–48 (Jan. 5, 1928), reprints the full text of this June 1927 address at Harvard.

Actually, Houghton was proposing, in the beginning, that America and Great Britain join in such a peace pledge. The treaty would be negotiated through normal diplomatic channels and an international conference and then be ratified by a referendum in each country. If similar plebiscites in other nations revealed public favor of the plan, they too could join the peace pact.[24] Coming at the time of the Kellogg-Briand negotiations and after several years of American discussion of the outlawing of war, the Houghton proposal sounded much like those renunciations of war plans. His speech and views were widely publicized in America, England, and Germany, becoming a subject for public debate and consideration.

After consistently rejecting the war referendum idea since 1916, the *New York Times* believed that Houghton's suggestion "should challenge the genius of modern democracy to find a way to put the proposal into practical effect." For two months thereafter readers informed the editors of their opinion on the matter.[25] Public leaders were hesitant to offer opinions in view of the popular response, but Washington correspondents discovered "no open disapproval" in the administration. Other newspapers that endorsed the proposal included the Boston *Herald,* New York *Telegram* and *World,* Brooklyn *Eagle,* and *Christian Science Monitor.* The last associated it, without supporting evidence, with "the level-headed New Englander" in the White House. As one paper pointed out, it indeed seemed as if the idea of popular control of foreign affairs, long regarded as "a piece of fantastic radicalism," was now respectable.[26]

Much of the favorable reaction to the 1927 Houghton war referendum proposal hinged upon his emphasis that "little groups of men called governments," not peoples, caused wars. His friend Oswald Garrison Villard, who had long presented this view of World War I, now congratulated himself, and Houghton, for being correct. The *Nation's* editor believed that Ambassador Houghton had uniquely, bravely, but accurately performed diplomatic "treason" by speaking of governments and diplomats as "little groups of men." After the failure of the Geneva Disarmament Conference later in 1927, Villard wrote Houghton often to encourage his continued effort for the "absolutely essential" proposal.[27]

In spite of generally favorable reaction to his Harvard speech, Houghton felt that editors and public alike partially misunderstood him.

[24]Ibid. Indeed, the advocates of the war referendum were so certain that the people would not vote for war that their program was an indirect outlawry of war plan.

[25]*New York Times,* June 25, 30, July 18, 31, and Aug. 7, 10, 1927. These letters favored Houghton's proposal 3 to 2.

[26]"To Put Wars to a Vote," *Literary Digest,* 94, No. 3 (1927), 8–9.

[27]"Ambassador Houghton Tells Some More Truths," *Nation,* 125 (1927), 32; Villard to Houghton, Aug. 2, 22, Sept. 15, 1927, Villard Papers. See also "Why War?" *Dearborn Independent,* n.d., in *The Herald of Peace,* 1, No. 2 (1927), 2, SCPC; Florence Brewer Boeckel,

He offered the proposal not only to America and England but also to the other "great self-governing powers," namely, France and Germany. Only Italy was absent from the group which he wished Secretary Hughes to include in a similar war referendum peace pact in 1922. His Harvard proposal also was not associated with the Allied debt, as in 1922. But no one, of course, at the time, and few since, knew of his important 1922 precedent attributed to Germany.[28]

The ambassador's 1927 war. referendum proposal received international attention in the press. The British Council of the World Alliance for Promoting International Friendship through the Churches and the Federal Council of the Churches of Christ in America were two internationalist-minded religious organizations that circulated reprints of Houghton's Harvard address. Villard's "Who Makes War in America?"—which relied heavily on Houghton's views as well as his own—publicized the recent proposals. The English Union of Democratic Control also carried the idea in its literature in 1928.[29] Apparently Ambassador Houghton, once again, had brought the war referendum to public attention throughout Europe and the United States. But this time he got no official governmental backing.

When Villard endorsed Houghton for vice president on a ticket with Franklin Roosevelt in 1928, the idea never caught fire. Instead, the ambassador was a New York Republican candidate for the United States Senate, and Roosevelt, of course, won the New York gubernatorial race. In Houghton's unsuccessful race, however, he emphasized his peace views and especially the war referendum–peace pact plan. Erroneously, some

---

Between War and Peace: A Handbook for Peace Workers (New York, 1928), p. 3. Pacifist minister John Haynes Holmes, who had accepted the war referendum plan as a member of preintervention peace groups, now objected to it. He acknowledged its "new and greater dignity" under Ambassador Houghton's sponsorship, but Holmes wanted to take the war power from politicians *and* people, making it a "crime" under any circumstances. See his review of Thomas Hall Shastid's *Give the People Their Own War Power* (1927), *Nation*, 125 (1927), 608.

[28] Wehberg, *Outlawry of War*, pp. 66–67, 112, does mention the "Cuno proposal" in his brief discussion of the Houghton address of 1927. Wehberg correctly believed that the latter showed the American public's support of the Briand proposal. Ferrell, *Peace in Their Time*, does not mention Houghton's 1927 address. See also Houghton to Villard, July 13, 1927, Villard Papers.

[29] Houghton, "War? Let the People Decide!" *Federal Council Bulletin*, 10, No. 7 (1927), 9–10; Houghton, "The Power of the People," *Goodwill: A Review of International Christian Friendship*, 3, No. 1 (1928), 20–23; Villard, "Who Makes War in America?" typescript, c. 1928, Villard Papers; *New York Times*, July 27, 1927; "The Peace of the World: A Summary of the Various Proposals Which Are Now Being Discussed" (London, 1928), Union of Democratic Control (England) Files, SCPC.

interpreted such emphasis as putting him at odds with Secretary of State Frank B. Kellogg's plan to outlaw war. Even so, neither Villard's efforts, the support of other pacifist editors (Paul U. Kellogg and Kirby Page), nor Houghton's speeches urging lower tariffs and the war referendum could win him enough votes.[30]

After the ambassador's return to America in 1929, he continued to speak for the war referendum at every opportunity. Active in peace and religious organizations, he considered a lecture tour for the Foreign Policy Association and addressed graduates on the war referendum at Syracuse, the University of Rochester, and Carnegie Institute of Technology. He became president of the Academy of Political Science, a trustee of the Carnegie Endowment for International Peace, and attended a preliminary Paris disarmament conference of religious and peace groups before the 1932 Geneva Disarmament Conference.[31] An interesting and dedicated peace worker, Alanson B. Houghton remained a serious spokesman for the war referendum plan in the 1930s.

Apart from its limited appeal to organized pacifism and significant individual support by men like Ambassador Houghton, the war referendum idea found its greatest number of friends in Congress during the interwar period. Between 1925 and 1935, after which congressional and pacifist interest reached its apogee, seventeen war referendum resolutions were introduced in Congress by nine senators and congressmen. Most of these were proposed constitutional amendments and did not receive much assistance from organized pacifism.[32]

A majority of these resolutions contained the same distinction, so prevalent in American thinking on other peace plans as well, between wars of aggression and defense. The war referendum idea appealed to some of its congressional sponsors because they doubted whether our intervention in 1917 was entirely an act of self-defense. In an atmosphere of historical revisionism on the reasons for America's entry in World War I, with its corresponding attack on munitions makers and economic "interests," the war referendum plan often provided congressmen a con-

[30]*Nation,* 127 (1928), 332, 389; Villard to Herbert Croly, Paul U. Kellogg, and Kirby Page, all Oct. 8, 1928, Page to Villard, Oct. 18, 1928, and Villard to Houghton, Nov. 13, 1928, Villard Papers; "Mr. Houghton's Little Plan," *New Republic,* 56 (1928), 342; Allen, *Fight for Peace,* p. 229.

[31]Houghton to Villard, June 7, 1929, Villard Papers; *New York Times,* June 17, Sept. 26, Dec. 14, 1930, June 10, Nov. 18, 25, and Dec. 14, 1931.

[32]The resolutions treated herein are from an examination of the congressional files in the National Archives, Record Groups 233 and 46, made on the basis of Edwin A. Halsey, comp., *Proposed Amendments to the Constitution of the United States Introduced in Congress from December 6, 1926, to January 3, 1941* (Washington, D.C., 1941). Of some 740 in this period, approximately 50 were proposed war referendum amendments.

venient way to talk about past errors in judgment. Under their war referendum amendments, therefore, defensive wars against attack or invasion, threatened or otherwise, in the continental United States or insular possessions, would not necessitate a referendum. For example, the later attack on Pearl Harbor would not have caused implementation of the amendment proposed in 1934 by Congressman Denver S. Church (Democrat, Calif.), who in 1916 had introduced the same plan. Among the resolutions which illustrated this defensive-aggressive distinction were also those of Congressmen John M. Evans (Democrat, Mont.) in 1926 and 1927 and Henry R. Rathbone (Republican, Ill.) in 1928.[33]

Another earlier war referendum sponsor, Senator Clarence C. Dill (Democrat, Wash.), reintroduced in 1926 the text of his 1918 and 1923 proposed amendments. He, too, made the distinction, and, like all of the other resolutions in the 1920s, his latest effort died in committee.[34] The only other senators to show interest in the war referendum between 1925 and 1930 were Progressive-Republican Robert M. La Follette, Jr., elected in 1925 on a platform that included the war referendum plan, and South Carolina Democrat Cole Blease. Prompted by Admiral Samuel McGowan, Blease announced in 1929 his intention to introduce a war referendum resolution if the Committee on Foreign Relations judged the plan feasible. His failure to do so may have thus indicated an adverse response by this committee.[35] Normally, however, these resolutions died a fast death in the respective judiciary committees of the Congress.

These proposed war referendum amendments also had in common the advisory feature the elder La Follette and others had applied earlier. Congress would retain the war-declaring power and could declare war at any time. However, in cases not "strictly defensive," which was never defined, such action of Congress would necessitate the direct advice of the electorate through a national referendum. The people would thereby "ratify and approve" such war declarations as appeared to indicate American "aggression." In this way the congressional prerogative would not be directly removed but would only, perhaps, be overruled by the people. Although often hidden, the implications were clear; sponsors of these resolutions believed that the people were more pacifist than

[33]House Joint Resolution 297, 73d Cong., 2d sess., Mar. 14, 1934 (Church), RG 233, NA; House Joint Resolution 152, Feb. 5, 1926 (Evans), "House of Representatives, Joint Resolutions, 1–379," 69th Cong., 1925–27, LC; House Joint Resolution 19, Dec. 5, 1927 (Evans), and House Joint Resolution 323, May 29, 1928 (Rathbone), "House of Representatives, Joint Resolutions, 1–435," 70th Cong., 1927–29, LC.

[34]Senate Joint Resolution 102, 69th Cong., 1st sess., Apr. 19, 1926, Records of the Senate, Record Group 46, NA.

[35]*Cong. Rec.,* 70th Cong., 2d sess., p. 3714 (Feb. 19, 1929).

congressmen and thought a greater extension of popular control in diplomacy was necessary to check minority "interests," whether executive, economic, or even congressional.

Sponsors often gave other reasons for their support, but the views of most of them would not contradict the above analysis. New York Republican Hamilton Fish, for example, claimed that his three 1929 war referendum resolutions would provide the logical complement to the Kellogg-Briand Pact. Fish was one of the leading isolationist congressmen and a severe opponent of Franklin Roosevelt later, always expressing fear of a future "warlike President."[36] Indeed, there was a close resemblance between the drive to outlaw war and the war referendum movement, and Ambassador Houghton, who had been involved in the Kellogg-Briand negotiations, supported the Fish proposals of 1929.

Another popular proposed constitutional amendment that pointed up the connection even more was that of Senator Lynn J. Frazier (Republican, N.Dak.). Introduced in 1926 and commanding congressional attention as well as that of the Women's Peace Union for some time, this proposal sought to make war "illegally impossible" by abolishing the war-making power entirely! It was in this respect more radical than the war referendum plan, which sought to transfer that power to the people, or the renunciation of war proposals of Levinson, Borah, or Briand. All of these plans sought to make future wars impossible; the difference was in the means utilized for this purpose. They disclosed a common lack of thought about concepts of national interest, the use of military force in diplomacy, or even the mechanics of the plans themselves. Yet the strength of the American desire for peace divorced from such considerations was indicated often in the interwar period. Certainly the two hearings granted the Frazier amendment and increasing popular and congressional favor of the war referendum plan were two such examples.[37]

In the 1930s, during President Hoover's administration and into the period of Franklin D. Roosevelt's New Deal, the war referendum plan entered upon better times. To the rich isolationist inheritance of the 1920s

[36] Ibid., pp. 1483–84 (Jan. 10, 1929); texts of his almost identical resolutions, Jan. 10, 11, and June 17, 1929, are in "House of Representatives, Joint Resolutions, 1–435," 70th Cong., 1927–29, and "1–536," 71st Cong., 1929–31, LC.

[37] The Frazier resolutions were introduced from 1926 to 1939. See U.S., Congress, Senate, 69th Cong., 2d sess., *Constitutional Amendment Making War Legally Impossible,* Hearing before a Subcommittee of the Committee of the Judiciary on Senate Joint Resolution 100, Jan. 22, 1927; U.S., Congress, Senate, 73d Cong., 2d sess., *Constitutional Amendment Making War Legally Impossible,* Hearing before a Subcommittee of the Committee of the Judiciary on Senate Joint Resolution 24, Apr. 14, 1934; and Women's Peace Union (1921–41) Records, SCPC. The Women's Peace Union also promoted the war referendum plan (Chatfield, *For Peace and Justice,* pp. 98, 143–44).

was now added a more sizable, intense, and united congressional isolationist bloc. Caused in part by the Great Depression and a wave of ag-
gressions in Europe, increased public demands "to keep America out of
war" replaced earlier demands, also translated into action by Congress,
"to keep out of the League." In truth, an "isolationist tornado" was form-
ing in 1930.[38]

Entering into this mood of the 1930s as leader of congressional war
referendum forces up to 1935 was Congressman James A. Frear (Republican, Wis.). He was in Congress from 1913 to 1934 and championed
the war referendum cause in six resolutions during his last four years. In
contrast to Hamilton Fish, Frear was a consistent friend of the New Deal
except in foreign policy matters. As one of many proponents of neutrality
legislation, Frear believed that the war referendum plan and anti-war-
profits legislation would preserve peace. Convinced of an imminent war in
Europe, he offered in 1931 two resolutions that clearly expressed
America's approach to peace during the entire interwar period.

One resolution urged an international conference of Kellogg-Briand
Pact signatories. Agreement would be sought on prohibiting loans and
war materials to belligerents and on declaring future wars only after
either (1) thirty days written notice or (2) submission of the question to
the electorate in a special referendum. These restrictions on declarations
of war, as usual, would not apply in cases of invasion or attack. The
proposed conference, furthermore, would seek to provide a one-year
moratorium on enlistments and a one-year naval holiday after the
conference. There was no provision for enforcing the proposed
agreements, except by moral force and public opinion, and no anticipation
of joint reaction to aggression among the signatories.

The other resolution proposed a war referendum amendment for the
United States. It retained previous advisory and self-defense features but
added an interesting anticonscription clause. Except in case of danger to
the "public safety," which was not defined, no forced military service
would be permitted, and then only on the North American continent.[39]

There was no better example of America's typically isolationist, self-
denying defense concepts of the interwar period. Like war referendum
proponents before and after him, Frear believed only in continental self-
defense. His was a limited-defense concept that sought to remove force
from diplomacy and to achieve peace by injecting into foreign affairs such
sanctions as popular control, moral force, and public opinion.

Frear often spoke of the necessity of "limited" national defense. But

---

[38] For background see Adler, *Isolationist Impulse,* pp. 219–29, and De Conde, *Isolation
and Security.*

[39] *Cong. Rec.,* 71st Cong., 3d sess., pp. 4628–31, 4650 (Feb. 11, 1931).

the overriding basis for his defense concept and war referendum work was his belief that neither Congress nor the Executive could be trusted to represent the people in such a crisis as a war decision. Profiteers, international bankers, military men, and "stupid statesmen" would be capable of "needless war blunders" without a war referendum amendment. He thus reintroduced his war referendum measure again in 1931, retaining the anticonscription feature, after discussing it before the War Policies Commission.[40]

From 1930 to 1932 there was an interesting but little-remembered example of congressional efforts to formulate public policy on the basis of public opinion. Seeking to prevent not war but "a recurrence of the conditions that in 1917–18 led to injustice, profiteering, and inefficiency," Congress investigated past wartime experience in the interest of promoting peace, equalizing burdens, and minimizing profits of war. This was done chiefly through a special War Policies Commission, comprised of cabinet members, senators, and congressmen. Its chief purpose was to recommend to Congress any constitutional amendments or other legislation needed to remove war profits, to provide for taking of private property for public use in wartime, and to stabilize prices in such an emergency. As a result of hearings conducted March 5 to 18 and May 13 to 22, 1931, the Commission's final report recommended only a constitutional amendment to remove any doubts as to congressional power to prevent profiteering and to stabilize prices in wartime. Many other suggestions by several war referendum advocates had been heard but unheeded during those hearings.[41]

[40]James A. Frear, *Forty Years of Progressive Public Service Reasonably Filled with Thorns and Flowers* (Washington, D.C., 1937), pp. 92–93, 99–104; House Joint Resolution 103, 72d Cong., 1st sess., Dec. 8, 1931, RG 233, NA.

[41]U.S., Congress, House, 72d Cong., 1st sess., House Document No. 163, *War Policies Commission Report,* which includes the hearings (cited hereafter as *WPC Report*). See also U.S., Congress, House, 72d Cong., 1st sess., House Document No. 264, *Final Report, War Policies Commission;* and U.S., Congress, House, 72d Cong., 1st sess., House Document No. 271, *Documents by War Policies Commission,* pp. 2, 5–6. The Commission resulted from American Legion efforts, begun in 1922, to assure more equitable distribution of the burdens of war. As Paul A. C. Koistinen points out, such concerns ironically were turned into support for industrial-mobilization planning by the War Department, which dominated the hearings. Elimination of war profits, therefore, was not given the emphasis many felt was needed, and opponents of army planning expressed fears of "the industrial-military ties resulting from department planning" ("The 'Industrial-Military Complex' in Historical Perspective: The Interwar Years," *Journal of American History,* 56 [1970], 828–30). An early account by Seymour Waldman, who was dissatisfied with the Commission's effort, sought to encourage "diagnosis of the whole problem, a study of the interlocking of our war mechanism and our economic system." See *Death and Profits: A Study of the War Policies Commission* (New York, 1932), pp. v, vii. Waldman was a journalist and an editor for the National Council for Prevention of War (Chatfield, *For Peace and Justice,* p. 165).

In addition to Congressman Frear, other spokesmen for the war referendum plan appearing before the Commission included Admiral Mc-Gowan and the pioneer legislative sponsor Richard Bartholdt. McGowan testified that he had removed from his 1923–24 Bok prize proposal, at the request of a Methodist minister, the requirement that individuals sign their ballots and serve at the front according to degrees of belligerency. He still believed that the war referendum plan had strong appeal to women, but did not think that it would have prevented World War I. Bartholdt later urged before the Commission the same peace program presented in 1913 and 1914—a small military establishment, the advisory referendum, government manufacture of munitions, and a total embargo of money and munitions to belligerents.[42] There was no better example of the persistence of his limited-defense concepts.

The lack of support for the war referendum by organized pacifism was clearly noted during the hearings. When leading pacifists like Socialist Norman Thomas, Dorothy Detzer, executive secretary of Jane Addams's Women's International League for Peace and Freedom, and American Peace Society Secretary Arthur Deerin Call testified, no reference was made to that peace plan. Dr. Thomas Hall Shastid, on the other hand, furnished lengthy testimony, replete with copies of his war referendum books and a record of his organizational efforts for the idea.[43]

Congressman Frear's testimony before the War Policies Commission repeated his opposition to sending American troops "by conscription abroad to fight Europe's battles." Here, in fact, was a basic attitude of most war referendum partisans. Their defense line started at the continental limits of the United States or, at the most, extended beyond only in a willingness to defend America's insular possessions by naval means. Frear especially objected to the views of "internationalists" who wanted "to police the world" with a large army. A defense establishment

[42] *WPC Report,* Mar. 9, 1931, pp. 73–85, 850–52, May 15, 1931, pp. 489–502. South Carolina Congressman John J. McSwain, a member of the Commission and friend of Mc-Gowan, did not sponsor a referendum resolution but spoke of McGowan's proposal in Congress late in December. See *Cong. Rec.,* 72d Cong., 1st sess., pp. 1055–56 (Dec. 21, 1931). McSwain's tireless interest in anti–war-profits legislation, even as chairman of the House Military Affairs Committee, 1932–36, is reflected in the large collection of his papers (Duke University Library) which do not contain any war referendum interest.

[43] *WPC Report,* May 19, 1931, pp. 612–66, May 20–21, 1931, pp. 722–59. Waldman fails to note interest in the war referendum plan by several witnesses. He identified most as industrialists or military men and agreed with Senator Dill, himself an advocate of the plan, who later described the work of the Commission as "like the mountain that labored and brought forth a mouse" (*Death and Profits,* pp. 136–37). See also John E. Wiltz, *In Search of Peace: The Senate Munitions Inquiry, 1934–1936* (Baton Rouge, La., 1963), pp. 14–15.

consisting of a "strong navy to police our own waters" and a referendum on war declarations, he thought, would prevent just that.[44]

The War Policies Commission hearings served as an important precedent to the more famous Senate Munitions Investigation directed by Senator Gerald Nye (Republican, N.Dak.), 1934–36.[45] During that time war referendum spokesmen like Frear, and even Senator Nye, added to their proposed war referendum constitutional amendments such anti–war-profits features as the two investigations seemed to justify. This feature, along with an inherent limited-defense concept, thus became central to future war referendum proposals. After all, what better way to insure equality of the public's wartime burdens and efficiency within the war machine than to prevent excess war profits by the "interests."

In 1934 Frear reintroduced his 1931 war referendum and anticonscription proposal with no change except a preamble that declared the Kellogg-Briand Pact "a scrap of paper." More important, however, the Judiciary Committee granted his resolution an "hour and a half" hearing on March 28, 1934. Hastily arranged, the hearing featured testimony of Frear, several college pacifists, congressmen, and Jeannette Rankin, former congresswoman and associate secretary of the National Council for Prevention of War. The hearing gradually became a sounding board for views that would soon dominate the Nye Committee's munitions investigation. Several Judiciary Committee members, including war referendum opponent Emanuel Celler (Democrat, N.Y.), even urged anti–war-profits legislation.

Evidently Frear had made an effort to unify war referendum sentiment around his resolution, for he received support from both Jane Addams and Samuel McGowan. Furthermore, plans for Senators Dill and Capper to testify failed only because they arrived too late. The Wisconsin congressman was also supported by Father Charles Coughlin. Although he received "sympathetic expressions" from "prominent members of the Administration," there was no clear endorsement of his resolution after a meeting with President Roosevelt, who urged Frear, nevertheless, to talk it over with Cordell Hull.[46]

[44] *WPC Report,* May 18, 1931, pp. 555–92; Frear, *Progressive Public Service,* p. 113.

[45] Nye entered the Senate in 1925 to fill Senator Ladd's seat, vacated by the war referendum sponsor's death. Background on the munitions investigation is in Wayne S. Cole, *Senator Gerald P. Nye and American Foreign Relations* (Minneapolis, 1962), pp. 60–76; and Wiltz, *In Search of Peace,* pp. 3–23, 117–19.

[46] Frear discussed his 1931 proposal before the Judiciary Committee in 1932 before the later hearing. Much of his correspondence with Chairman Hatton W. Sumners is in House files on House Joint Resolutions 103 (Dec. 8, 1931), 217 and 218 (Jan. 5, 1934), RG 233, NA. See also U.S., Congress, House, 73d Cong., 2d sess., *Amend the Constitution with Respect*

As a result of the March 28, 1934, hearing on Frear's resolutions, he introduced on April 2 and April 12 two revised war referendum amendments. The only changes were additions of anti–war-profits clauses. Whenever war became imminent, the president, under the revised Frear proposals, would conscript for public use "public and private war properties, yards, factories, and supplies, together with men and employees necessary for their operation." For use of these properties in the war effort, the government would return annually only 4 percent "profit," based on local tax values the preceding year. Frear's preamble clearly disclosed the ultimate source of these changes—recent testimony in the Congress had confirmed, he believed, an unholy connection between arms manufacturers and governments.[47] (Senator Nye was seeking investigation of that connection at the time.) Thus began a new theme and an additional feature contained in future war referendum interest and increased congressional support.

Actually that theme had seen earlier emphasis by the more radical individual sponsors of the war referendum idea. The elder La Follette had pointed up the relationship in 1916 and 1917 and again during the early twenties when he engaged in an individual study of the munitions industry. But the activities of the War Policies Commission and Senator Nye's approaching investigation, plus unusual public interest, increased that emphasis and made it respectable in the mid-1930s. Restudy of World War I convinced Americans that "taking the profits out of war," after thorough investigation of "war interests," would eradicate the war problem.

Senator Nye himself introduced a proposed constitutional amendment incorporating Frear's exact text April 19, 1934. It provided a referendum on war, the anticonscription clause, and the anti–war-profits feature. Nye, who had endorsed the war referendum idea in 1925, successfully had his bill referred to his own special munitions committee.[48]

Other war referendum resolutions inspired by current interest in the munitions investigation included those of Congressman George B. Terrell (Democrat, Tex.) and Senator Marvel M. Logan (Democrat, Ky.). Terrell clearly stated in his proposed constitutional amendment that no profit should derive from munitions sales nor were interest-bearing bonds to be

---

to *Declarations of War,* Hearings before the Committee on the Judiciary . . . Mar. 28, 1934, and Frear, *Progressive Public Service,* p. 312.

[47] House Joint Resolution 313, 73d Cong., 2d sess., Apr. 2, 1934, RG 233, NA; House Joint Resolution 321, 73d Cong., 2d sess., Apr. 12, 1934, RG 233, NA; and Frear, *Progressive Public Service,* pp. 121–22.

[48] Original text of the Nye resolution is an edited copy of Frear's last bill. See Senate Joint Resolution 104, 73d Cong., 2d sess., Apr. 19, 1934, RG 46, NA; Cole, *Nye,* pp. 120–22, mentions only Nye's later (1937–39) war referendum resolutions.

issued to prosecute a future war. Taxes were enough to do the job, he believed. Senator Robert M. La Follette, Jr., and the Wisconsin Legislature endorsed the Logan measure on the basis of the Nye investigation.[49]

Always heretofore sporadic and usually uncoordinated, the war referendum movement had reached, once more, an important juncture. Offsetting a lack of organized pacifist interest were endorsements of the idea during the Bok Peace Contest, individual support by private citizens, and Ambassador Houghton's continuing interest. More important, congressional interest had increased between 1926 and 1934. As forecasts of war in Europe and Asia became more frequent and were confirmed by events in the next five years, the war referendum plan demanded national attention as never before. Isolationism, enjoying its greatest popularity from 1935 to 1941, took many forms. Not insignificant were the thirty-three war referendum resolutions introduced in Congress.

[49]House Joint Resolution 283, 73d Cong., 2d sess., Feb. 24, 1934 (Terrell), RG 233, NA; Judiciary Committee folder on Senate Joint Resolution 7, 74th Cong., 1st sess., Jan. 4, 1935 (Logan), containing supporting correspondence, RG 46, NA. Public hearings of the Nye Committee did not begin until Sept., 1934, *after* all of the above resolutions except Logan's. His first resolution for an investigation was Feb. 8, 1934. See Cole, *Nye,* pp. 69–73.

CHAPTER VIII

The Ludlow Amendment and Fortress Defense

UNDER THE LEADERSHIP of Louis Ludlow in the 1930s many Americans believed more than ever that a constitutional amendment providing for a popular referendum before foreign wars offered the best hope for peace. Whereas thirty-one war referendum resolutions were introduced in Congress from 1914 to 1935, thirty-three more appeared between just 1935 and 1941. These proposals, which were seen as threatening executive leadership in the form of the proposed Ludlow Amendment, are best remembered as representing the most immature diplomacy of the thirties.[1] Most historians, treating only the January 10, 1938, test vote on the Ludlow plan, see it as a foolhardy scheme, as representative of the peace-at-any-price mood, and as an ultra-isolationist measure.[2] Some writers have overlooked the war referendum device in this period entirely, and others have misrepresented it. Historians and others (including the Department of State) have asserted or implied that *any* declaration of war would have required a popular vote under the Ludlow plan.[3] Yet the

[1]Additional treatment of the Ludlow Amendment is in the author's "The Ludlow Amendment: The War Referendum Idea, 1935–1941," M.A. Thesis, Georgia 1963.

[2]For example, see Robert A. Divine, *The Reluctant Belligerent: American Entry into World War II* (New York, 1965), pp. 48–49; Adler, *Isolationist Impulse,* pp. 159, 172, 247; Dexter Perkins, *The New Age of Franklin Roosevelt: 1932–45* (Chicago, 1957), pp. 101–2; Allan Nevins, *America in World Affairs* (New York, 1942), p. 115; Robert Alan Dahl, *Congress and Foreign Policy* (New York, 1950), p. 24; Daniel S. Cheever and H. Field Haviland, Jr., *American Foreign Policy and the Separation of Powers* (Cambridge, 1952), p. 88; Basil Rauch, *The History of the New Deal* (New York, 1944), p. 316; Richard Bolling, *Power in the House: A History of the Leadership of the House of Representatives* (New York, 1968), p. 142; Julius W. Pratt, *Cordell Hull, 1933–44* (New York, 1964), II, 451; and Rexford G. Tugwell, *The Democratic Roosevelt* (Garden City, N.Y., 1957), pp. 469–470.

[3]Among those overlooking the Ludlow Amendment are: Samuel F. Bemis, *A Diplomatic History of the United States* (New York, 1965); Frank Freidel, *America in the Twentieth Century* (New York, 1970); Holbert N. Carroll, *The House of Representatives and Foreign Affairs* (Boston, 1966); James A. Robinson, *Congress and Foreign Policy-Making* (Homewood, Ill., 1967); Charles C. Tansill, *Back Door to War: The Roosevelt Foreign Policy, 1933–1941* (Chicago, 1952); Louis Henkin, *Foreign Affairs and the Constitution* (New York, 1975); and Charles A. Beard, *American Foreign Policy in the Making, 1932–40: A Study in Responsibilities* (New Haven, 1946). Writers who misrepresent the Ludlow proposal include Nevins, *America in World Affairs,* pp. 115; idem, *The New Deal and World Affairs: A Chronicle of International Affairs, 1933–1945* (New Haven, 1950), p. 132; Nevins and Louis

proposal, as presented by its leading sponsor, Indiana Democratic Congressman Louis Ludlow, did *not* require a referendum in case of attack or invasion. Ludlow favored the war referendum device as a means of limiting the defense establishment and of reducing executive use of force in diplomacy. Additionally, he believed that his measure offered a challenge to the tendency of Congress itself to abdicate war powers to the Executive. But the Ludlow Amendment chiefly expressed a fortress concept of defense that struck at the heart of executive leadership and Franklin Roosevelt's own emerging defense concept and foreign policy attitudes.[4]

Ludlow's interest in the war referendum device originated with the American debate on intervention in World War I. As a Washington correspondent in the House press galleries at the time, persistent congressional and popular agitation influenced him. During the war he reported for several Ohio newspapers the interest in it among some of the state's Washington delegation. Although never especially concerned with the historical development of the war referendum idea, Ludlow stated in 1938 that his interest began "about the time I was doing war work some twenty years ago." His personal friendship during the war with William Jennings Bryan and Vice President Thomas Marshall, both of whom advocated the war referendum, also intensified his interest. Ludlow's earliest known public support of the plan, however, came as a newspa-

---

M. Hacker, *The United States and Its Place in World Affairs, 1918–1943* (Boston, 1943), p. 400; Foster Rhea Dulles, *Twentieth Century America* (Boston, 1945), p. 482; idem, *America's Rise to World Power, 1898–1954* (New York, 1955), p. 183; Frederick Lewis Allen, *Since Yesterday: The Nineteen-Thirties in America, September 3, 1929–September 3, 1939* (New York, 1940), p. 324; William L. Langer and S. Everett Gleason, *The Challenge to Isolation, 1937–1940* (New York, 1952), p. 14; Donald F. Drummond, *The Passing of Neutrality, 1937–1941* (Ann Arbor, Mich., 1955), p. 59; Divine, *Reluctant Belligerent,* p. 48; Manfred Jonas, *Isolationism in America, 1935–1941* (Ithaca, N. Y., 1966), p. 37; and Charles Chatfield, "Alternative Antiwar Strategies of the Thirties," *American Studies,* 13 (Spring 1972), 87. See also U.S., Department of State, *Peace and War: United States Foreign Policy, 1931–1941* (Washington, D.C., 1942), p. 52.

[4]For fuller treatment of Ludlow's personal background and the congressional debates on the proposed Ludlow Amendment, see Richard Dean Burns and W. Addams Dixon, "Foreign Policy and the 'Democratic Myth': The Debate on the Ludlow Amendment," *Mid-America,* 47 (1965), 288–306, and Walter R. Griffin, "Louis Ludlow and the War Referendum Crusade, 1935–1941," *Indiana Magazine of History,* 44 (1968), 267–88, which does not rely on records of the SCPC. Jonas, *Isolationism,* pp. 159–66, relates the Ludlow proposal to the "devil theory of war" and, like Robert A. Divine, *The Illusion of Neutrality* (Chicago, 1962), pp. 219–20, correctly points out the erroneous impression of some historians who regard the issue in 1938 as adoption of the proposed amendment. The issue was to compel the Rules Committee to permit full floor debate of the measure.

perman during 1924, at the time of Democratic and Progressive party endorsement of it.[5]

By temperament and outlook, moreover, Louis Ludlow was fitted to lead the war referendum cause. Beginning his career as a Washington correspondent in 1901, his reporting during the progressive era made a strong impression. He championed any "instrumentalities for registering the popular will" and praised, for example, the popular election of senators. As a journalist believing that "the greatest of all forces in regulating the world is public opinion," Ludlow favored extended popular controls in government generally. In fights against monopoly and inefficiency in government, he considered rule by the people "a sacred American principle."[6]

Unconsciously, perhaps, Ludlow acknowledged his affinity with Bryan when he described himself in 1924 as a "Democrat nationally and a Republican internationally." He confessed that he had no trouble keeping "his politics on fairly straight until Woodrow Wilson began to project America into the international sphere," proclaiming the United States as the "partner and paymaster for all of the unruly, trouble-breeding" nations of the world. Wilson he likened to the schoolmaster who jumped into every foreign quarrel to regulate or punish some "bad kid." Ludlow's speeches and books, even as a newspaperman, reveal another basis for his isolationist viewpoint. During an interview with former President Benjamin Harrison, Ludlow was told, "We have no commission from God to police the world."[7] This dictum, as well as his disappointment with Wilsonian progressivism abroad, strongly influenced his attitudes concerning foreign affairs and peace.

After a long and successful career as a Washington correspondent, recognized by his election as National Press Club vice president, Louis Ludlow was elected to Congress by the Indianapolis district in 1928.[8]

[5]Louis Ludlow to John R. Mackie, Sept. 29, 1938, Louis L. Ludlow Papers, Indiana University Library, Bloomington, Ind. Ludlow's autobiography, covering most of his newspaper career, records his 1924 support for the plan (*From Cornfield to Press Gallery: Adventures and Reminiscences of a Veteran Washington Correspondent* [Washington, D.C., 1924], p. 405).

[6]Ludlow, *Washington Correspondent*, pp. 404–5; "Louis Ludlow's Scrapbooks" (non–war referendum), 31 vols., 1903–48, VI, 1005, XIV, 2083, Ludlow Papers.

[7]Ludlow, *Washington Correspondent*, pp. 400–401.

[8]After Ludlow became president of the club (when its elected officer moved from Washington), he became less "reticent and retiring," took speech lessons, and turned toward congressional politics (Homer Dodge, "Louis Ludlow Developed Statesman's Technique as Head of Press Club," *Goldfish Bowl* [National Press Club, Washington, D.C., n.d., reprinted in *Cong. Rec.*, 78th Cong., 2d sess., A725–26 (Feb. 15, 1944)]; interview, Mrs. Herbert Pillen, Ludlow's secretary for twenty years, Washington, D.C., July, 1965; "Changing His Estate," editorial, *New York Times*, Nov. 13, 1928).

Confident of a decade of progress toward peace, the Indiana Democrat praised the decline of the rule of force and the appearance of the Kellogg-Briand Pact, disarmament in naval categories, and the continuing influence of William Jennings Bryan. "Highly armed nations, like individuals who pose as walking arsenals," Ludlow wrote, "are not likely to keep the peace."[9] He did not immediately, however, initiate his own efforts in America's interwar search for peace or provide leadership for the war referendum plan.

Ludlow often credited James A. Frear of Wisconsin with leadership of the drive before he took over. When Frear retired from Congress in 1934, Ludlow requested literature and speeches on the subject and asked if he might continue the "great cause," one which he thought "should not be allowed to lapse."[10] It was with Frear's blessings that Ludlow introduced his first war referendum and anti–war-profits resolution January 14, 1935. It proposed a constitutional amendment which provided:

SEC. 1. Except in the event of attack or invasion the authority of Congress to declare war shall not become effective until confirmed by a majority of all votes cast thereon in a Nation-wide referendum.

SEC. 2. Whenever war is declared the President shall immediately conscript and take for use by the Government all the public and private war properties, yards, factories, and supplies, together with employees necessary for their operation, fixing the compensation for private properties temporarily employed for the war period at a rate not in excess of 4 percent based on tax values assessed in the year preceding the war.[11]

A more immediate influence upon Ludlow's philosophy of foreign affairs, however, was the Senate Munitions Investigation headed by North Dakota Senator Gerald P. Nye. Earlier sponsors of war referendum resolutions, including Frear and Nye, had included anti–war-profits clauses in their war referendum bills. Yet, as Ludlow later put it, attention on the Nye hearings had left the war referendum proposal "a defunct baby" needing "the breath of life."[12] Although few writers, as a result, have related the origins of the Ludlow Amendment to the Nye

[9]"Ludlow's Scrapbooks," VI, 1004–5, III, 369, Ludlow Papers.

[10]Ludlow to Frank B. Kellogg, May 23, 1935, Ludlow Papers; Ludlow to Frear, Nov. 20, 1934, in Frear, *Progressive Public Service,* pp. 122–23.

[11]*Cong. Rec.,* 74th Cong., 1st sess., p. 430 (Jan. 14, 1935), and p. 514 (Jan. 16, 1935). Supporting correspondence is in File on House Joint Resolution 89, 74th Cong., 1st sess., Accompanying Papers Files, Judiciary Committee, RG 233, NA.

[12]U.S., Congress, Senate, 76th Cong., 1st sess., *War Referendum:* Hearings before a Subcommittee of the Committee on the Judiciary . . . May 10, 11, 12, 17, 18, 19, 24, and 31, 1939, p. 105. Nye endorsed the war referendum idea in 1925 and introduced his first war referendum bill before the munitions investigation.

investigation, the committee's conclusions certainly prompted the renewed enthusiasm of Louis Ludlow for the war referendum.[13] Along with his long-standing disapproval of American intervention in World War I, the Nye investigation, which further questioned that decision, was the most important influence upon Ludlow's thinking about foreign affairs and his actions on behalf of the war referendum in 1935.

Ludlow presented his 1935 resolution, in his words, "to save civilization from the munitions manufacturers" and called upon the people "to crystallize" the Senate findings by securing the war referendum to the Constitution, along with its anti–war-profits clause. In his request for presidential support, Ludlow cited the "constant danger of the United States being forced into war by the rapacity and greed of the munitions makers." He wrote Senator Nye in 1935, praising his committee's exposure of the munitions makers' activities. The next year he directly requested Senator Nye's support.[14] In an article published in *World Affairs* and radio addresses on the two major networks, Ludlow further revealed economic motives for the resolution.[15] The first two years of his efforts, in fact, saw an equal emphasis upon the anti–war-profits clause as well as extensive use of Nye Committee testimony in his speeches and correspondence.

Ludlow's effort in 1935 consisted chiefly of a personal letter campaign, first with President Franklin D. Roosevelt and the State Department. Although he may have met with Assistant Secretary of State R. Walton Moore, a meeting with Roosevelt apparently did not occur. He urged his proposed constitutional amendment upon the president as a "fitting capsheaf to [his] great program of social benefits" and in "the interest of jus-

[13]For example, see Harold H. Sprout, "Ludlow Resolution," in James Truslow Adams, ed., *Dictionary of American History* (New York, 1940), III, 313; Stephen and Joan Raushenbush, *The Final Choice: America between Europe and Asia* (New York, 1937), and *War Madness* (Washington, D.C., 1937), pp. 174–76; and Cole, *Nye,* pp. 120–21. John E. Wiltz, *In Search of Peace,* does not even mention the war referendum proposals of the period.

[14]*Cong. Rec.,* 74th Cong., 1st sess., p. 430 (Jan. 14, 1935), p. 514 (Jan. 16, 1935); public letter from Ludlow, Mar. 8, 1935, in "War Referendum Scrapbooks," 8 vols., 1935–48, I, 40–41, Ludlow Papers; Ludlow to Roosevelt, Jan. 21, 1935, President's Personal File 2007, "Louis Ludlow" (hereafter cited as PPF 2007), Franklin D. Roosevelt Library, Hyde Park, N.Y.; Ludlow to Nye, Feb. 2, 1935, and July 1, 1936, Ludlow Papers. Senator Nye in 1934, 1937, and 1941 sponsored war referendum resolutions but never became otherwise attached to the Ludlow campaign.

[15]Ludlow, "To End the Profits in Wars," *World Affairs,* 98 (1935), 36–42; press release for radio address, CBS, May 4, 1935, "War Referendum Scrapbooks," I, 14, Ludlow Papers; *Cong. Rec.,* 74th Cong., 1st sess., pp. 3763–64 (Mar. 15, 1935), reporting his Mar. 12 NBC radio address.

tice."[16] Ludlow received support for his resolution from former Secretary of State Frank B. Kellogg and an offer of assistance in securing international agreement to the war referendum idea from Salmon O. Levinson, Chicago lawyer and father of the outlawry-of-war idea. Realizing the need of organized publicity and monetary support, Ludlow unsuccessfully solicited the help of Henry Ford. Ludlow's extensive 1935 correspondence, containing many letters which he typed himself, was his primary method of publicizing his war referendum resolution.[17]

By June such untiring personal labor, illustrated by his two-month correspondence with Judiciary Committee Chairman Hatton Sumners, resulted in hearings before a subcommittee of the House Judiciary Committee. On June 19, 1935, a three-hour hearing featured the testimony of Ludlow and other supporters but gave little impetus to the campaign except as it encouraged Ludlow.[18] He later readily acknowledged the popular sentiment behind his proposal but admitted that it was "an unorganized sentiment" and that he lacked the means and opportunity to build an effective organization. When the Committee on the Judiciary took no action on the bill before adjournment of the first session of the Seventy-fourth Congress, Ludlow's war referendum correspondence nevertheless continued. After introduction, February 26, 1936, of a discharge petition early in the second session, the congressman's letter-writing campaign increased further as the effort became for him "a fight for humanity."[19]

The 1935 hearing revealed early but limited public support from the peace movement. Dorothy Detzer, executive secretary, and her Women's International League for Peace and Freedom had supported Ludlow even before the hearing. Frederick J. Libby's National Council for Prevention of War began to report on Ludlow's activities and to consider support of

[16]Ludlow to Roosevelt, Jan. 21, 1935, and Louis McH. Howe to Ludlow, Jan. 24, 1935, PPF 2007, Roosevelt Papers; Ludlow to Moore, May 12, 1935, Moore to Ludlow, May 13, 1935, Ludlow Papers. There is no reference to the Ludlow proposal in the R. Walton Moore Papers, Franklin D. Roosevelt Library, Hyde Park, N.Y.

[17]Kellogg to Ludlow, May 21, 1935, Ludlow to Kellogg, May 23, 1935, Levinson to Ludlow, Apr. 17, 1935, and Ludlow to Ford, May 18, 1935, Ludlow Papers. Ludlow's correspondence for 1935 fills 20 folders in eight boxes. See also "Petitions Protesting Military Preparedness," 74th Cong., 1st sess., Committee on the Judiciary, RG 233, NA.

[18]See House Joint Resolution 167, 74th Cong., 1st sess., Accompanying Papers Files, Judiciary Committee, RG 233, NA; and U.S., Congress, House, 74th Cong., 1st sess., *Hearing before subcommittee No. 2 of the Committee on the Judiciary, on H.J. Resolution 167,* . . . June 19, 1935, which reprints much of his 1935 correspondence.

[19]Ludlow to Harry N. Jones (constituent), Mar. 13, 1936, Ludlow Papers; Ludlow's public letter, June 23, 1936, "War Referendum Scrapbooks," I, 115, Ludlow Papers. On the petition to discharge his bill, see *Cong. Rec.,* 74th Cong., 2d sess., pp. 2868–69 (Feb. 26, 1936), pp. 4507–8 (Mar. 27, 1936).

his resolution in its journal, *Peace Action.* The Indiana World Peace Committee and the consensus-minded Emergency Peace Campaign were other peace organizations actively interested in 1935. In Chicago the Fellowship of Reconciliation heard retired Marine General Smedley Butler blast bankers and munitions makers in his plea for support of the Ludlow proposal. Consistently denying that the war referendum proposal was a pacifist measure, Ludlow nevertheless welcomed and cultivated support from the organized peace movement.[20]

The brief hearings also marked the beginning of interest by educators and organized labor, culminating in consideration of the measure by the United Mine Workers and John L. Lewis in the summer of 1936. In May 1936 Ludlow's efforts received the support of William F. Bigelow, editor of William Randolph Hearst's popular *Good Housekeeping* magazine.[21] The appeal to women, always emotional, whether in the peace movement or not, proved most effective. Bigelow's conversion to the cause, therefore, was an important turning point for Ludlow, providing publicity and other influence.

Early changes in the war referendum resolution, for example, resulted from Ludlow's correspondence with numerous individuals, including Bigelow. In 1935 he deleted the provision that employees be conscripted to operate public and private war properties, though retaining the major portion of the anti–war-profits section. He wrote Senator Nye that the provision might be antagonistic, a reaction noted in earlier correspondence with leaders of the Indiana Council on International Relations and the Women's International League for Peace and Freedom. Ludlow sought Bigelow's advice in 1936 concerning a plan to split the war referendum and anti–war-profits clauses. Alanson B. Houghton, former United States ambassador to Germany and Great Britain and himself a war referendum advocate in the 1920s, also favored dropping the clause, as had Salmon O. Levinson. Bigelow, furthermore, encouraged Ludlow to seek Senate support for a similar bill and suggested that the congressman

[20]*Hearing, 1935,* p. 42; James P. Mullin of the Emergency Peace Campaign to Ludlow, Apr. 19, July 15, 1936, Ludlow Papers; *Peace Action,* 1 (Mar. 1935), 5; ibid., 1 (June 1935), 12; ibid., 2 (July 1935), 8; ibid., 2 (Nov. 1935), 14; *Peace Digest* (Van Nuys, Calif.), 4 (Summer 1935), 9–10. Interest shown by the Emergency Peace Campaign, a coalition of peace groups, was significant since, as Chatfield maintains, "Never had the peace movement been so united or so closely in touch with the people as it was during the Emergency Peace Campaign" (*For Peace and Justice,* p. 271).

[21]*Hearing, 1935,* pp. 61–106; Lewis to Ludlow, Sept. 10, 1936, "War Referendum Scrapbooks," I, 120B, Ludlow Papers; William F. Bigelow, "A Peace Amendment," *Good Housekeeping,* May 1936, p. 4, and "Mine Eyes Have Seen the Glory," ibid., June 1936, p. 4.

ascertain President Roosevelt's feeling on the proposed constitutional amendment. The editor conferred on his own with his magazine's owner, William Randolph Hearst, concerning the proper senator to approach for assistance.[22] Although Ludlow and Bigelow apparently never met personally during the entire war referendum campaign, their extensive correspondence indicates close collaboration on the measure.

Bigelow's direct influence was evident in late December 1936, when Ludlow sent a memorandum to the president requesting an interview for discussion of the war referendum plan. Citing Roosevelt's own 1933 remarks as the "text" of his communication, that "war by governments" must be changed to "peace by peoples," Ludlow urged careful consideration of the war referendum in advance of the annual message and preparation of the next session's legislative program. Ludlow cited popular support for the war referendum measure, requested Roosevelt's endorsement "to complete the democratic processes by democratizing the war power," and commented on its impact upon national defense. As he saw it, "Such a referendum would interfere in no way with adequate national defense. It has no reference to the size of the Army and Navy but only to the method of declaring war. I am personally a believer in strong national defense." Roosevelt thanked Ludlow for his "interesting" letter, but no meeting of the two men occurred.[23]

When the second session of the Seventy-fourth Congress adjourned in the summer of 1936, only seventy-two members of the House of Representatives had signed the discharge petition to force the Ludlow proposal out of committee. Yet this "fine nucleus of fighting support," as he called the group, encouraged Ludlow, whose reelection in 1936 also turned in part on the war referendum issue. Realizing that his proposal lacked wide popular interest and aware that domestic New Deal legislation still commanded the attention of the Congress and public, Ludlow spent much of the year preparing his major vehicle for war referendum publicity. His book *Hell or Heaven* appeared early in 1937. Relying heavily upon the Nye Committee's recent revelations, as well as his own progressive-type "conspiracy concepts," Ludlow insisted that economic

[22]Ludlow to Nye, Feb. 9, 1935, Ludlow to E. J. Unruh, Feb. 6, 1935, Ludlow to Dorothy Detzer, May 20, 1935, Ludlow Papers; *Hearing, 1935,* p. 42; Ludlow to Bigelow, Apr. 9, Nov. 16, Dec. 12, 1936, Bigelow to Ludlow, Nov. 20, Dec. 7, 1936, Ludlow Papers; Houghton to Ludlow, Sept. 15, 1936, and Levinson to Ludlow, Apr. 17, 1935, ibid.

[23]Ludlow to Roosevelt, Dec. 21, 1936, "War Referendum Scrapbooks," I, 129–30, Ludlow Papers, and Official File 274, "Constitution of the United States" (hereafter cited as OF 274), Roosevelt Papers; Roosevelt to Ludlow, Dec. 29, 1936, ibid.; and Bigelow to Ludlow, Jan. 7, 1937, Official File 3084, "War Referendum" (hereafter cited as OF 3084), Roosevelt Papers.

influences were "continually dragging nations into wars." Yet he consistently stressed that his referendum plan did not restrict the building of a "strong and adequate national defense."[24] His defense concept, which sought to limit rather than to deny totally the use of force in diplomacy, appeared more and more in connection with his advocacy of the war referendum.

By the opening of the Seventy-fifth Congress early in 1937, Ludlow had decided to drop the anti-war-profits clause from his resolution, introduced again February 5. William F. Bigelow was again chiefly responsible, believing this proposal less valuable than the war referendum and more technical and debatable. On the twentieth anniversary of the 1917 war declaration, April 6, 1937, Ludlow added to his campaign arsenal a new discharge petition, beginning for the second time an effort to secure 218 signatures necessary to force the bill out of the Judiciary Committee. Testimony to Ludlow's personal success and to rising popular approval of the measure were the names of 120 members of the House who signed the petition in less than two months.[25]

In that time, Ludlow drew the aid of pacifist Frederick J. Libby, head of the National Council for Prevention of War (NCPW), Harold Knutson (Republican, Minn.), who on his own initiative wrote all Republican members for petition signatures, and former war referendum sponsor Hamilton Fish, ranking New York Republican on the House Foreign Affairs Committee. The Libby organization became the center of a vast peace literature and educational effort for Ludlow's proposal through its lobbying activities in Washington and its widely circulated monthly bulletin, *Peace Action.* One typical NCPW press release, noting publisher Frank E. Gannett's support of the war referendum, went to

[24]*Cong. Rec.,* 74th Cong., 2d sess., p. 10755 (June 20, 1936); *New York Times,* Nov. 29, 1936; "War Referendum Scrapbooks," I, 137–47, Ludlow Papers; "Ludlow's Scrapbooks," XXIV, 3754–60, ibid.; Ludlow, *Hell or Heaven* (Boston, 1937), pp. ii, 4, 18–30, 58–71, 133, 138. Publication of Ludlow's book was aided by the National Council for Prevention of War, according to Chatfield, *For Peace and Justice,* p. 283.

[25]Ludlow to Bigelow, Feb. 17, 1937, and Bigelow to Ludlow, Feb. 19, 1937, Ludlow Papers; *Cong. Rec.,* 75th Cong., 1st sess., p. 947 (Feb. 5, 1937), p. 3198 (Apr. 6, 1937); *New York Times,* Apr. 7, 1937; form letter, Ludlow to Members of the House, Apr. 6, June 7, 1936, "War Referendum Scrapbooks," II, 167, 200–201, Ludlow Papers; Ludlow had the assistance of the National Council's Jesse MacKnight and Stephen Raushenbush in the discharge petition effort (Chatfield, *For Peace and Justice,* p. 283). See also Ludlow's radio address, CBS June 9, 1937, in *Cong. Rec.,* 75th Cong., 1st sess., Appendix, pp. 1401–4 (June 9, 1937). Ludlow found the South apathetic, with no signers "from Virginia, the Carolinas, Georgia, and Florida" (Ludlow to Bigelow, July 24, 1937, Ludlow Papers).

"400 country weeklies" and "200 labor" papers.[26] Ludlow also used the radio to publicize his proposal, and Oswald Garrison Villard of the *Nation* furnished valuable support in articles, speeches through the Emergency Peace Campaign, and in a personal letter campaign to members of Congress in the spring of 1937.[27]

Despite the encouraging progress of the discharge petition and the war referendum campaign generally, Ludlow felt the need of greater publicity. William Randolph Hearst pledged his papers' support but never got them into action, and Ludlow later stated, in fact, that the most unfair criticism of his plan came from the Hearst papers. He had long held the support of the Indianapolis *Times* and other Indiana papers, but his proposal seldom had received attention by the *New York Times*.[28] Ludlow began to think, therefore, of organizing a national coordinating body to direct his campaign.[29]

Ludlow also took advantage of a crisis atmosphere created by Japan's undeclared war against China in the summer of 1937. As American neutrality policies came under closer congressional scrutiny, rising support for the war referendum became apparent. Taking hope from increased public interest and the 185 signatures acquired on the discharge petition, Ludlow believed by the end of the 1937 session of Congress that his resolution would eventually "make democracy a fact as well as a theory."[30] Impetus to the campaign resulted also from endorsement of the proposal by the Young Democrats of America, presided over at its Indianapolis convention by President Roosevelt's son, James. Factions of the American Legion convention in New York, as well as a few separate Le-

[26] Ludlow to Fish, July 2, 1937, Ludlow Papers; "War Referendum Scrapbooks," II, 210B, 214–14B, ibid.; by June 1937 a booklet—*The Ludlow Referendum*—by associate editor Florence Brewer Boeckel was available. See also Libby to Ludlow, Apr. 2, 1937, and Jesse M. MacKnight to Ludlow, June 5, 1937, Ludlow Papers; *Peace Action,* 3 (Feb. 1937), 7, 8; ibid., 3 (Apr. 1937), 3–4 and one-page supplement; ibid., 3 (May 1937), 2–3; ibid., 3 (June 1937), 3, 8.

[27] *Nation,* 143 (1936), 335; Villard to Ludlow, Apr. 12, 18, 29, 1937, Ludlow Papers. Ludlow received responses to Villard's letters as well as copies of several Villard letters to congressmen (Villard to Walter M. Pierce, Apr. 4, 1937, ibid.).

[28] Ludlow to Hearst, May 19, June 4, 1937; Hearst to Ludlow, June 3, 1937; Ludlow to Bigelow, July 24 and Dec. 16, 1937, Ludlow Papers. Also *Hearing, 1935,* p. 100; and J. K. Winkler, *W. R. Hearst* (New York, 1928), p. 277.

[29] Ludlow to Bigelow, May 26, 1937, Ludlow Papers. Correspondence in September and October especially dealt with this. See Ludlow to Maury Maverick, Sept. 16, 1937, ibid., on Ludlow's search for southern support.

[30] *Cong. Rec.,* 75th Cong., 1st sess., pp. 7709–11 (July 27, 1937) and Appendix, p. 2334 (Aug. 21, 1937).

gion posts, also supported the Ludlow Amendment before the fall of 1937.[31]

The undeclared war between Japan and China produced hundreds of letters to the president in favor of neutrality and withdrawal from China of American nationals and naval forces. The isolationist press, which also urged withdrawal of troops, and peace organizations became alarmed over the possibility of American involvement. The Women's International League for Peace and Freedom deplored "a single soldier or marine or war vessel" on Chinese soil or waters. In a letter to the president, Ludlow praised Roosevelt's earliest public statements, especially his warning to Americans remaining in Chinese danger zones, and reported that his own mail was in support of the president. Surprisingly, the Hoosier congressman made no reference to his war referendum plan; rather, he urged that 7,780 American nationals in China not be allowed to jeopardize peace for 130 million Americans. Roosevelt's reply, which was noncommittal and prepared in the State Department, indicated the administration's continuing respect for isolationist sentiment such as Ludlow represented.[32]

After Roosevelt's October 5, 1937, Chicago Quarantine Speech, in which the president asked peace-loving nations to "quarantine" aggressor nations, differences between Ludlow and Roosevelt became more apparent and the president's truce with the isolationists ended. Ludlow's immediate reaction to the speech was to urge invocation of the 1937 Neutrality Act and to press harder toward formation of a national organization to direct the war referendum campaign.[33] Stephen Raushenbush,

[31]*Cong. Rec.,* 75th Cong., 3d sess., p. 5281 (Apr. 11, 1938) and Appendix, p. 2347 (Aug. 21, 1937).

[32]World Peaceways, the Women's International League for Peace and Freedom, the National Council for Prevention of War, Fellowship of Reconciliation, and the Committee on Militarism in Education joined in a telegram to Roosevelt, Sept. 8, 1937, expressing opposition to involvement in China and to "waging undeclared wars." See also Hannah Clothier Hull to Roosevelt, Aug. 20, 1937; Charles A. Beard to Roosevelt, Aug. 18, 1937; Ludlow to Roosevelt, Sept. 11, 1937; Roosevelt to Ludlow, Sept. 16, 1937; and Cordell Hull to Roosevelt, Sept. 16, 1937, Official File 150–C, "China–Chinese-Japanese War," Box 5 (1937), Roosevelt Papers.

[33]"War Referendum Scrapbooks," II, 238, Ludlow Papers, and *New York Times,* Oct. 11, 1937. Active work to organize the national committee began in September "under the auspices of Congressman Louis Ludlow" and not the National Council for Prevention of War, as Chatfield suggests. See press release, National Council for Prevention of War, Nov. 27, 1937, National Committee for the War Referendum Papers, SCPC; Ludlow to John R. Mackie (Berkeley, Calif.), Sept. 29, 1938, Ludlow Papers; and Chatfield, *For Peace and Justice,* pp. 283–84. William Allen White served on the committee but declined the honorary chairmanship due to age and illness; Ludlow then turned to retired Army General William

former head counsel of the Nye Committee and now chosen by Ludlow to direct the National Committee for the War Referendum, first acted to coordinate the congressional petition campaign with the existing publicity efforts of the National Council for Prevention of War. When Roosevelt on October 12 called a special session of Congress to meet on November 15, 1937, to deal with the sudden economic recession, Raushenbush and Ludlow received an unexpected advantage. It appeared they now might force a debate on the war referendum resolution sooner than planned. Although Senator Harry Truman publicly disapproved of the measure, Senators Robert M. La Follette, Jr., Bennett Clark, and Arthur Capper introduced separate resolutions proposing either a war or conscription referendum. Furthermore, a poll by the American Institute of Public Opinion revealed that 73 percent of those polled were in favor of the Ludlow war referendum resolution.[34] By the end of November 1937, with 194 signatures on the discharge petition and discussion of the proposal on the floor of the House a definite possibility, the war referendum plan required one-third of the work of Ludlow's congressional office.[35]

At this point an unforeseen crisis in the Far East intervened, offering opponents of the measure a solid foundation for their attack and presenting Ludlow with an insoluble dilemma. An unexpected result of the Japanese attack on the American gunboat *Panay,* December 12, was renewed interest in the war referendum and sudden completion of the discharge petition on December 14.[36] The administration, however, eager to defeat the measure quickly and without unnecessary publicity, dropped

---

C. Rivers (Ludlow to White, Sept. 18, 29, Oct. 5, and Nov. 20, 1937, Series C, Box 269, William Allen White Papers, LC). Also see White to Ludlow, Nov. 8, Ludlow to Rivers, Dec. 9, and Rivers to Ludlow, Dec. 11, 1937, Ludlow Papers. Ludlow reported 26 directors of the National Committee for the War Referendum in *Cong. Rec.*, 75th Cong., 2d sess., p. 244 (Nov. 22, 1937).

[34]*New York Times,* Oct. 13, 1937; *Peace Action,* 4 (Nov. 1937), 3–4; "War Referendum Scrapbooks," II, 245, 247–48, Ludlow Papers; *Cong. Rec.,* 75th Cong., 2d sess., p. 24 (Nov. 16, 1937), p. 61 (Nov. 17, 1937) and Appendix, p. 185 (Nov. 24, 1937); Homer E. Socolofsky, *Arthur Capper: Publisher, Politician, and Philanthropist* (Lawrence, Kan., 1962), p. 181; George Gallup and Saul Forbes Rae, *The Pulse of Democracy* (New York, 1940), p. 315.

[35]Ludlow revealed this figure in a CBS radio address, "Ballots before Bullets," Nov. 29, 1937 (*Cong. Rec.,* 75th Cong., 2d sess., Appendix, pp. 244–45, 255 [Nov. 30, 1937]; "War Referendum Scrapbooks," III, 308, Ludlow Papers).

[36]*Cong. Rec.,* 75th Cong., 2d sess., pp. 1517–18 (Dec. 14, 1937), and *New York Times,* Dec. 15, 1937. See also Manny T. Koginos, *The Panay Incident: Prelude to War* (Lafayette, Ind., 1967). Frederick J. Libby overstates his organization's role in taking credit for completion of the discharge petition (*To End War,* p. 146).

plans announced the day before to hold hearings on the proposal.[37] Judiciary committeeman Emanuel Celler, chairman of the subcommittee which had held the three-hour 1935 hearing on the war referendum, typified opposition at this time in a letter to Oswald Garrison Villard. When he stated that the proposal was "bound to embarrass and hamper President Roosevelt in the negotiations concerning the *Panay*," Celler adequately expressed the adverse impact of the crisis.[38] Judiciary Chairman Sumners, who obviously felt responsibility for not blocking discharge of the bill, echoed this sentiment. In unusually lengthy correspondence with Texas constituents, he expressed opposition to the war referendum idea generally and to the timing of the Ludlow measure especially.[39]

Ludlow, who now expected consideration of the discharge motion on the House floor early in the next session, accelerated the pace of his campaign. His persistence was remarkable. According to House rules, the merits of the war referendum amendment could not be debated at length until a favorable vote on his motion to discharge the committee from further consideration of the bill.[40] So Ludlow aimed all his efforts at that short preliminary debate on the discharge motion.

As he continued radio addresses and other publicity, the opposition developed rapidly. Walter Lippmann, who asserted that the proposal would "forbid the President to use diplomacy to prevent war," and Arthur Krock of the *New York Times,* who emphasized the paralyzing effect of the measure on national defense and executive initiative in foreign policy, were strong in their opposition and typical of the eastern press.[41] As yet, however, the administration did not "take the fight in behalf of the resolution seriously," distracted by the special session and the *Panay* crisis. Secretary of State Hull, in a press conference December 15,

---

[37] Failure to hold hearings did not upset Ludlow. In an earlier letter to Stephen Raushenbush, he had urged that they concentrate on the petition rather than work for hearings, which he considered a favorite device "to kill legislative proposals" (Ludlow to Raushenbush, Dec. 2, 1937, Ludlow Papers).

[38] Celler to Villard, Dec. 14, 1937, in *Cong. Rec.,* 75th Cong., 2nd sess., Appendix, pp. 494–95 (Dec. 15, 1937). Samuel B. Pettengill of Indiana favored a delay of the test vote following the *Panay* attack (*Cong. Rec.,* 75th Cong., 2d sess., p. 1847 [Dec. 18, 1937]).

[39] Letters are in House Joint Resolution 199, 75th Cong., 1st sess., Accompanying Papers Files, Judiciary Committee, RG 233, NA.

[40] *Cong. Rec.,* 75th Cong., 2d sess., pp. 1516–17 (Dec. 14, 1937). Most writers have reported, in error, that the 1938 vote was on the proposed constitutional amendment rather than the discharge motion.

[41] *New York Times,* Dec. 14, 16, 17, 1937. Cordell Hull sent a copy of Lippmann's article to a critic to indicate "two sides to the question" (Hull to Howard N. Bream, Dec. 20, 1937, Box 42, Folder 101, Cordell Hull Papers, LC).

merely opposed the Ludlow Amendment as a peace measure, unable to see its "wisdom or practicability." The president registered his first public opposition to the measure at a regular press conference December 17. Replying negatively to a question as to whether the referendum idea was consistent with representative government, Roosevelt's answer, according to the press, reflected definite opposition and dissatisfaction that the discharge petition was completed just as the *Panay* question came before the administration.[42]

More interested in reviving his earlier plan for a naval quarantine of Japan, however, the president began secret talks with British Ambassador Lindsay the night of December 16. Along with Secretary of State Hull, the two men discussed American public opinion, with Hull less certain of public support for any future joint American-British naval blockade of Japan. The next day, December 17, Roosevelt discussed with his cabinet his quarantine plan and executive powers "to prevent war" and engage in hostilities without a declaration of war.[43] In view of the recent progress of Ludlow's discharge petition and popular support for withdrawal from China, this discussion is all the more remarkable. The president, although leading an administration divided over policy and over how to read public opinion, was momentarily unconcerned about the Ludlow Amendment. He referred in the cabinet meeting to Italian and Japanese evolution of a "technique of fighting without declaring war," posing the question "Why can't we develop a similar one?" He continued: "We want to develop a technique which will not lead to war. We want to be as smart as Japan and as Italy. We want to do it a modern way."[44] The president obviously did not appreciate at this time, early in the *Panay* crisis, the full impact of the Ludlow proposal.

[42]*Congressional Digest,* 18 (Feb. 1938), 37; *New York Times,* Dec. 16, 18, 1937; Department of State, *Press Releases,* Jan. 15, 1938, p. 100. Before the *Panay* crisis and completion of Ludlow's discharge petition, when Congressman Hatton Sumners earlier had phoned the White House concerning whether the Ludlow Amendment should go to committee for hearings, the White House showed no interest and allowed Sumners to act on the matter without talking to Secretary Hull (White House Memorandums for Mr. [Marvin H.] McIntyre, Dec. 9, 1937, OF 274, Box 5, Roosevelt Papers). See also Sumners to Denys P. Myers, Dec. 9, 1937, House Joint Resolution 20, 75th Cong., 1st sess., Accompanying Papers Files, Judiciary Committee, RG 233, NA.

[43]John McVickar Haight, "Franklin D. Roosevelt and a Naval Quarantine of Japan," *Pacific Historical Review,* 40 (1971), 209-11.

[44]John Morton Blum, ed., *From the Morgenthau Diaries: Years of Crisis, 1928-1938* (Boston, 1959), p. 489; Anthony Eden, *The Memoirs of Anthony Eden: Facing the Dictators* (Boston, 1962), p. 616, cites a "strong isolationist lobby" which prevented an early Anglo-American response to the *Panay* crisis but does not identify it as behind the Ludlow proposal.

When the special session of Congress adjourned December 22, 1937, former Secretary of State Henry L. Stimson had actually made the most thorough and best-stated attack against the war referendum plan. In a letter to the *New York Times,* he labeled it as experimental, destructive of representative government, and later called it the "high point in the prewar self-deception of the American people."[45] William T. Stone and Raymond Leslie Buell of the Foreign Policy Association also suggested that the Ludlow Amendment was an important issue of national policy, regardless of the *Panay* attack. Stone saw it as the symbol of "instinctive popular distrust of power-politics diplomacy." It was to Buell the final ingredient of the policy of "New Isolationists," the policy of insulation from "other people's wars." Stone believed that the January vote would be a test of how President Roosevelt could hope to carry Congress in the direction of internationalism.[46] When the National Committee for the War Referendum approached Denys P. Myers to support the proposal, he wrote Sumners concerning what he called the "latest form of legislative racketeering." Research Librarian of the Fletcher School of Law and Diplomacy and Director of Research, World Peace Foundation, he charged that Ludlow was appealing to emotions and attempting to create an "artificial public voice."[47]

It was a representative of the peace forces who actually pressed for stronger administration opposition to Ludlow. Clark Eichelberger, who was National Director of the League of Nations Association, a peace group of world cooperationists, appealed for a week that the State Department counter isolationist radio addresses. He suggested speakers, offered to help prepare addresses himself, and discussed tactics with Norman H. Davis following Hamilton Fish's radio speech December 21. Since Fish had referred to the president as "a dictator who was conducting foreign affairs without any notice or consultation with Congress," Eichelberger pressed Hull further and even furnished the State Department with the draft of a speech. After review by five State Department officials, Hull finally joined in approval, and the speech was delivered December 28 by House Foreign Affairs Committee Chairman Samuel D.

[45]*New York Times,* Dec. 22, 1937; Henry L. Stimson and McGeorge Bundy, *On Active Service in Peace and War* (New York, 1947), pp. 303, 307, 313. Other bipartisan opposition included that of former Republican presidential candidate Alf Landon and his running mate in 1936, Frank Knox (*New York Times,* Dec. 22, 23, 1937).

[46]*Foreign Policy Bulletin,* 17 (Dec. 10, 1937), 3; ibid. (Dec. 24, 1937), 2–4; Buell, "The Failure of Isolation," *Nation,* 145 (1937), 709–10; Buell, *Isolated America* (New York, 1940), pp. 66–68.

[47]Myers to Sumners, Dec. 6, 1937, File on House Joint Resolution 20, 75th Cong., 1st sess., Accompanying Papers Files, Judiciary Committee, RG 233, NA.

McReynolds. In this way the internationalist viewpoint was encouraged. The fact that the speech was "prepared in the State Department" was to be kept confidential, and in a tactic which became typical, Eichelberger and the others failed to note that the Ludlow Amendment would not apply in case of attack.[48]

Such activity as this, led by international cooperationists within the peace movement, was designed to calm fears but actually helped make the Ludlow Amendment a divisive issue in the recently successful coalition efforts of pacifists and nonpacifists. Eichelberger and Frederick Libby were both on the steering committee of the National Peace Conference but divided on the Ludlow Amendment.[49] Although the consensus-minded Emergency Peace Campaign endorsed the measure, many of its member peace organizations and leaders opposed it. But Clark Eichelberger's opposition initiative was most important. By mid-December he had created within the 1935–37 neutralist coalition of pacifists and peace advocates a Committee for Concerted Peace Efforts. This new group, which included, among others, his own League of Nations Association and the National Committee on the Cause and Cure of War, sought to counteract demands for strict neutrality and to support international cooperation against aggressors.[50] On the Ludlow Amendment issue, his efforts served to awaken the administration to the dangers of the measure.

Ludlow had remained in Washington during the Christmas recess, working for consideration of the proposed war referendum amendment on its own merit, chiefly through the newly formed National Committee for the War Referendum and the technique of the penny petition. He was gratified by support from the National Council for Prevention of War, World Peaceways, the Fellowship of Reconciliation, the Emergency Peace Campaign, and the Women's International League for Peace and Freedom.[51] But Ludlow was unable to remove the war referendum plan from its crisis setting. Since 1935 he had stressed it as a means for more democratic control of foreign policy. Now he reaffirmed that it was

[48] Memorandums for the Secretary, Dec. 15, 16, 17, 21, 22, with Press Release, Committee for Concerted Peace Efforts, Dec. 15, 1937, attached, Box 42, Folder 101, Cordell Hull Papers. See also Hugh R. Wilson to Hull, Dec. 27, 1937; and Memorandum to Sumner Welles, Dec. 28, 1937 (with copy of McReynolds's speech attached), ibid.

[49] Chatfield, *For Peace and Justice,* p. 112.

[50] Ibid., p. 284.

[51] The committee believed that passage of the Ludlow Amendment in the coming session would provide ratification by early 1939 (Press Release, National Committee for the War Referendum, Dec. 22, 1937, OF 3084, Roosevelt Papers, and "War Referendum Scrapbooks," IV, 452A, Ludlow Papers). See also *New York Times,* Dec. 23, 26, 1937.

offered in good faith well before the current international threat to the peace, but he and his supporters were forced into a defensive position.[52] Supporting peace organizations sought to challenge opposition arguments that the measure was "not in accord with representative government" by pointing to the 1924 Democratic party platform, which endorsed international agreement to the war referendum plan.[53] It was impossible, however, to disassociate the Ludlow Amendment from the *Panay* crisis, especially as films of the attack arrived in the country and were shown to large theater audiences.

Neither the opposition nor Ludlow himself fully realized at the time that the debate on the war referendum also turned on different defense concepts. The Ludlow Amendment was never a matter of isolationism at any price for many of its supporters and especially for Ludlow. Liberal isolationists who favored a limited defense—use of military power for national self-defense only—supported Ludlow. Like him, they desired to limit the military establishment to a level adequate to defense of the homeland. Before the *Panay* crisis, Ludlow wrote: "If we are wise we will keep up our defenses but will stay at home and attend to our own business and keep out of foreign entanglements." Later an interview in the *Indianapolis Star* quoted Ludlow: "I shall vote for a navy that would cause warring nations to think twice before attacking us, but I regret it like the dickens that other nations force us to do it."[54]

Other representatives of the limited-defense concept included retired General Smedley D. Butler, who supported the Ludlow Amendment as a member of the National Committee for the War Referendum and in speeches advocating withdrawal of American military forces from areas outside the continental United States. Early in 1937 retired Major-General Johnson Hagood had argued that America should stay at home behind its "natural fortress" and keep out of foreign entanglements.[55]

[52]*New York Times,* Dec. 29, 1937. California Congressman Jerry Voorhis wrote Assistant Secretary of State Francis B. Sayre to criticize the "tremendous drive" being made to defeat the measure and to explain that he supported it before the hostilities in China as "democratic and just." Sayre's response denied *any* State Department opposition activity since Hull's earlier statement (Voorhis to Sayre, Dec. 24, 1937, and Sayre to Voorhis, Dec. 28, 1937, Decimal File [DF] 711.0011 War Referendum/1, Records of the Department of State, Record Group 59, NA).

[53]Press Release, joint peace organizations, Dec. 30, 1937, "War Referendum," Vertical File, SCPC.

[54]Ludlow to H. A. Dinius (constituent), Oct. 14, 1937, Ludlow Papers; *Indianapolis Star,* Jan. 9, 1938, in "War Referendum Scrapbooks," IV, 576, Ludlow Papers.

[55]*Peace Digest,* 4, No. 2 (1935), 9–10; Quincy Howe, *England Expects Every American to Do His Duty* (New York, 1937), pp. 205–7; Hagood, *We Can Defend America* (New York, 1937), reviewed in *Saturday Review of Literature,* Jan. 30, 1937, pp. 10–11.

Ludlow's attempt to insulate America from foreign wars through the war referendum, therefore, expressed a popular American attitude in the 1930s. As Hagood colorfully stated it in 1936 and 1937, many Americans believed in America's impregnability and sought to erect a "hog-proof fence around America."[56]

Support for the proposed constitutional amendment in early January 1938 continued in radio addresses, *Good Housekeeping,* and among peace organizations. General Butler, who had just concluded a speaking tour of states in the Northeast, Middle Atlantic, and Far West, believed that the Ludlow resolution was "the most popular piece of legislation before Congress."[57] At the same time, opposition of the administration came alive. As the day for the test vote, January 10, approached, the administration finally began to bring its total force against the measure. For example, Assistant Secretary of War Louis Johnson spoke, at Roosevelt's direction, against the war referendum plan before businessmen in Los Angeles.[58]

Ludlow and proponents of the amendment in Congress also worked early in January on minor revisions of the Ludlow bill. The third session of the Seventy-fifth Congress was only three days old when Hamilton Fish informed the House of some intended revisions. Operation of the proposed war referendum would not occur in case of attack by any non-American nation in the Western Hemisphere, a change made necessary, Fish explained, by the Monroe Doctrine and certain treaties guaranteeing United States support in Latin America against foreign invasions. Fish announced another contemplated change making the referendum inoperative in case of attack upon American ships on the high seas. Al-

[56]*New York Times Book Review,* Jan. 31, 1937, p. 6.

[57]Radio addresses were by Democratic Congressmen Herman P. Kopplemann (Conn.) and Herbert S. Bigelow (Ohio) (*Cong. Rec.,* 75th Cong., 3d sess., Appendix, p. 25 [Jan. 5, 1938], pp. 86–87 [Jan. 10, 1938]). See also Mary Roberts Rinehart, "Before the Drums Beat," *Good Housekeeping,* Jan. 1938, pp. 24–25, 158–59; *Peace Action,* 4 (Jan. 1938), 1, 3–4, 8; *Christian Science Monitor,* Weekly Magazine Section, Jan. 5, 1938, pp. 1–2, for a debate-article by Ludlow and David J. Lewis (Democrat, Md.), the latter an early opposition spokesman for the administration; and *Cong. Rec.,* 75th Cong., 2d sess., p. 250 (Nov. 22, 1937). For reports of Butler's tour, see National Council for Prevention of War, press release, Jan. 1, 1938, "War Referendum," Vertical File, SCPC.

[58]Johnson's two California speeches, Jan. 5, are reported in "War Referendum Scrapbooks," IV, 549–51, Ludlow Papers; *Cong. Rec.,* 75th Cong., 3d sess., Appendix, pp. 126–28 (Jan. 17, 1938). Ludlow charged in 1948 that Roosevelt had sent Johnson on the tour purposely to block the war referendum (ibid., 80th Cong., 2d sess., p. A4853 [Aug. 4, 1948]) and later Hull referred to Johnson's Los Angeles University Club address as a key source of administration opposition (Hull to Senator Carl Hayden, Jan. 26, 1938, DF 711.0011 War Referendum/14, RG 59, NA).

though Ludlow favored a delay of the test vote in the belief that additional support would result, a caucus of about sixty of the signers of the discharge petition agreed not to postpone the vote scheduled for Monday, January 10. The revisions Fish had announced the previous day were approved, thus "enlarging" Ludlow's underlying "homeland" defense perimeter to include the hemisphere. These revisions, according to the *New York Times,* gave Ludlow's forces a fighting chance on the eve of the showdown vote.[59]

In the House on January 7 a brief debate on the proposal placed Jerry Voorhis (Democrat, Calif.), Everett Dirksen (Republican, Ill.), and Pete Jarman (Democrat, Ala.) in defense of the measure and Rules Committee Chairman John O'Conner (Democrat, N.Y.) in opposition. Jarman insisted that "neither the Far Eastern situation in general nor the sinking of the *Panay* in particular" had influenced a majority of the signers of the petition. Yet he reported a conversation with an embassy attaché who believed the petition was "filed" soon after the *Panay* attack rather than April 6, 1937! During this debate Judiciary Committee Chairman Hatton W. Sumners (Democrat, Tex.) typically expressed the feelings of many who respected Ludlow's hard work but opposed the bill. Not sure of how to attack, Sumners simply stated: "We all love Louis Ludlow. He is wrong this time."[60]

Others believed Ludlow right. Frank P. Graham, president of the University of North Carolina, endorsed the war referendum with its recent modifications. He believed that American acceptance of the proposal would challenge other nations and that participation of the people in war-and-peace decisions would "be a step toward the development of a league of peoples in behalf of peaceful international cooperation and collective security."[61] This indicated that Clark Eichelberger had not yet won all such peace advocates away from Ludlow. The National Committee for the War Referendum made its last prevote appeal at this point. Chairman Rivers defended the plan against charges of interference with national defense and the State Department. The committee also released a letter supporting the war referendum plan from Senator Robert M. La Follette, Jr., who especially appealed for House and Senate debate, "at

[59]*Cong. Rec.,* 75th Cong., 3d sess., p. 122 (Jan. 6, 1938), p. 196 (Jan. 7, 1938); *New York Times,* Jan. 8, 1938.

[60]*Cong. Rec.,* 75th Cong., 3d sess., pp. 163–65, 188–89, 192–96, 200 (Jan. 7, 1938) and Appendix, p. 9 (Jan. 4, 1938); *New York Times,* Jan. 8, 1938. "The Ludlow Amendment," *Christian Century,* Jan. 5, 1938, offers a good analysis and opposition statement ("War Referendum," Vertical File, SCPC).

[61]Press Release, Jan. 8, 1938, National Committee for the War Referendum Papers, SCPC. For support by 200,000 teachers in the National Education Association and 30,000 teachers in the American Federation of Teachers, see press release, Jan. 7, ibid.

length, for weeks, for months, if necessary." La Follette believed that an adverse vote on the discharge motion coming before the House January 10 would be, in effect, a "gag rule."[62]

As Congress recessed for the weekend, administration opposition intensified. Speaker Bankhead held an afternoon press conference and mentioned but did not elaborate on opposition by Hull and Roosevelt. He probably had Roosevelt's letter, drafted by Undersecretary Sumner Welles, January 6, which he later used in the debate of January 10. Bankhead also charged that there were alien influences behind the Ludlow Amendment, illustrating obvious alarm within the opposition forces.[63] Hull in an open letter to his right-hand man in the House, Foreign Affairs Committee Chairman Samuel D. McReynolds, repeated his opposition to the proposal, earlier stated in a press conference in mid-December 1937.[64] The pattern of opposition was completed by an effective *New York Times* editorial on January 10, by Postmaster General James A. Farley's day-long telephone campaign directed at all Democratic members of the House, by Democratic whip Patrick J. Boland's canvass of the House, and by Ludlow's loss of southern ally Maury Maverick. After these efforts, the administration claimed to have a "good working majority" in the House with which to prevent further progress of the bill.[65]

Details of the administration effort were not known immediately by Ludlow and his supporters.[66] Major-General Rivers, chairman of the National Committee for the War Referendum, wrote Farley January 6 ap-

[62]Ibid., Jan. 9, 1938, National Committee for the War Referendum Papers, SCPC; and La Follette to Rivers, Jan. 5, 1938, ibid.

[63]*New York Times,* Jan. 8, 1938; Sumner Welles to Roosevelt, Jan. 6, 1938, Official File 24, "Speaker of the House of Representatives, 1933–45," Box 1, Roosevelt Papers. By this time State Department Legal Advisor Green Hackworth had also prepared a background paper, "Power to Declare War," Jan. 7, 1938, in which he reviewed the origins of congressional war-declaring powers and concluded there was "no suggestion by anyone that the power to declare war should be left in the people" (DF 711.0011 War Referendum/19, RG 59, NA).

[64]*New York Times,* Jan. 9, 1938; Hull to McReynolds, Jan. 8, 1938, in Department of State, *Press Releases,* Jan. 15, 1938, p. 100. Hull later wrote that "we determined to fight it at the outset" (of the ratification process) (Hull, *The Memoirs of Cordell Hull* [New York, 1948], I, 563).

[65]*New York Times,* Jan. 10, 1938; James A. Farley, *Behind the Ballots* (New York, 1938), pp. 361–62; Hull, *Memoirs,* I, 564. Maverick later acknowledged that Roosevelt asked him to influence liberals against the measure (Richard B. Henderson, *Maury Maverick: A Political Biography* [Austin, Tex., 1970], pp. 171–72). His earlier support was noted in Maverick to Ludlow, July 1, 1935, cited in *Hearing, 1935,* p. 62.

[66]Ludlow did know of Boland's Jan. 5 canvass. Its purpose was to give Speaker Bankhead information before a prevote White House conference (Jennings Randolph [Democrat, W.Va.] to Ludlow, Jan. 5, 1938, "War Referendum Scrapbooks," IV, 541, Ludlow Papers).

pealing for full discussion of the matter by Congress and requesting his influence to prevent any "extreme obstructionist strategy." After the test vote, the press stressed the role of Farley against the Ludlow Amendment, reporting "an almost unprecedented application of argument, appeal and pressure from the administration." The New Jersey delegation, for example, got calls from Mayor Frank Hague of Jersey City requesting votes against the war referendum plan. According to Farley's later report to the president, he telephoned 110 congressmen and reached 78, one "just about the time of the roll call." When Farley noticed after the January 10 vote that only four of those not contacted voted with the administration, he assumed that they "knew why I was calling and were dodging the telephone."[67]

Ludlow spent the weekend working on final revisions of the proposed constitutional amendment with the congressional steering committee appointed late in December. The committee met on January 9 to put the proposal into the form in which it would be presented the following day. Also active during the weekend were the five peace organizations already behind the measure—the National Council for Prevention of War, World Peaceways, the Fellowship of Reconciliation, the Women's International League for Peace and Freedom, and the Emergency Peace Campaign. On the evening of January 9 a dress rehearsal for the short debate of the next day even took place. In a radio debate Congressman Celler, who repeated Bankhead's charge of alien influence behind the amendment, challenged former clergyman and then Congressman Herbert S. Bigelow (Democrat, Ohio) of the pro-referendum forces.[68]

After almost three years of concentrated effort for the war referendum, Louis Ludlow must have been only mildly enthusiastic and hopeful when the time arrived for the House to consider his discharge motion. The tone of Ludlow's introductory statement on January 10, 1938, reflected his uncertainty and lack of hope, for he simply offered the war referendum as a permanent "future" policy and then quickly turned over the proposal for debate. Any remaining hope must have surely been

[67]Rivers and A. F. Whitney to Farley, Jan. 6, 1938, OF 274, Box 5, Roosevelt Papers; Committee for the War Referendum to "Organizations supporting the war referendum," Jan. 11, 1938, "War Referendum," Vertical File, SCPC; Libby, *To End War,* p. 146; Farley to Cordell Hull, Jan. 11, 1938, attaching copies of Memorandum to Roosevelt, Jan. 10, and Farley to Roosevelt, Jan. 11, 1938, Box 42, Folder 102, Cordell Hull Papers. The latter memorandum was a lengthy listing of congressmen by name and response to Farley's call.

[68]*New York Times,* Jan. 9, 10, 1938; *Cong. Rec.,* 75th Cong., 3d sess., Appendix, p. 207 (Jan. 10, 1938); and Press Release, open letter to House members, Jan. 10, 1938, in "War Referendum," Vertical File, SCPC. On direct pacifist pressure on Secretary Hull, see DF 711.0011 War Referendum/4 and 6, RG 59, NA.

destroyed when he observed Bankhead leave the Speaker's stand to come to the floor of the House in a show of his highly refined political strategy. The Speaker's next act was the last demonstration of force the administration needed to wreck the chances for discharge of the proposed constitutional amendment. To the 247 members present in the House, Bankhead read a letter, prepared in the State Department January 6, 1938, in which President Roosevelt stated:

I consider that the proposed amendment would be impracticable in its application and incompatible with our representative form of government. . . .Such an amendment to the Constitution as that proposed would cripple any President in his conduct of our foreign relations, and it would encourage other nations to believe that they could violate American rights with impunity.

I fully realize that the sponsors of this proposal sincerely believe that it would be helpful in keeping the United States out of war. I am convinced it would have the opposite effect.[69]

This letter, although frequently overlooked as such, was a milestone in the administration campaign to educate the public away from what Secretary Hull regarded a "rigid form of isolationism."[70] Hull, Undersecretary Welles, who prepared the letter, and Roosevelt, who was suggesting increased executive initiative and control of diplomacy, agreed that the Ludlow Amendment typified such rigid isolationism.

After Bankhead's dramatic play for defeat of Ludlow's discharge motion, Fish then carried the fight for it by reading the revised war referendum resolution. Of course it could be voted on only if the discharge vote succeeded. Regarding it the "greatest peace proposal" in the last eighteen years, Fish read the revised draft of the Ludlow Amendment:

SECTION 1. Except in case of attack by armed forces, actual or immediately threatened, upon the United States or its Territorial possessions, or by any non-American nation against any country in the Western Hemisphere, the people shall have the sole power by a national referendum to declare war or to engage in warfare overseas. Congress, when it deems a national crisis to exist in confor-

---

[69]Roosevelt to William B. Bankhead, Jan. 6, 1938 (copy), OF 3084, Roosevelt Papers; Samuel I. Rosenman, ed., *The Public Papers and Addresses of Franklin D. Roosevelt* (New York, 1938–50), VII, 36–37; *Cong. Rec.,* 75th Cong., 3d sess., p. 277 (Jan. 10, 1938). Bankhead had requested statements from Roosevelt and Hull. See also Department of State, *Press Releases,* Jan. 15, 1938, pp. 99–100, and Welles to Roosevelt, Jan. 6, 1938, DF 711.0011 War Referendum/9A, RG 59, NA.

[70]Hull also testified to the intensive character of the administration's opposition in *Memoirs,* I, 563–64.

mance with this article, shall by concurrent resolution refer the question to the people.[71]

Fish was followed by brief speeches supporting the measure by several Democrats and an opposition speech by Texas Democratic leader Sam Rayburn, who argued that discharge of the bill would be the "most tremendous blunder" in congressional history.[72]

Conducted in a "tense atmosphere" of crowded galleries, the debate saw frequent disorder on the floor and slashing attacks by administration leaders. At one point Speaker Bankhead rebuked occupants of the galleries for applauding Congressman Fish. The brief but hard-fought battle nevertheless ended quickly with announcement of a close roll call vote. Cutting across party lines to muster every possible vote against the resolution, the administration won 209 to 188. Two ill congressmen, rolled into the chamber in wheelchairs, attended the session long enough to answer the roll call in opposition to the motion. Only 247 members were counted after Rayburn's earlier claim that a quorum was not present, but in the course of the twenty-minute debate, 162 additional members came into the House chamber. A shift of only eleven votes would have discharged the resolution for consideration.[73]

Ludlow left the Capitol without making a statement, a reflection of his personal disappointment and doubt over further developments. Although Republican Hamilton Fish promised to carry the fight into the primaries and fall congressional elections, Ludlow made no organized effort to make the war referendum a campaign issue.[74] Supporting peace forces claimed the vote was a "warning to the government" that "dictatorial control of foreign policy" would produce a popular response in the fall elections. "The exhibition today of presidential control of Congress in peacetime shows clearly that Congress cannot be counted upon to check the Administration in any war crisis."[75] Later Ludlow held the January 10

[71]*Cong. Rec.,* 75th Cong., 3d sess., p. 278 (Jan. 10, 1938).

[72]Ibid., pp. 278–82 (Jan. 10, 1938); *New York Times,* Jan. 11, 1938.

[73]*New York Times,* Jan. 11, 1938; *Cong. Rec.,* 75th Cong., 3d sess., pp. 282–83 (Jan. 10, 1938). Newspaper clippings for Jan. 10 and 11, 1938, on the defeat are in "War Referendum Scrapbooks," IV, 585–91, and V, 601–19, 643–98, Ludlow Papers. Arthur M. Schlesinger, Jr., *The Imperial Presidency* (Boston, 1973), p. 98, erroneously maintains that the war referendum effort "died away" after this defeat.

[74]On appeals to make the war referendum a national campaign issue, see Ludlow's correspondence, Feb. 14, 1938, and other correspondence, Jan. 11 to Mar. 3, 1938, Ludlow Papers.

[75]Press Release, National Council for Prevention of War, Women's International League for Peace and Freedom, World Peaceways, Fellowship of Reconciliation, Jan. 11, 1938, "War Referendum," Vertical File, SCPC.

defeat only a "temporary set-back," hoping that the war referendum amendment could be considered on its merits in an unprejudiced atmosphere. He also apparently considered an effort, led by William C. Lee, and the Popular Government League, to secure adoption of the Ludlow Amendment by prior ratification in the states, assuming that Congress would eventually submit such a proposal. Although Lee requested the aid of the Women's International League for Peace and Freedom and those congressmen and senators in favor of the proposal, this was never pushed by Ludlow.[76]

Despite the administration's satisfaction over the president's handling of the *Panay* crisis and its victory against Ludlow, evident in the fact that fifty-two Democrats were among the fifty-five petition signers who voted against discharge, there was no celebration. Postmaster General Farley routinely referred the vote on the Ludlow resolution to the president, who, in turn, instructed Secretary of State Hull: "I think you had better keep this. It is an interesting list."[77] It was at best a narrow and uncomfortable victory for Roosevelt, and not a mandate for incautious internationalism or complete executive control over diplomacy.

The president did subsequently order three cruisers to Singapore, advance American naval maneuvers three weeks, and transfer the fleet from the Atlantic to the Pacific. He also quietly returned to his plan for a naval quarantine of Japan and received the first French request to purchase American planes.[78] At the same time, and in addition to these actions, he expressed his own defense concepts in further reaction to the proposed Ludlow Amendment. In a private letter to his son James, Roosevelt faulted the proposal as a misuse of the referendum and thought the defense concept behind it untenable. The president believed that national defense was a day-to-day problem which necessitated executive leadership. "National defense represents too serious a danger, especially in these modern times where distance has been annihilated, to permit delay and our danger lies in things like the Ludlow Amendment which ap-

[76] Lee to Dorothy Detzer, Feb. 3, 1938, enclosing copy of Lee to supporters of the Ludlow Amendment, Jan. 31, 1938, Box 27, Women's International League for Peace and Freedom Papers, SCPC. Lee wanted, in addition to the war referendum, a "brake on naval expansion" and an embargo.

[77] Farley to Roosevelt, Jan. 21, 1938, referred to in Roosevelt to Hull, Jan. 25, 1938, OF 274, Box 5, Roosevelt Papers, and Box 42, Folder 102, Cordell Hull Papers.

[78] American–British Admiralty talks with Captain Royal E. Ingersoll were near completion when the Ludlow vote came (Haight, "Roosevelt and a Naval Quarantine of Japan," pp. 219–24). On Roosevelt's meeting with French Senator Baron Amaury de La Grange, January 15–16, 1938, and the president's early air power planning, see Haight, *American Aid to France, 1938–1940* (New York, 1970).

peal to people, who, frankly, have no conception of what modern war, with or without declaration of war, involves."[79] The clear implication in this letter was that Roosevelt already believed it impossible to maintain national defense on the basis of Ludlow's popular concept of continental or even hemispheric defense limits. Mere defense of the homeland, which limited the use of force in diplomacy, was not a valid concept in Roosevelt's opinion.

Nevertheless, the president was slow to make public his own continued opposition to the Ludlow Amendment. When one of his secretaries, Stephen Early, reported plans for a "widespread campaign of propaganda in the schools and colleges" to keep the matter alive and to secure its ultimate passage, the president again referred the opposition tactics to Secretary Hull. Early believed it advisable to "prepare a paper which will clearly set forth the reasons why the Ludlow Resolution was opposed, should continue to be opposed, etc.," distributing this to colleges and congressmen. In notifying Hull of the president's desires, Early added that it would not be necessary to name the author or department preparing the paper.[80]

Early's request for an administration paper produced the longest official statement on the Ludlow proposal yet. Although never publicly acknowledged, it was written in the Division of European Affairs headed by Jay Pierrepont Moffat, who also answered most of the public correspondence on the war referendum issue. After reviewing the Constitutional Convention debate and recent war declarations, the author of the statement concluded that it had not been the president, State Department, or Congress but "public clamor" which had taken America into war, especially World War I. The Ludlow Amendment, it was argued in classic overstatement, would reduce the president to a "mere figurehead," would blind and "make a mockery" of the navy and army, and would rob the State Department of its influence. Then the author of the statement got to the central issue between Roosevelt and Ludlow—their contrasting defense concepts. The referendum plan would permit an invading force to penetrate the present defense line, "a periphery touching on three supporting points of territory, at Panama, Hawaii and Alaska, at a distance of more than 2,000 miles from our American mainland."[81] Ludlow, of course, believed that he had altered his proposal to

[79]Roosevelt to James Roosevelt, Jan. 20, 1938, Elliott Roosevelt, ed., *F.D.R., His Personal Letters, 1928–1945* (New York, 1947–50), II, 750–51.

[80]Early to Roosevelt, Jan. 24, and Early to Hull, Jan. 25, 1938, OF 3084, Roosevelt Papers.

[81]Department of State, Division of European Affairs, "The War Referendum as a Menace to Peace," n.d., 13 pages, enclosed with Early to Hull, Jan. 25, 1938, DF 711.0011 War Referendum/14½, RG 59, NA.

answer such an objection; it would not apply in cases of invasion of the American homeland or territorial possessions. But opponents, who supported greater executive discretion and international cooperation against aggressors, looked toward an extended defense perimeter—beyond Ludlow's or even the administration front line of defense then acknowledged. The State Department paper clearly envisioned defense-at-a-distance and faulted the defense concept inherent in the Ludlow Amendment.

Roosevelt, however, remained reluctant to challenge openly the limited defense posture of Ludlow and his supporters. This request for an administration paper, which was never released by the State Department, actually reflected well the greater alarm of certain congressmen. Chief among them was House Judiciary Chairman Sumners. On February 3 Sumners had delivered his own position statement before the House of Representatives and was satisfied his was an adequate explanation of administration views.[82] But late in February he still insisted upon "some statement prepared for emergencies." On March 1 Sumners further reported to Roosevelt's office that since "this propaganda business" could be expected to increase in the not very distant future, he was prepared to offer "a little resistance before the pressure gets too great."[83] Thus was expressed the heat of the earlier battle over the Ludlow Amendment and the desire to be better prepared in the future.

Although most historians have begun and ended the war referendum story with the January 1938 vote, Ludlow soon pressed for the reform again, confident he had made a valuable contribution to peace and democracy.[84] Continuing to base his efforts on his defense attitudes, Ludlow worked simultaneously on a Senate version of the plan, questioned Hull on administration defense planning, and asked Roosevelt to call a naval holiday and Washington peace conference. Ludlow's letter to Hull, dated February 7, 1938, was typical of the grilling Congress often gave the secretary. Hull henceforth refused to be party to military planning regardless of the relationship to diplomacy. Prompted by leaks in London and the United States concerning the naval quarantine of Japan[85]

[82]Early to James Dunn, and White House Memo to Early, Feb. 14, 1938, OF 3084, Roosevelt Papers. See *Cong. Rec.*, 75th Cong., 3d sess., pp. 1477–80 (Feb. 3, 1938) for Sumner's speech.

[83]Sumners to Early, Feb. 28, and Sumners to Marvin H. McIntyre, Mar. 1, 1938, OF 3084, Roosevelt Papers. McIntyre promised only to place a copy of Sumner's congressional speech before Roosevelt, and Early had felt since about Feb. 14 that an administration statement was no longer needed (McIntyre to Sumners, Mar. 2, 1938, ibid.).

[84]*Cong. Rec.*, 75th Cong., 3d sess., p. 5281 (Apr. 11, 1938), pp. 9240–42 (June 14, 1938) and Appendix, p. 207 (Jan. 10, 1938).

[85]Walter Millis, with Harvey C. Mansfield and Harold Stein, *Arms and the State: Civil-*

and by Roosevelt's request for increased naval appropriations, Ludlow asked Hull whether naval increases were necessary for national defense of the homeland and our distant possessions. He especially inquired whether some units had already been committed for use in other parts of the world in cooperation with other nations. Hull, in a reply made public February 10, stated that there was no intention to engage in warfare anywhere and further defended administration defense policy. Later in his memoirs, Hull cited the Ludlow letter as an example of the "suspicion that dogged our every step toward international cooperation."[86]

Not satisfied with Hull's assurances, Ludlow introduced on March 8, 1938, a resolution proposing action by the president to halt the country's advances toward "the brink of war." Specifically, Ludlow wanted Roosevelt to seek international agreement to a naval holiday until January 1, 1940, and a Washington peace conference of naval powers to discuss limitation of armaments. Apparently, he had in mind a peace conference similar to the Washington Naval Conference of 1921–22.[87] Ludlow also supported Ohio Congressman Frank C. Kniffen's unsuccessful effort to amend the second Vinson naval expansion bill in order to establish a naval frontier, or what Ludlow called a "zone of defense." He nevertheless voted for the naval expansion bill March 21, and on April 11 renewed his commitment to the war referendum measure itself. Earlier he had supported the group of twelve senators, led by Robert La Follette, Jr., who introduced a measure similar to the Ludlow Amendment February 25, 1938.[88] Thus he preferred still to work for peace by "adequate defense" and the war referendum, insisting that the people be allowed

---

Military Elements in National Policy (New York, 1958), p. 33; Haight, "Roosevelt and a Naval Quarantine of Japan," pp. 224–25.

[86]"War Referendum Scrapbooks," VI, 812–22, Ludlow Papers; *Cong. Rec.,* 75th Cong., 3d sess., Appendix, pp. 587–88 (Feb. 14, 1938); Hull, *Memoirs,* I, 573–75; *New York Times,* Feb. 13, 1938. Hull's last opposition to the war referendum was in a speech before the National Press Club, Mar. 17. He conferred with Norman H. Davis about that speech shortly after Ludlow's inquiry about naval defense policy, and Davis suggested a more emphatic opposition to the war referendum (Davis to Hull, Feb. 28, 1938, and copy of Hull, "Our Foreign Policy," address before the National Press Club, Mar. 17, 1938, Box 42, Folder 103, and Box 94, Cordell Hull Papers).

[87]*New York Times,* Mar. 9, 1938; *Cong. Rec.,* 75th Cong., 3d sess., Appendix, p. 913 (Mar. 8, 1938).

[88]Kniffen had supported the Ludlow Amendment earlier and sought to define the naval frontier "as extending from Bering Strait to the western end of the Aleutian Islands, to the Hawaiian Islands, to American Samoa, to Panama, to the Virgin Islands, and to the eastern extremity of the State of Maine." See *Cong. Rec.,* 75th Cong., 3d sess., pp. 2410–11 (Feb. 25, 1938), p. 3337 (Mar. 14, 1938), pp. 3701, 3703 (Mar. 18, 1938), p. 3767 (Mar. 21, 1938), p. 5281 (Apr. 11, 1938).

more influence—not less—in determining objectives of American foreign policy.

This activity of Ludlow intensified fears of opponents, including Congressman Sumners, who informed Hull that he had 10,000 copies of his earlier address against the Ludlow Amendment. Hull acknowledged receipt of 100 copies and indicated he was "keeping in touch with this situation." Sumners also continued to defend his opposition to the Ludlow Amendment in letters to constituents. Since he pictured the people as warlike and administration figures as pacific, he was confident to rely on diplomacy as "our first line of defense against war." Regarding the Ludlow proposal an "idle gesture," he seemed willing to abdicate the war-declaring powers of Congress to the Executive entirely.[89]

Ludlow continued his fight for the reform after adjournment of Congress and during the summer and fall of 1938, impressed especially by the 68 percent Gallup poll measure of war referendum interest in September.[90] As Senator William E. Borah (Idaho) declared he would support the measure if broader discretionary powers were given the president in foreign affairs or if arms expansion was not stopped, the war referendum amendment loomed large again as a potential threat to Roosevelt.[91] The Indiana congressman surprised no one, therefore, when he filed a discharge petition to free his own war referendum bill, introduced January 10, 1939, early in the new session. As a further indication of his homeland defense concept, Ludlow also introduced a conscription referendum resolution early in 1939.[92]

Even before Ludlow introduced his bill or the discharge petition, Judiciary Chairman Hatton Sumners, alarmed by what he thought was a

[89]Sumners to Hull, Feb. 28, 1938, and Hull to Sumners, Mar. 7, 1938, DF 711.0011 War Referendum/14½, RG 59, NA; Sumners to Mrs. J. W. Belton, Jan. 20, 1938, in File on House Joint Resolution 199, 75th Cong., 1st sess., Accompanying Papers Files, Judiciary Committee, RG 233, NA.

[90]Gallup and Rae, *Pulse of Democracy,* p. 315. Ludlow's National Committee for the War Referendum, with resources of eighty dollars, became inactive in March 1938, although when Raushenbush resigned in May, Ludlow secured National Council for Prevention of War assistant Jesse MacKnight as the new acting secretary for the war referendum headquarters (Raushenbush to Ludlow, May 30, 1938, Ludlow Papers).

[91]*New York Times,* Dec. 4, 1938; Borah to G. Krause, Feb. 28, 1938, Borah Papers, which also contain press clippings for the period of his interest. He believed the measure needed revision in 1938 and finally, in May 1939, rejected the war referendum as "unworkable." Maddox does not mention Borah's earlier interest in the war referendum (1925 and 1927) or the attention he paid to the Ludlow Amendment.

[92]*Cong. Rec.,* 76th Cong., 1st sess., p. 185 (Jan. 10, 1939), p. 2681 (Mar. 13, 1939) and Appendix, p. 1541 (Apr. 19, 1939), p. 2195 (May 23, 1939), pp. 3876–77 (Aug. 4, 1939); "War Referendum Scrapbooks," VII, 979–83, Ludlow Papers; and Ludlow, "Whither Are We Drifting?" *Vital Speeches of the Day,* 5 (1939), 369–71.

growth of popular interest in the plan, had contacted the State Department once more. He expected the fight to be "more difficult" and asked approval of his earlier opposition statement, made "at the Secretary's suggestion." He further requested that he be recognized as the leader of House opposition forces. About this time Sumners received a petition from Ludlow Amendment supporters in his home district of Dallas and renewed also his personal campaign against the measure. He still believed it would embarrass the administration and challenge the diplomatic process created to handle difficult internal problems.[93]

Increased congressional interest in the war referendum plan produced long May hearings in the Senate, where La Follette and eleven other senators still sponsored a bill using the exact text of Ludlow's 1938 measure.[94] Neither the hearings nor Ludlow's renewed efforts, however, produced success for war referendum forces. Rather, the 1939 publicity provoked President Roosevelt's longest statement against it, during a March 7 press conference, and a decline of 10 percent in public support for the plan. In response to a question, the president stated that the proposed Ludlow Amendment "might very easily" impair defense of the nation. He commented especially on the problem of defining war, noting that undeclared wars would offer the United States a special problem under the proposed constitutional amendment. He favored the representative system in decisions of war and peace but believed the commander in chief had the right and power to defend the nation under attack without congressional action. When one member of the press apparently misunderstood the Ludlow Amendment, indicating that it "would seem to apply in the event of an attack on the continental United States," Roosevelt made no effort to correct the error.[95]

During the spring and summer of 1939 the administration continued to fight, behind the scenes, both the war referendum plan and proposals for public referendums on conscription outside the United States. The War Department reviewed such proposed legislation for the Bureau of the

[93]Joseph C. Green, Memorandum, Jan. 5, 1939, DF 711.0011 War Referendum/15, RG 59, NA; Sumners to Claud Walker, Jan. 6, 1939, File on House Joint Resolution 89, 76th Cong., 1st sess., Accompanying Papers Files, Judiciary Committee, RG 233, NA.

[94]"War Referendum Scrapbooks," VII, 995–998A, 1009, Ludlow Papers. Ludlow's correspondence from March to May 1939 does not indicate close work with La Follette, but there apparently was still wide public support of the measure in Ludlow's mail. The committee nevertheless reported the La Follette bill unfavorably (*War Referendum, Hearings, 1939; Senate Reports, Miscellaneous,* III, Reports 749, 750).

[95]The Gallup poll showed 58 percent favoring the measure (*New York Times,* Mar. 8, 1939). The press conference is in Personal Papers Files 1-P, Press Conferences, vol. 13, Box 233, Roosevelt Papers.

Budget, which then advised the House Judiciary Committee to oppose the legislation.[96] Opposition was never actually due to potential costs or the impact upon the administration budget but to strategic considerations. In a similar review of the La Follette group's war referendum measure in the Senate, the State and War Departments recommended an unfavorable Judiciary Committee report.[97] These actions, in which Cordell Hull participated, often recalled earlier opposition to the Ludlow Amendment, illustrating the administration's still cautious approach in trying to counter the neutralist bloc in Congress. The administration clearly differed with Ludlow and his associates on defense concepts but respected their popular appeal.

Once the European war broke out, however, the administration campaign combined with events to frustrate Ludlow and his supporters further. In the special session of Congress which followed the outbreak of war, Ludlow opposed cooperation with Great Britain in regard to cash-and-carry neutrality, fought repeal of the arms embargo, and urged Roosevelt instead to mediate in Europe.[98] Ludlow and La Follette failed on October 27, 1939, during an administration revision of neutrality legislation, to include an advisory war referendum when the Senate defeated the idea 73 to 17.[99] For the second time in less than two years, the Congress—this time the Senate—voted down the war referendum idea, which was remarkably persistent but obviously weakened.

In 1940 Ludlow lost the support of Hamilton Fish, who turned wholly to the conscription referendum plan; William Bigelow and his magazine; and former member of the National Committee for the War Referendum William Allen White, who turned to the Committee to Defend America by Aiding the Allies. White felt the principle was still sound but had

---

[96]"Referendum for declaration of war and/or sending American troops overseas (1/5/39)," Series 39.1, Folder R70 (1), Files on House Joint Resolution 66, 76th Congress, 1st session, Records of the Bureau of the Budget, Record Group 51, NA.

[97]File on Senate Joint Resolution 84, 76th Congress, 1st session, ibid. When conscription referendum proposals were introduced in 1940 and 1941, this review process continued to result in reports against the measures. As congressmen sought to give more force to their own Selective Service Act provision against use of troops outside the Western Hemisphere and American possessions, State and War Department efforts against such conscription referendum proposals were an expression of the emerging defense-at-a-distance strategy. See Files on House Joint Resolution 408, 76th Cong., 3d sess., ibid.; Senate Concurrent Resolution 7, 77th Cong., 1st sess., ibid., and Cordell Hull to Senator Carl Hatch, May 16, 1939, DF 711.0011 War Referendum/25, RG 59, NA.

[98]*New York Times,* Oct. 7, 10, 1939; *Cong. Rec.,* 76th Cong., 2d sess., pp. 485–88 (Oct. 16, 1939), p. 1389 (Nov. 3, 1939).

[99]*Cong. Rec.,* 76th Cong., 2d sess., p. 773 (Oct. 24, 1939), pp. 986–99 (Oct. 27, 1939); *New York Times,* Oct. 28, 1939.

doubts if "we are faced with a totalitarian world." He continued: "In this world of terror, I am not sure whether time spent holding elections would not be better spent in those defenses which can only be put up in a state of war."[100] With the enthusiasm of peace organizations also less evident, Ludlow appealed directly for the first time to youth groups, notably the Junior Chamber of Commerce and Young Democrats of America.[101] His major efforts, however, were to win endorsements in national party platforms. In this he received support from Senator Nye, Norman Thomas, and Oswald Garrison Villard, but he seemed to work closely only with Senator Burton K. Wheeler.[102] Correspondence on this project, once again heavy, reflected public fear of American involvement in war as well as Ludlow's own conviction that the president's leadership was taking the country toward war. Ludlow believed that any revision of neutrality in 1939 granting the president more discretion would lead to "going the entire way later on." In 1940 Ludlow predicted that "the next year will be a very important one in American history," with America choosing whether to enter the war or to "keep out of foreign entanglements, devoting our future to a rehabilitation of our own country, economically and morally."[103]

Ludlow introduced his last war referendum resolution in January 1941, but his chief interest by then had shifted to opposing the administration's Lend-Lease bill. He made no major speech in the House solely on the war referendum in 1941, made no effort to support actively Senator Arthur Capper's referendum resolution, and only briefly encouraged a Senate ad-

[100]Ludlow to Mrs. Margaret Daly, Feb. 1, 1940; Bigelow to Ludlow, Nov. 28, 1939; Ludlow to White, Dec. 23, 1940, Ludlow Papers; and White to Ludlow, December 28, 1940, White Papers.

[101]The Junior Chamber of Commerce agreed to discuss the proposal in its Executive Committee, but no further action is known (Chamber letter to Ludlow, Mar. 6, 1940, Ludlow Papers). Appeals Dec. 27, 1940, to Joseph P. Kennedy and Herbert Hoover evoked only a noncommittal reply from Kennedy (Kennedy to Ludlow, Jan. 2, 1941, ibid). Ludlow also failed to win the support of Roy Howard and the Scripps-Howard newspapers from late 1939 to 1941 (Arthur Capper to Ludlow, Dec. 18, 1939, and Howard to Ludlow, Jan. 2, 1941, ibid.).

[102]The war referendum was not incorporated into party platforms in 1940, but Democrats reflected the Ludlow kind of homeland defense attitudes by pledging not to send American forces to foreign lands except in case of attack. On Ludlow's efforts, see Nye to Ludlow, Apr. 10, 1940; Thomas to Ludlow, Apr. 16, 1940; Villard to Ludlow, June 17, 1940; Ludlow to Wheeler, July 11, 1940; and Ludlow to Robert F. Wagner, chairman of the Democratic Platform Committee, July 11, 1940, Ludlow Papers.

[103]Ludlow to Mrs. Charles E. Thomas (constituent), Sept. 27, 1939, and Ludlow to unnamed Canton, Ohio, citizen, Apr. 24, 1940, ibid.

visory war referendum proposal that was discussed in the summer of 1941 by the America First Committee.[104] During the war years Ludlow returned to the war referendum idea, offering it in 1945 for consideration in long-range postwar peace plans. Always desirous of more popular control of foreign policy, he had sought in 1943 a Committee on Peace Aims representing government, labor, and religion. By the end of the war Ludlow had accepted limited American involvement in world affairs in his support of the United Nations organization, but he still looked to the day when the Charter could be amended to include international agreement to the war referendum plan.[105]

Slow to lose faith in limited-power isolationism, Louis Ludlow admitted only upon retirement in 1948 that it was "too late for war referendums."[106] Until then, he well represented those Americans who in the thirties turned away from international schemes in favor of national plans for keeping out of war. Not a symbol of isolationism-at-any-price, the war referendum device appealed chiefly to those who favored a concept of defense, narrow in application and relatively inexpensive to the taxpayer, which sought use of limited military power for national self-defense only. Ludlow desired to limit the military establishment to what was necessary for defense of the homeland. He never envisioned a wider defense perimeter than the Western Hemisphere and frequently spoke of America's impregnability. "No nation is coming to attack us," he argued.[107] The war referendum plan, inoperable in the unlikely case of attack or invasion of the homeland, therefore, would insulate America

---

[104]*Cong. Rec.,* 77th Cong., 1st sess., p. 20 (Jan. 3, 1941), pp. 422–23 (Jan. 30, 1941), pp. 616–17 (Feb. 5, 1941), p. 2178 (Mar. 11, 1941); Robert E. Wood to Ludlow, Feb. 11, 1941, and Ludlow to Wood, Feb. 14, 1941, Ludlow Papers. In 1941 the Senate war referendum proposal was supported by the National Council for Prevention of War and the Keep America Out of War Congress as well as by America First. See Chatfield, *For Peace and Justice,* pp. 321–22; Stephen A. Thernstrom, "Oswald Garrison Villard and the Politics of Pacifism," *Harvard Library Bulletin,* 14 (Winter 1960), 149; and Wayne S. Cole, *America First: The Battle against Intervention, 1940–41* (Madison, Wis., 1953), pp. 56–61.

[105]*Cong. Rec.,* 78th Cong., 1st sess., p. 1685 (Mar. 8, 1943), pp. A2681–A2687 (June 1, 1943); ibid., 79th Cong., 1st sess., pp. 805–12 (Feb. 5, 1945), p. 7890 (July 20, 1945), pp. A3320–A3321 (July 5, 1945). As early as 1937 Ludlow hoped for acceptance of the referendum by other nations. See Ludlow to Ramsay MacDonald, Jan. 2, 1937, and Ludlow to David Lloyd George, Jan. 2, 1937, Ludlow Papers.

[106]*Cong. Rec.,* 80th Cong., 2d sess., p. A4853 (Aug. 4, 1948).

[107]Ludlow to C. F. Hansing, Oct. 11, 1937, Ludlow Papers. This popular view was also expressed by Hanson Baldwin, *American Mercury,* 47 (1939), 267; Charles A. Beard, *The Devil Theory of War* (New York, 1936), p. 120; Buell, *Isolated America,* pp. 66–68; and Hagood, *We Can Defend America.*

from what he regarded the unnecessary foreign wars, or what he called the offensive, or "policy," wars. He called for "adequate defense" in terms of a navy for coastal defense primarily and believed a large defense establishment was incompatible with popular government: "I stand ready to vote all of the multiplied billions that may be needed for home defense but I sincerely and truly believe that we should be thinking of America first." In 1938 he typically stated: "I am for a strong and adequate navy for defense and for nothing else. . . .We should keep our defense navy at home and not send it to far-away Singapores."[108]

Ludlow favored the war referendum as a means of limiting not only the defense establishment but the executive's use of force in diplomacy as well. He felt that Congress by 1941 had "abdicated to the Executive in respect to international relations." There appeared "to be no responsibility left in Congress as far as international relations are concerned." "We have centralized," he concluded, "all war activities and have placed all of the controls in the President."[109] Yet it was not the differences between Ludlow and President Roosevelt, and their supporters, over who should direct American foreign policy that was so significant for postwar America. Their conflict on defense concepts, symbolized in the fight over the Ludlow Amendment, was the underlying issue at the time and the more important matter for the future.

The war referendum amendment struck at the heart of executive leadership and discretion in foreign affairs. It was Ludlow's alternative for congressional abdication of war powers to the Executive. But Ludlow's popular "fortress," or homeland, defense concept was a greater potential obstacle to Roosevelt's own emerging defense-at-a-distance concept. The president only gradually became the recognized national spokesman for this concept, but as early as 1935 he had indicated the direction of his thinking in comparison with limited-power isolationists like Louis Ludlow. "They," he wrote to Colonel House, "imagine that if the civilization of Europe is about to destroy itself through internal strife, it might just as well go ahead and do it and that the United States can stand

---

[108]*Indianapolis Star,* Jan. 21, 1941, in "Ludlow's Scrapbooks," XXVI, 4127, Ludlow Papers; *Cong. Rec.,* 75th Cong., 3d sess., p. 3703 (Mar. 18, 1938).

[109]Ludlow to W. C. Dennis (president, Earlham College), May 5, 1941, Ludlow Papers. In a radio address over CBS June 9, 1937, Ludlow had expressed a strong personal faith in the president as a friend of peace but warned against the tendency of Congress to abdicate powers to the Executive (*Cong. Rec.,* 75th Cong., 1st sess., Appendix, pp. 1401–4 [June 9, 1937]).

idly by."[110] Ludlow operated, however, on the basis of former President Benjamin Harrison's earlier advice: "We have no commission from God to police the world." Viewed with Ludlow's consistent opposition to discretionary neutrality legislation and his favoring a total wartime embargo, the war referendum device—with its underlying faith in the people—made him one of the foremost limited-power isolationists of the thirties.

[110]Roosevelt to Edward M. House, Sept. 17, 1935, President's Personal File 222, Roosevelt Papers.

Conclusion

IN AND OF itself the history of the war referendum approach to peace has been neglected simply because the peace plan did not become law. As a legislative proposal and a persistent peace proposition for over twenty five years, however, it was one of the most interesting failures in modern American history. Its disparate sponsors and the equally varied forms they gave it made the war referendum plan relevant to many of America's major experiences at home and abroad. Its significance, therefore, belies America's failure to adopt it.

Of basic significance was the fact that it never stood alone. The war referendum proposal usually was tied to antipreparedness, liberal pacifism, domestic progressivism, civil liberties, internationalism, anti–war-profits or neutrality legislation, or related national movements and interests. Its affinity with America's reform impulses was frequently as important as its relation to antiwar attitudes. Nurtured by the preparedness struggle of 1914–16, support for the war referendum plan was strong in progressive ranks both in Congress and in the organized peace movement. Chances of a national decision on war declarations especially appealed to the women's suffrage movement and to women generally, even after the Nineteenth Amendment. The progressives' attack on domestic monopoly and special interests, as well as their faith in direct democracy, brought them to the war referendum plan as an expression of similar goals in diplomacy. La Follette's Progressive party interest in 1924 and support of the Ludlow Amendment by liberal isolationists before World War II further demonstrated its close relation to American liberalism.

Many liberal partisans of this proposal often confessed a fear for future domestic reform and civil liberties without peace through referendum. Only when that fear became most intense, as during an international crisis, did their plan become a peace-at-any-price measure. Even then, as before American intervention in World War I, some sponsors urged limited war or armed neutrality to protect American interests. Like the anti-imperialists before them, liberal antimilitarists wanted America to serve as the world's foremost democratic model—at peace with the world and engaged in domestic reform.

After progressives, led by William Jennings Bryan, failed before 1918 in securing this reform, they, and others, turned toward international application of the war referendum principle. Again, the proposal seldom stood apart from other international developments or peace proposals. It was tied to the debate on the League Covenant, outlawry of war proposals, and international economic problems. Interest shown the war referendum plan by Secretary of State Charles Evans Hughes in 1922–23, in his attempt to forestall the Ruhr crisis, marked another significant attempt, although heretofore neglected by historians, to secure international agreement to the plan. Furthermore, it represented the single time when the American government officially but indirectly endorsed the proposal.

Finally, in the 1930s the plan reached its apogee in legislative endorsement. Though unknown to historians generally, or even to Louis Ludlow himself, congressional interest in 1935–41 enjoyed a generous inheritance from the 1920s. For two decades the plan had been tied to neutrality, anti–war-profits legislation, munitions embargoes, and self-denying defense attitudes. Thus, again, the proposed war referendum amendment to the Constitution was an isolationist measure typical of the times. Yet it remained for some, including Ludlow, a symbol of sincere liberal motives, especially faith in the people.

The referendum's greatest significance lay in its translation into concrete form of two ideals basic to America's domestic and diplomatic traditions. Most war referendum proponents saw little or no distinction between foreign and domestic politics. Why not then extend greater popular control to foreign affairs? Since use of force, it was maintained, served no advantage in American domestic political practice, why resort to force in diplomacy? Law prevailed at home, so why not abroad? Domestic rejection of force and reliance upon law and public opinion pointed to the war referendum plan in diplomacy.

War in this scheme of thinking resulted from deliberate choice. There was no such thing as an "inevitable conflict." It was, furthermore, typical of the progressives' attempt to root out the domestic and international "conspiracy," considered the basis of most problems. What better solution than the progressives' faith in popular control? If war came by blunders or conspiracies, then it might be prevented by assuring free choice. And who was more deserving to exercise that choice directly than the people who would fight in the war?

The typical war referendum proponent held that wars in the past resulted from only the choice of selfish autocrats to gain power and glory. Wars of this type were fought by other nobles and mercenaries who would share the booty. Later kings ordered their subjects to war when the conflict held no profit for the vast majority of soldiers. When even diffusion of responsibility for war into representative legislatures failed to prevent conflicts, many liberals then turned to the war referendum plan. With democracy thus fully operative, the people could at least express their obvious opposition to war if not postpone or even prevent it.

From the anti-imperialist precedents at the turn of the century until World War II, many Americans, therefore, urged unusually ambitious peace and reform programs. Yet in urging only a "homeland" defense and the war referendum idea, they revealed more than merely a lack of faith in representative government or distrust of executive leadership in foreign affairs. They had little understanding of the national interest or the mechanics of foreign affairs. In a sense they sought to make America safe for progressivism by outlawing war and reforming traditional diplomatic machinery.

But not even in the days before overkill and billion-dollar defense budgets was such a program realistic. America could not be both a partner to international peace and domestic progress without assuming its share of the responsibility for maintaining peace. War did have a close relationship to national interest as well as to national reform ideals. A nation might have to fight, as Woodrow Wilson had concluded, because the right is more precious than peace. War came not always by choice but by necessity, forced upon the nation against its will. That was the lesson of the war referendum for American ideals and diplomatic practice. And that was the lesson of other more familiar, but no more typical, American peace efforts during the twentieth century.

On the other hand, the questions posed by war referendum sponsors still remain unanswered. Their errors in judgment by no means suggest an easy choice between collective security and isolationism. Perhaps America will yet find the essential "middle way" between the demands for national unity, action, and military power and the often conflicting ideals of individual choice, popular control, and peaceable reform. Certainly no nation in the world is today better equipped to conduct a workable foreign policy derived both from popular control and the use of force. Although the limits to such bases in diplomacy have been suggested by the sporadic appeals for a war referendum, the two are not necessarily incongruous.

Indeed, the ideals of a war referendum approach to peace remain strong and at times quite vocal. One could surmise, for example, what Louis Ludlow and earlier war referendum proponents would say about the late Walter Lippmann's 1965 statement that Americans are "not the policemen of mankind." Efforts to restore a balance between congressional and executive branches concerning powers and responsibilities for foreign affairs have led to the National Commitments Resolution of 1969 and the War Powers Act of 1971. Also, in 1971, the war referendum plan itself, in the familiar form of a proposed constitutional amendment, reappeared in Congress. Congressman John Rarick (Democrat, La.) with Robert L. Leggett (Democrat, Calif.) and Parren J. Mitchell (Democrat, Md.) as cosponsors, introduced the People Power over War Amendment.[1] This proposal used the exact text of the earlier Ludlow Amendment. As before, however, the difficulty in the referendum approach to peace comes in applying a sound principle to uncompromising facts. Within a world in which modern warfare often defies choice or total reliance upon force, no nation can stand alone either in isolationism or as policeman of the world.

[1]Walter Lippmann on CBS Reports, Feb. 22, 1965; U.S., Congress, Senate, 91st Cong., 1st sess., Senate Committee on Foreign Relations Report 129, *National Commitments Report . . . to accompany S. Res. 85, April 16, 1969;* U.S., Congress, Senate, 92d Cong., 1st sess., Senate Committee on Foreign Relations, *Hearings . . . on War Powers Legislation, March 8, 9, 24, and 25, April 23 and 26, May 14, July 26 and 27 and October 6, 1971;* and *Cong. Rec.,* 92d Cong., 1st sess., pp. 9052–53, 9065 (Apr. 1, 1971). The war referendum plan was supported by New Left spokesman Mark Raskin of the Institute for Policy Studies in 1973. See Raskin, "The Erosion of Congressional Power," reprinted ibid., 93d Cong., 1st sess., pp. 5523–29 (Feb. 27, 1973).

Bibliography and Abbreviations

Index

Bibliography and Abbreviations

Books, articles, and unpublished theses and dissertations—all secondary sources used in this study—are fully cited in footnotes. This section lists only those primary sources that were used most heavily.

Unpublished Personal Papers

Athens, Ga. University of Georgia Library
    William Henry Fleming Collection
Bloomington, Ind. Indiana University Library
    Louis L. Ludlow Papers
Cambridge, Mass. Harvard University Library
    Oswald Garrison Villard Papers
Durham, N.C. Duke University Library
    Samuel McGowan Papers
    John Jackson McSwain Papers
Hyde Park, N.Y. Franklin D. Roosevelt Library
    R. Walton Moore Papers
    Franklin D. Roosevelt Papers
Madison, Wis. State Historical Society of Wisconsin
    James A. Frear Papers
New York, N.Y. Columbia University Library
    Randolph Silliman Bourne Papers (microfilm)
Princeton, N.J. Princeton University Library
    Warren Worth Bailey Papers
Swarthmore, Pa. Swarthmore College Peace Collection.   SCPC
    Henry Wadsworth Longfellow Dana Papers
Washington, D.C. Library of Congress, Manuscript Division.   LC
    William E. Borah Papers
    William Jennings Bryan Papers
    James M. Cattell Papers
    Charles Evans Hughes Papers
    Cordell Hull Papers
    Judson King Papers
    Robert M. La Follette and Burton K. Wheeler Collection
    Robert Latham Owen Papers
    Amos R. E. Pinchot Papers
    Louis F. Post Papers
    William Allen White Papers

West Branch, Iowa. Herbert Hoover Presidential Library
    William R. Castle Papers

Other Manuscripts

Durham, N.C. Duke University Library
    Socialist Party of America Papers
Swarthmore, Pa. Swarthmore College Peace Collection.   SCPC
    American Conference for Democracy and Terms of Peace Files
    American Foundation Files
    American League Against War and Fascism Files
    American League to Limit Armament Files
    American Neutral Conference Committee Papers
    American Peace Congress Files
    American Peace Society Papers
    American Union Against Militarism Records (microfilm).   AUAM
        Records
    Church Peace Union Records
    Collegiate Antimilitarism Committee Files
    Committee for Democratic Control Papers.   CDC Papers
    Emergency Anti-War Committee (Chicago) Papers
    Emergency Peace Committee of Massachusetts Files
    Emergency Peace Federation Papers
    National Committee for the War Referendum Papers
    People's Council of America Papers (microfilm).   PCA Papers
    Union of Democratic Control (England) Files
    Woman's Peace Party Collection.   WPP Collection
    Women's International League for Peace and Freedom Papers
    Women's Peace Union Records
Washington, D.C. National Archives.   NA
    Records of the Bureau of the Budget. Record Group 51
    Records of the Department of State. Decimal File, 1910–29. Record Group
        59
    Records of the House of Representatives. Accompanying Papers Files and
        Petitions, Committee on the Judiciary; Committee Papers, Committee on
        Foreign Affairs; and Joint Resolutions and Original House Bills. Record
        Group 233
    Records of the Senate. Original Bills and Resolutions. Petitions and Memo-
        rials Referred to Committees. Record Group 46

Printed Government Documents

Halsey, Edwin A., comp. *Proposed Amendments to the Constitution of the
    United States Introduced in Congress from December 6, 1926, to January 3,
    1941*. Washington, D.C.: Government Printing Office, 1941.

United States. Congress. *Congressional Record.* Proceedings and Debates of the 63d Congress, 1913, through the 77th Congress, 1941. Washington, D.C.: Government Printing Office, 1913–1941.

United States. Congress. House, 54th Congress, 2d Session. House Document No. 353, part 2, *The Proposed Amendments to the Constitution of the United States during the First Century of Its History.* Washington, D.C.: Government Printing Office, 1897.

———, 64th Congress, 2d Session. *Emergency Peace Federation.* Hearings, House of Representatives, Committee on Foreign Affairs, February 22, 1917. Washington, D.C.: Government Printing Office, 1917.

———, 64th Congress, 2d Session. *Referendum on Declaration of War.* Hearings before the Committee on Foreign Affairs, House of Representatives, on House Resolution 492, February 17, 1917. Washington, D.C.: Government Printing Office, 1917.

———, 72d Congress, 1st Session. House Document No. 163, *War Policies Commission Report.* Washington, D.C.: Government Printing Office, 1931.

———, 72d Congress, 1st Session. House Document No. 264, *Final Report, War Policies Commission.* Washington, D.C.: Government Printing Office, 1932.

———, 72d Congress, 1st Session. House Document No. 271, *Documents by War Policies Commission.* Washington, D.C.: Government Printing Office, 1932.

———, 73d Congress, 2d Session. *Amend the Constitution with Respect to Declarations of War.* Hearings before the Committee on the Judiciary, House of Representatives, Subcommittee No. 1, on House Joint Resolution 217, House Joint Resolution 218 (Also House Joint Resolution 313 subsequently introduced as a result of suggestions made at Hearing), March 28, 1934. Washington, D.C.: Government Printing Office, 1934.

———, 74th Congress, 1st Session. *Hearing before Subcommittee No. 2 of the Committee on the Judiciary, on House Joint Resolution 167,* Proposing an Amendment to the Constitution of the United States with Respect to the Declaration of War and the Taking of Property for Public Use in Time of War, June 19, 1935. Washington, D.C.: Government Printing Office, 1935.

United States. Congress. Senate, 69th Congress, 1st Session. Senate Document No. 93, *Proposed Amendments to the Constitution of the United States Introduced in Congress from December 4, 1889, to July 2, 1926.* Washington, D.C.: Government Printing Office, 1926.

———, 76th Congress, 1st Session. *War Referendum.* Hearings before a Subcommittee of the Committee on the Judiciary, on Senate Joint Resolution 84; a Joint Resolution Proposing an Amendment to the Constitution of the United States for a Referendum on War, May 10, 11, 12, 17, 18, 19, 24, and 31, 1939. Washington, D.C.: Government Printing Office, 1939.

———, 85th Congress, 1st Session. Senate Document No. 65, *Proposed Amendments to the Constitution of the United States, Introduced in Congress from December 6, 1926, to January 3, 1957.* Washington, D.C.: Government Printing Office, 1957.

———, 90th Congress, 1st Session. *Separation of Powers.* Hearings before the Subcommittee on Separation of Powers of the Committee on the Judiciary, July

19, 20, August 2, and September 13 and 15, 1967. Washington, D.C.: Government Printing Office, 1967.

United States. Department of State. *Foreign Relations of the United States, Diplomatic Papers, 1937.* 5 vols. Washington, D.C.: Government Printing Office, 1954.

_____. *Foreign Relations of the United States: Japan: 1931–1941.* 2 vols. Washington, D.C.: Government Printing Office, 1943.

_____. *The Lansing Papers, 1914–1920.* 2 vols. Washington, D.C.: Government Printing Office, 1939.

_____. *Papers Relating to the Foreign Relations of the United States, 1922.* Vol. II. Washington, D.C.: Government Printing Office, 1938.

_____. *Peace and War: United States Foreign Policy, 1931–1941.* Washington, D.C.: Government Printing Office, 1942.

_____. *Press Releases, 1938.* Washington, D.C.: Government Printing Office, 1938.

Newspapers and Contemporary Journal Files

Anti-Imperialist League (Boston). *Annual Reports,* 1899–1919
Atlanta Constitution, 1937–38
Atlanta Journal, 1937–38
Collier's, 1916
Commoner, 1915–17, 1919, 1920
Current Opinion, 1917
Dial, 1917
Greenville (S.C.) *News,* 1924
Herald of Peace, 1927–28
Harvey's Weekly, 1920–21
Independent, 1916–17
International Conciliation, 1910, 1913–14
La Follette's Magazine, 1916–18
Let the People Vote on War: A Journal Devoted to the People's Peace Movement, 1919
Literary Digest, 1917, 1925, 1927, 1937–38
Nation, 1917, 1924, 1927–28, 1936–38
National Council for Prevention of War. *News Bulletin,* 1924–34
_____. *Peace Action,* 1934–40
New Republic, 1914–17, 1928, 1937–38
New York Times, 1915–17; 1919–20; 1922–23; 1927–33; 1935–41
Ohio State Journal, 1916–17
Outlook, 1906
Peace Digest: Quarterly Review of World Literature on Peace, 1933–41
Public: A National Journal of Fundamental Democracy and a Weekly Narrative of History in the Making, 1917

Seven Arts, 1917
Survey, 1915–17
Times (London), 1922–23
World Tomorrow, 1929

Published Memoirs, Letters, Addresses, Books and Articles

Addams, Jane. *Peace and Bread in Time of War.* 1922; rpt. New York: King's Crown Press, 1945.

———, Emily G. Balch, and Alice Hamilton. *Women at The Hague: The International Congress of Women and Its Results.* New York: Macmillan, 1915.

Allen, Henry T. *My Rhineland Journal.* Boston: Houghton Mifflin, 1923.

Ashurst, Henry F. *A Many-Colored Toga: The Diary of Henry Fountain Ashurst.* Tucson: Univ. of Arizona Press, 1962.

Barnett, James D. "Referendum on War." *Open Court* (Chicago), 39 (1925), 109–14.

Bartholdt, Richard. *From Steerage to Congress: Reminiscences and Reflections.* Philadelphia: Dorrance and Co., 1930.

Beasley, Robert E. *A Plan to Stop the Present and Prevent Future Wars; Containing a Proposed Constitution for the General Government of the Sovereign States of North and South America.* Rio Vista, Calif.: Published for the author, 1864.

Bell, Julian, ed. *We Did Not Fight, 1914–1918: Experiences of War Resisters.* London: Cobden-Sanderson, 1935.

Benson, Allan L. *A Way to Prevent War.* Girard, Kan.: Appeal to Reason, 1915.

Bigelow, Herbert S. *The Religion of Revolution.* Cincinnati: Daniel Kiefer, 1916.

Bigelow, William F. "A Peace Amendment." *Good Housekeeping,* May 1936, p. 4.

———. "Mine Eyes Have Seen the Glory." *Good Housekeeping,* June 1936, p. 4.

———. "Let's Vote before We Fight." *Good Housekeeping,* Feb. 1937, p. 4.

Boeckel, Florence Brewer. *Between War and Peace: A Handbook for Peace Workers.* New York: Macmillan, 1928.

Bourne, Randolph S. *History of a Literary Radical and Other Essays.* Ed. Van Wyck Brooks. New York: B. W. Huebsch, 1920.

———. *Untimely Papers.* Ed. James Oppenheim. New York: B. W. Huebsch, 1919.

———. *War and the Intellectuals.* Ed. Carl Resek. New York: Harper and Row, 1964.

———. *The World of Randolph Bourne, an Anthology.* Ed. with an introduction by Lillian Schlissel. New York: Dutton, 1965.

———, comp. *Towards an Enduring Peace: A Symposium of Peace Proposals and Programs, 1914–1916.* New York: American Association for International Conciliation, 1916.

Bryan, Charles. *Governor Bryan Recommends that a Resolution Be Passed Memorializing Congress to Submit an Amendment to the Constitution Requir-*

ing a Referendum of the People before a Declaration of War, Unless the Country Is Invaded. Lincoln, Neb.: Kline Pub. Co., 1923.

Bryan, William Jennings, and Mary Baird Bryan. *The Memoirs of William Jennings Bryan.* Philadelphia: United Publishers of America, 1925.

Buell, Raymond Leslie. *Isolated America.* New York: Knopf, 1940.

Burgh, James. *Political Disquisitions.* 3 vols. Philadelphia: Bell and Woodhouse, 1775. Microcard.

Capper, Arthur. "Let the People Decide." *Vital Speeches of the Day,* 4 (1938), 165–66.

Colborne, Hubert C. S. "World Referendum and War." *Foreign Affairs* (London), 4 (Aug. 1922), 40.

––––––. "Referendum and Wars." *Foreign Affairs* (London), 4 (Jan. 1923), 132.

––––––. "The German Offer to Stop War by Referendum." *Foreign Affairs* (London), 5 (July 1923), 14–15.

D'Abernon, Edgar V. *The Diary of an Ambassador.* 3 vols. Garden City, N.Y.: Doubleday, Doran, 1929–30.

Democratic Party. *Official Report of the Proceedings of the Democratic National Convention, 1924.* Indianapolis: Bookwalter-Ball-Greathouse, 1924.

Detzer, Dorothy. *Appointment on the Hill.* New York: Holt, 1948.

Eastman, Max. *Love and Revolution: My Journey through an Epoch.* New York: Random House, 1964.

Farley, James A. *Behind the Ballots.* New York: Harcourt, Brace, 1938.

Fleming, William H. *The Tariff, Civil Service, Income Tax, Imperialism, the Race Problem, and Other Speeches.* Atlanta: A. B. Caldwell, 1908.

Foreign Policy Bulletin (New York), 7 (Dec. 1937), and (Jan. 1938).

Foster, John. *A Sermon Preached Before the Ancient and Honourable Artillery Company, in Boston, June 5, 1809; Being the Anniversary of Their Election of Officers.* Boston: Munroe, Francis and Parker, 1809.

Frear, James A. *Forty Years of Progressive Public Service Reasonably Filled with Thorns and Flowers.* Washington, D.C.: Associated Writers, 1937.

Grew, Joseph C. *Turbulent Era: A Diplomatic Record of Forty Years, 1904–1945.* Ed. Walter Johnson. 2 vols. Boston: Houghton Mifflin, 1952.

High, Stanley. "Peace, Inc." *Saturday Evening Post,* Mar. 5, 1938, p. 8.

Houghton, Alanson B. "War? Let the People Decide!" *Federal Council Bulletin: A Journal of Religious Cooperation and Interchurch Activities,* 10, No. 7 (1927), 9–10.

––––––. "The Power of the People." *Goodwill: A Review of International Christian Friendship,* 30, NS 1 (1928), 20–23.

Howe, Frederic C. *Why War?.* New York: Scribner's, 1916.

Hull, Cordell. *The Memoirs of Cordell Hull.* 2 vols. New York: Macmillan, 1948.

Jordan, David Starr. *The Question of the Philippines.* Palo Alto, Calif.: Graduate Club of Leland Stanford Junior University, 1899.

La Follette, Belle Case, and Fola La Follette. *Robert M. La Follette.* 2 vols. New York: Macmillan, 1953.

Lansing, Robert. *War Memoirs of Robert Lansing.* Indianapolis: Bobbs-Merrill, 1935.

Lape, Esther Everett. *Ways to Peace: Twenty Plans Selected from the Most Representative of Those Submitted to the American Peace Award for the Best Practicable Plan by Which the United States May Co-operate with Other Nations to Achieve and Preserve the Peace of the World.* New York: Scribner's, 1924.

Ludlow, Louis. *From Cornfield to Press Gallery: Adventures and Reminiscences of a Veteran Washington Correspondent.* Washington, D.C.: W. F. Roberts Co., 1924.

———. "To End the Profits in Wars." *World Affairs,* 98 (Mar. 1935), 36–42.

———. *Hell or Heaven.* Boston: Stratford Co., 1937.

———. "Whither Are We Drifting?" *Vital Speeches of the Day,* 5 (1939), 369–71.

———, and David J. Lewis. "Referendum on Making War?" *Christian Science Monitor,* Weekly Magazine Section, Jan. 5, 1938, pp. 1–2.

Marshall, Edison, Gerald P. Nye, Florence B. Boeckel, Rose Wilder Lane, and Louis Ludlow. "Who Shall Say When We Shall Go to War?" *Good Housekeeping,* Mar. 1939, p. 24.

Moore, John Bassett. *The Collected Papers of John Bassett Moore.* 7 vols. New Haven: Yale Univ. Press, 1944.

Norris, George W. *Fighting Liberal: The Autobiography of George W. Norris.* New York: Macmillan, 1945.

Pinchot, Amos R. E. *History of the Progressive Party, 1912–1916.* Ed. with biographical introduction by Helene Maxwell Hooker. New York: New York Univ. Press, 1958.

Raushenbush, Stephen. *War Madness.* Washington: National Home Library Foundation, 1937.

——— and Joan. *The Final Choice: America between Europe and Asia.* New York: Reynal and Hitchcock, 1937.

Report of the Sixteenth Annual Meeting of the Lake Mohonk Conference on International Arbitration, May 18th, 19th, and 20th, 1910. Lake Mohonk, N.Y.: Lake Mohonk Conference, 1910.

Report of the Eighteenth Annual Lake Mohonk Conference on International Arbitration, 1912. Lake Mohonk, N.Y.: Lake Mohonk Conference, 1912.

Report of the Twenty-second Annual Lake Mohonk Conference on International Arbitration, May 17th, 18th, and 19th, 1916. Lake Mohonk, N.Y.: Lake Mohonk Conference, 1916.

Roosevelt, Elliott, ed., assisted by Joseph P. Lash. *F. D. R., His Personal Letters, 1928–1945.* 4 vols. New York: Duell, Sloan and Pearce, 1947–50.

Rosenman, Samuel I., ed. *The Public Papers and Addresses of Franklin D. Roosevelt.* 13 vols. New York: Macmillan, 1938–50.

Schurz, Carl. "Manifest Destiny." *Harper's New Monthly Magazine,* 87 (1893), 737–46.

———. *Speeches, Correspondence, and Political Papers of Carl Schurz.* Ed. Frederic Bancroft. 6 vols. New York: Putnam's, 1913.

Shastid, Thomas Hall. *The Only Way.* Duluth, Minn.: Conopus, 1926.

———. *Give the People Their Own War Power.* Ann Arbor, Mich.: George Wahr, 1927.

——. *How to Stop War-Time Profiteering.* 2d ed. Ann Arbor, Mich.: George Wahr, 1937.

——. *My Second Life.* Ann Arbor, Mich.: George Wahr, 1944.

Slayden, Ellen Maury. *Washington Wife: Journal of Ellen Maury Slayden from 1897–1919.* New York: Harper and Row, 1963.

Stillman, James W. *Republic or Empire? An Argument in Opposition to the Establishment of an American Colonial System.* Boston: George H. Ellis, 1900.

Stimson, Henry L., and McGeorge Bundy. *On Active Service in Peace and War.* New York: Harper, 1947.

Villard, Oswald Garrison. *Fighting Years: Memoirs of a Liberal Editor.* New York: Harcourt, Brace, 1939.

Wald, Lillian D. *Windows on Henry Street.* Boston: Little, Brown, 1933.

Waldman, Seymour. *Death and Profits: A Study of the War Policies Commission.* New York: Brewer, Warren, and Putnam, 1932.

"The War Referendum Proposal." *Congressional Digest,* 17 (1938), 37–64.

Wheeler, Burton K., with Paul F. Healy. *Yankee from the West.* Garden City, N.Y.: Doubleday, 1962.

Wheeler-Bennett, John W., and Frederic E. Langermann. *Information on the Problem of Security, 1917–1926.* London: George Allen and Unwin, 1927.

White, William Allen. *Politics: The Citizen's Business.* New York: Macmillan, 1924.

Wilson, Woodrow. *The Public Papers of Woodrow Wilson.* Ed. Ray Stannard Baker and William E. Dodd. 6 vols. New York: Harper, 1925–27.

Index